DECISIONS, DECISIONS!

After the flurry and excitement of graduation is over, you'll inevitably be faced with the question, "What's next?" The college-to-first-job transition period involves a number of major decisions, and while this may be a time of uncertainty, *The Smith College Job Guide* shows you how it can also be a time of wonderful opportunities. With its whole-person approach to career planning, *The Smith College Job Guide* demonstrates how looking for your first job can be an education in success—laying that all-important foundation of job-hunting and career-building skills that you will recycle, adapt, and expand throughout your professional life.

Elizabeth Tener has created a warm and enlightening resource that will provide you with all the practical advice and information you need to land that perfect job. There's no need to go it alone. Just let *The Smith College Job Guide* support you in your quest for the right career!

THE SMITH COLLEGE JOB GUIDE

Elizabeth Tener, a Smith College graduate, is a freelance journalist. She has contributed a regular careers column to *Self* magazine and her articles have appeared in *YM*, *McCall's*, *Women's Day*, *Readers' Digest*, *Family Circle*, and *Cosmopolitan*. Senior editor of *Co-Ed* magazine for eight years, Tener's articles have won her numerous awards from the Educational Press Association of America. She is currently a psychotherapy resident at the Blanton-Peale Institute in New York City.

THE SMITH COLLEGE JOB GUIDE

HOW TO FIND AND MANAGE YOUR FIRST JOB

Elizabeth Tener

with the Smith College Career Development Office

Introduction by Barbara Reinhold, Ed.D., Director of the Smith College Career Development Office

A PLUME BOOK

PLUME
Published by the Penguin Group
Penguin Books USA Inc., 375 Hudson Street,
New York, New York 10014, U.S.A.
Penguin Books Ltd, 27 Wrights Lane,
London W8 5TZ, England
Penguin Books Australia Ltd, Ringwood,
Victoria, Australia
Penguin Books Canada Ltd, 2801 John Street,
Markham, Ontario, Canada L3R 1B4
Penguin Books (N.Z.) Ltd, 182-190 Wairau Road,
Auckland 10, New Zealand

Penguin Books Ltd, Registered Offices:
Harmondsworth, Middlesex, England

First published by Plume, an imprint of New American Library,
a division of Penguin Books USA Inc.

First Printing, June, 1991
10 9 8 7 6 5 4 3 2 1

REGISTERED TRADEMARK—MARCA REGISTRADA

LIBRARY OF CONGRESS CATALOGING IN PUBLICATION DATA:
Tener, Elizabeth.
The Smith College job guide : how to find and manage your first job / Elizabeth Tener ; introduction by Barbara Reinhold.
p. cm.
ISBN 0-452-26626-2
1. Job hunting—Handbooks, manuals, etc. 2. Career development—Handbooks, manuals, etc. 3. Vocational guidance for women—Handbooks, manuals, etc. 4. College graduates—Employment—Handbooks, manuals, etc. I. Title.
HF5382.7.T46 1991
650.14'02'02—dc20 90-26050
CIP

Printed in the United States of America
Designed by Eve L. Kirch

In loving memory of my aunts
Elizabeth Fisher Trimble, Class of 1932
and
Martha Fisher Hubbell, Class of 1935
The first career women I knew

Contents

Acknowledgments ix

Introduction by Barbara Reinhold, Ed.D. xiii

Part One. Self-Assessment

Chapter 1. Not a Path but a Process: *A Whole-Person Approach to Career Planning* 3

Chapter 2. Discovering Who You Are 15

Part Two. Exploring Options

Chapter 3. The Art of Creative Floundering: *Getting Prepared for Your Job Search* 45

Chapter 4. Mini-Jobs That Test the Current 67

Part Three. Conducting a Search

Chapter 5. Basic How-To's of Career Research 93

Chapter 6. The Hand-Crafted Job Search 127

Chapter 7. Winning Resumes, Intriguing Cover Letters 155

Chapter 8. Job Interviews 199

Chapter 9. Evaluating Your Job Offers and Getting the Deal You Want 233

Part Four. Using Your Job to Create Further Opportunities

Chapter 10. Starting Off Smart 251

Chapter 11. Your Professional Cornerstone: *Good Work Habits* 263

Chapter 12. Managing Up: *How to Get Along with Your Boss and Coworkers* 281

Appendix A. Information Sources for Profit-Making Organizations 301

Appendix B. Resources for Researching Nonprofit Organizations 308

Acknowledgments

The up-to-the-minute information, the state-of-the-art services, and the breadth of resources offered to students and alumnae by the Smith College Career Development Office make it arguably the best of its kind in the country. This is neither an accident nor an overnight success story. It reflects Smith College's longstanding dedication to women and their rightful and central place in the world of work, and is the result of a gathering and refining process that has taken place over many years.

When I first approached Barbara Reinhold, Director of the CDO, with the idea for this book almost four years ago, I found her to be a wonderful source of enthusiasm, up-to-date thinking, and original ideas. On subsequent visits to the CDO, I was impressed with the feeling of competence and gentle energy that seemed to hum through all three floors of the quaint New England–style building it inhabits on the Smith campus. This was not only a place to learn to write resumes or to sign up for on-campus interviews. It was a place that, whatever your age or experience, you were encouraged to view yourself as a whole person, with values, skills, abilities, and potential all your own, and to approach your life work through that wholeness. I hope I have conveyed some of that feeling in this book.

During the course of the writing I had many occasions to talk to the CDO counselors and staff on the telephone to round out my ideas, confirm my intuitions, get feedback on my approach. Many times current staff members would refer to the research, compilations, ideas of past staff and students. Therefore, I would like to acknowledge and thank not only current staff people who so patiently answered my questions but also people who serve in different capacities at Smith and people no longer there whose work remains an important part of the Smith CDO contribution: Joanna Donahue, Richard Loebl, Nancy Steeper, Gisela Bonde, June Delaney, Nancy Hill, Terry Michael, Beverly Catnoir, Miranda Rose Ring, Norma Packard, Judy Johnson Palmer, Paula Giovanelli, Marta Staiti, Jane Sommer, Carrie Hemenway, Renee Hill, Amy Hoffman, Lucy Freeman Greenberg, Merle Norman, Janet McNeill, Charles Johnson, Mary Albro, Robert Jay Ginn, Deborah Orgera, and Jan Black.

I would also like to thank people who were willing to share with me the story of their career growth or who kindly offered me the benefit of their expertise: Lynn Staudacher, Roger Parson, Richard Shaedle, Laurel Toubey, Susanne Parente, Rhoda Frindell Green, and Kate Wendleton. Georgia Donati, the supervising librarian at the Job Information Center of the Mid-Manhattan Branch of the New York Public Library, helped me sort through the voluminous literature on this subject, made many timesaving suggestions, and provided the basis for this book's appendices. My friend Kit Brewster spent a day or two with me further refining the bibliography.

And, since I've stressed so many times in this book the importance of developing a support network to keep you on track in your career and your life, I want to express my deepest gratitude to all those special angels in mine: my parents, Richard and Wilma Tener, who have shown touching faith, eager interest, and solid support through all my career changes; and Frank Alagna, Sue Bloland, Elizabeth Forst, Joan Iaconetti, Patricia Pike, and Miriam Velez, who nudged me along when I got hopelessly stuck. A toast or three are also due to the fellow sufferers in my Tuesday Night Writers' Group and the people at St. Michael's Church.

This project would never have flown without the ministrations of my ever-engaging and persuasive agent, Meg Ruley of the Jane Rotrosen Agency (whose world-class networking sells my book ideas in record time), and a bouquet also to Rosemary Ahern, my editor at New American Library, for her kind words about my words, and the spare and graceful touch of her editorial pen.

—Elizabeth Tener

New York City
October 1990

Introduction
by
Barbara Reinhold, Ed.D.

Aren't there enough career books already? Indeed, at first glance it's hard to argue with that. Upon closer inspection of the volumes on the shelf, however, you'd find mostly two categories: books about self-assessment and books about job-search strategies.

The hard part (and the part that sends people scurrying to counselors and expensive career-testing firms) is that nebulous, creative, terrifying place between assessment and search—the place where you try to put it all together.

This is where you figure out what to do with a major in religion, a love of sports, and fluency in three languages, or how to combine a double major in computer science and history with a flair for color and design.

This is the point in the career-exploration process where "inside" information (your own talents and preferences) and "Outside" realities (the facts about requirements for and rewards in particular fields and functions) come together to suggest career possibilities for you. It is elusive, but fascinating. And Elizabeth Tener has captured it very well indeed.

What's a Good Job?

"I have to have a good job before graduation. It doesn't matter that much what it is, so long as it makes me feel that this hard work was worth it. It'll also be a graduation present to my family for the sacrifices they made for me to come here. So, I want to find out how to interview for corporate jobs that pay really well."

The intense senior sitting in my office desperately wanted me to approve her plan to jump into interviews with the first round of fast-paced on-campus recruiters, without any real self-assessment and introspection on her part. It was hard not to agree that this would be the logical culmination of her demanding liberal arts education, but I had no choice. "You're going too fast," I said quietly. "You've left out the most important steps in this process. Let's start over and talk about *you*."

At colleges like Smith, where the career office is an active resource for students and alumnae alike, conversations like this one happen often. At the Smith College Career Development Office (CDO), trained counselors and an array of both written and nonprint materials are available to help in the slow, painstaking, but ultimately exhilarating process of finding out what type of work will allow you to continue developing, intellectually and personally, in the years after graduation. But not all colleges have made the choice to offer their graduates this costly resource. And so, when Smith alumna Elizabeth Tener decided to write a book that could make this in-depth approach to career exploration available to all career searchers, the Smith CDO was delighted to assist her in sharing our materials and strategies with you. And we are very pleased with the clarity, sensitivity, and spirit of ever-unfolding opportunity which Elizabeth has woven into this book.

Because Smith has been the country's largest liberal arts college for women for more than one hundred years, we have been concerned mostly with the career choices of women, even though the career office is crowded on Sunday afternoons with men from other colleges who extend their weekend stays to use our career resources before heading back to their own campuses.

For the 1990s and the turbulent years beyond, however, men's and women's careers will look more alike than ever before. "Oh yes," you might be saying, "women's lives and careers will look more like men's." But actually the reverse is true. Men's careers have begun to have the same twists and turns which women's lives have traditionally had.

Given the volatile, global political economy you are entering today, exploring different alternatives in response to external changes and balancing the demands of work and personal life effectively have become the most basic survival tools for both men and women. Organizations grow, shrink, get restructured, or add and drop services or products with dizzying frequency. The old pattern of declaring your career choice at graduation time and sticking with it for a lifetime (the tried and true "male model") fits fewer and fewer people's experience every day.

At Smith we put it this way: "The career track has been replaced forever by the career trampoline!" The good news is that this book can coach you well in this emerging art of career gymnastics.

Women's career choices have sold lots of media space in the past several years, as women of all ages have wrestled with the new set of conflicting mandates and opportunities emerging in their lives. Unfortunately, gender issues reported in the press often give off more heat than light. The research underlying much of what has been written reveals two heartening and one problematic observation: First, the good news:

- In the past twenty years, women have made remarkable gains in all careers and fields of study. Just as women now surpass males in the percentage of students enrolled in higher education, in this decade it is likely that 50 percent of the positions in most formerly male-dominated fields will be held by women.

• Still, discrimination and antifemale backlash will be part of the scenery in your current career drama. In research conducted at Smith recently, two-thirds of high-achieving alumnae of all ages reported that they had experienced gender discrimination. Women must be constantly vigilant of the ways in which organizations and individuals can diminish the effectiveness of some of our brightest and most forthright young women, and figure out ways to manage that tendency. That's the bad news, obviously, but there's a compensatory trend in sight.

• Men have also begun to be concerned about having a quality life and a better balance of career and personal experiences. We know now that the sexist assumptions locking women *out of* certain places has for too long also locked men *into* certain roles. For the 1990s and beyond, there are signs that men and women will be working together to ensure each other's support for very individualized career options, organized around their own talents and interests rather than on jaded old norms based on gender, race, or lifestyle.

Who's in Charge of Your Career?

A critical concept for the next decade is "employability," as discussed by Harvard Business School professor and author Rosabeth Kanter in her ground-breaking book, *When Giants Learn to Dance.* Employability implies a 180-degree turnabout in how employers and employees view their responsibilities to each other and to themselves. Traditionally, loyalty to an organization has carried with it an implicit promise of security and protection for employees, in such givens as seniority and retirement benefits.

In our current economy, however, it is important for you to know that the critical factors in a new style of security are not seniority and retirement benefits, but rather being able to move and change easily. "Right-sizing," the euphemistic term for expanding and contracting quickly in response to market realities, has become a management prerogative. It requires that all employees learn to take care of themselves by paying very careful attention to their own employability.

Employability is your protective state of readiness to shift gears, your ability to move yourself into new positions, either inside or outside your current organization. It means that you will have to be up-to-date at all times, well-connected via various networks, and engaged in constant replenishing of your information and skills bank. It also assumes that you will stay self-aware, anticipating and even enjoying the fact that your values, interests, and needs will shift (usually without your permission) with each passing year. Learning how to look honestly inside yourself as you graduate from college (or into a new life of some type) is the first real test of this self-assessment function that you'll need to use continually for the rest of your life.

The Only Constant Is Change

As you start on your search for an exciting new way to use your education, it's important to remember that even if you land the perfect job immediately, your career will need to be fine-tuned regularly. Many of the articles and books about career development and renewal use the metaphor of air travel and course correction. Did you know, for instance, that most commercial airliners are off course almost 90 percent of the time? Only a computerized course correction capability on each airliner keeps us from bumping into each other in the crowded airways. That same habitual surveillance (asking questions about what's really going on inside yourself and in the office) and responsiveness to changes you encounter in your work environment will need to be your constant companions in whatever job you choose.

This need for lifelong fine-tuning is one of the reasons

why colleges are increasingly asked to offer career transition services for alumnae. At Smith, alumnae and their families bring us an interesting array of career transitions about which to counsel them. In the recent past, we've talked to all of the following (and many more):

- The two-years-out analyst who chose corporate finance for the salary and lifestyle she thought she wanted, but who now has decided that she wants to work in a more service-oriented organization.
- The forty-year-old sculptor returning to Smith to take two years of basic sciences to prepare for application to medical school.
- The fifty-two-year-old Smith husband considering leaving a lucrative career as a divorce lawyer to study for a counseling degree.
- The seventy-two-year-old retired teacher just finishing her doctoral degree in future studies and planning to start another career.

On and on it goes. Who knows just when one of these turnabouts might poke its way into your life? The good news is that the ideas in this book are "one size fits all." In order for the book to guide you all your life—at twenty-two, forty-two, and sixty-two—all you need to do is to *stay aware* of your own needs, values, interests, and feelings. Feelings? Yes; despite the claims by some that career planning is primarily an exercise in logic, your emotions will always provide essential evidence in solving career dilemmas. When you stay aware of all those subjective elements, each spiral of reassessment yields richer and richer personal rewards.

Another new reality that probably doesn't get talked about much by people who may be advising you is the importance of smaller organizations and the many different opportunities they provide. Even though 89 percent of potential nongovernment employers have less than twenty people, new job seekers seem to assume that the larger, brand-name organizations, in both the profit and not-for-profit sectors, offer the best shot at a "good job." Of course, a "good job" is a relative term. What would be good for you might be horrible for your roommate. Actually, your best bet is to consider many kinds and sizes of organizations and to see which ones feel right to you.

It's been said of family life that being born into a family is like happening in on a party that's already in full swing and frantically trying to figure out how to fit in there. Well, the same is true for entering a new organization: You'll find both a "family" and a party that started without you. Some people find it much easier to get started at a smaller party, where the roles are often less distinct and the tasks more varied.

Other people feel much more comfortable at a larger party, where the roles are sometimes more clear-cut and patterns more established. The important thing, though, is to start out intent on finding a party that suits you, no matter what the size or name recognition of a particular organization. At this point, you'll need to rely much less on logic than on your intuition. Again, it's what feels right to you that you'll want to consider most. At Smith, we often caution job seekers, who are frequently told what they should do from interested family and friends, that "if the should doesn't fit, don't wear it."

Career Advice from Mind and Body

It would be short-sighted to write about careers without considering the impact of the *self-fulfilling prophecy.* With your jobs, as with all other parts of life, what you expect is what you'll get.

Psychological hardiness, a concept developed by University of Chicago researchers Suzanne Kobasa and Salvatore Maddi, describes people who expect to get positive results and are able to handle stress. Hardy people show this strength in three ways, by manifesting:

- An openness to change
- A feeling of involvement in what they're doing
- A sense of control over their own lives

Studies have proven again and again that people who expect to get sick do, people who expect relationships to disappoint them are disappointed, and employees who expect to have trouble at work experience trouble. In short, things will only go as well as your mind allows you to believe that they will.

Therefore, if you're having trouble imagining that things will work out as you'd like, you're probably setting yourself up for disappointment. Perhaps you could find a few friends to form a "Great Results Support Group," to encourage each other in really appreciating your strengths and believing that you each will find work that suits you.

Another important and often ignored factor in managing your career has surfaced in the relatively new field of psychoneuroimmunology. What does that mean? In one word, *bodymind:* the inextricable connection between physical and emotional well-being.

Doing work you don't enjoy or not being able to use the particular skills and talents you have (either in your career or personal life) will, in time, make you sick. You've probably heard that the late Norman Cousins was able to cure himself of several potentially fatal illnesses by laughing at funny old movies for hours at a time. Or perhaps you've read that twenty minutes of watching a comic video can improve the output of your immune system. But did you know that boredom, depression, meaninglessness, and lack of stimulation actually depress your immune system, and hence make you much more susceptible to all kinds of illness?

If you do work you don't like because the pay is good, or if you try to work in a place where your values and personal style don't fit, your immune system will take a beating every day, at inevitable cost to your general health. And, as if that's not enough, while your physical symptoms are *increasing*, your self-esteem will be *decreasing* rapidly. People trying to do work that doesn't fit them end up moaning to themselves, "What's wrong with me?" Our answer is, "There's nothing wrong with *you*. You've just allowed yourself to get stuck in work that doesn't nourish you. You're starving in your job."

It's unfortunate but true, then, that many people have sickening jobs—a fate this book is designed to prevent. But if the work you choose excites you, seems worthwhile to you, and allows you to get paid for doing things you consider fun, then your work will keep you healthy.

Gender is a factor here too. Unfortunately, little girls were often taught to look out for others and play supporting roles while little boys were groomed for stardom. At job search time, those old supporting-role tapes in some young women's unconscious minds keep them from aiming high enough or campaigning with enough vigor.

It has been noted by some observers of gender and work, for instance, that in the 1990s there may actually be more opportunities open for women than there are self-confident, assertive, psychologically hardy women to claim them as their own. Should that sad situation materialize, it would be a great loss for everyone, not only for employees but also for employers (who need all the bright, well-educated people they can get.)

The likelihood that women might not be prepared to move into the positions which have now been opened up for them is much greater for women who have not had the kind of support and assistance in career-strategizing which is so much a part of a women's college like Smith. Here, the emphasis is on teaching women to appreciate their strengths and to expect the most from themselves. Through the collaborative efforts of the alumnae association and the CDO, Smith students and alumnae of all ages have immediate on-line access to more than sixteen thousand career and educational advisers in fields all over the globe. These women form what we call "the ageless women's network," a group of honest, enthusiastic, and savvy Smith graduates eager to share their secrets and support with other Smith women moving in, out, and through a wide range of educational experiences. Though it's not possible for everyone to go to Smith and reap the benefits of the CDO, it is possible for women everywhere to commit to taking themselves seriously and champion their own causes in the decade ahead.

We've talked about lots of concepts which are pressing in on you in this decade of change—economic volatility, gender role shifts, employability, introspection, course corrections, self-fulfilling prophecies, and even bodymind theory. These are the themes of the future. The seeds for finding and sustaining career satisfaction in these rapidly changing times have all been carefully planted in the chapters of the *Smith College Job Guide* by Elizabeth Tener. I know you'll enjoy harvesting these ideas in your own career life, season after season.

PART ONE

SELF-ASSESSMENT

CHAPTER

1

Not a Path but a Process:

A Whole-Person Approach to Career Planning

If college graduation is bearing down on you and suddenly the question "What next?" seems very real and very scary—congratulations. If graduation's over, you've said goodbye to your classmates, and suddenly you don't know *who* you are—congratulations. If you went all out to get into that management training program, you were accepted, and *now* you panic—congratulations. You're going through one of the most important transition periods of your life, and all of these feelings are entirely appropriate and to be expected.

The stretch of time just after college (it can last several months or several years) when you search for, find, and adjust to your first full-time job is a major demarcation zone between one way of life and another. You're relinquishing your identity as a youngster, as a student, as a child in your parents' home—an identity that you've grown used to and one that has been to some extent imposed on you by others. At the same time you're building a new concept of yourself as a valuable, contributing adult. And you must build it largely from scratch—from your gifts and your skills and your potential. You'll be testing that self-concept out in the world, to see how well it flies. As you research, explore, and begin to get an idea of a career you think you'd like, you'll discover a world filled with people, activities, values, and vocabulary that are strange to you, and you'll be leaving behind some comfortable attitudes and familiar habits. Furthermore, you'll have gone from being a confident college senior to being a confused beginner all over again. The people around you will know more than you do, and this is bound to make for crises of confidence and moments of discouragement.

The college-to-first-job transition period can have its lonely and uncertain moments, but it needn't be that way all the time. This period presents wonderful opportunities to meet people who can help and support you now and in the future. You'll also be laying a foundation of job-hunting and career-building skills that you'll expand, adapt, and recycle throughout your life. You'll need them because . . . and here's the surprise . . . unlike past generations, people working in the 1990s and early twenty-first century will have several "first jobs" in the course of their lifetimes. Here are the kinds of "first jobs" you might look forward to:

The first job after school or college. This is where you are now, looking for the traditional sort of first job right after college. You're leaving your life as a full-time student and joining the "real world" of nine-to-five employed people who are making a living and paying the bills.

The first job after a long while. Many women and some men take time away from the workplace while their children are young. Returning to work after the kids are out on their own, or after a divorce or family financial difficulty has made a job a necessity, can be like starting all over again. People in this situation may feel confused and undertrained when they see the technological changes that have occurred in their field. They may not have had a chance to launch a real career earlier, or they may not have worked at all. At any rate, that first day at work after all those years at home will definitely have that "first job" feeling.

The first job in a new career field. If you're beginning your working life now, the U.S. Department of Labor, Bureau of Labor Statistics, says you'll change careers four times. Not jobs, *careers.* The latest trend: beginning a new career after retirement. The decision to change careers is a difficult one that often comes after a long period of reappraisal, especially when it involves added education and/or a reduction in pay or status. But if it's the right move, a new career feels like a new beginning—challenging and energizing. A new career may call on entirely new skills, expose you to different sorts of people, and discipline you in a brand-new working style. There's a good chance it will feel like a first job.

The first job you really love. Some people fall into unsuitable jobs because of financial necessity or inadequate self-assessment and slog along in them for years, not feeling that they're making as effective a contribution as the people around them. Or they've taken a passive, hit-or-miss approach to job hunting, accepting their first job offer or perhaps working for a relative they feel indebted to. Then they decide to take their career more seriously, do some inner searching, and spend some time investigating several fields that really engage their interest. When they finally find the spot they've so consciously and painstakingly sought out, and the fit is good, they'll discover that going to work will have a whole new meaning for them.

Although almost every "first job" seeker, regardless of her age, can get something of value from this book, the *Smith College Job Guide* is written primarily for you, the new college graduate. Its suggestions for pacing yourself and taking interim jobs are designed to lower transition anxiety and give you the confidence to wait for the job you really want. The self-discovery exercises and research how-tos will help you precisely match your skills and interests with a job in which you can grow. Perhaps most important are the networking strategies, because learning to work with other people—to ask for their support, receive it with appreciation, and pass that help on to others—will be of great value to you long after you land that first job. Working well with others is essential to long-term career building; it's a carefully nurtured skill of all truly successful people. But this book does not confine itself simply to the job campaign. It offers advice about making the most of the job once you have it, demystifying everything from difficult bosses to office politics to on-the-job etiquette to self-promotion.

Career-Sculpting Techniques—Your Portable Security in an Insecure World

There's no doubt about it—the art and science of job hunting and career building has taken a giant step into the spotlight in the past fifteen years. Hundreds of books are devoted to its innumerable subtleties. Job counselors, career coaches, industrial psychologists, and outplacement consultants are full of helpful (or sometimes merely expensive) advice on researching job fields, networking, practicing door-opening techniques, and sharpening your self-awareness, your intuition, and your resume. Sometimes it seems you need more smarts and skills to *find* the job than you do to *keep* the job. Why is this discipline suddenly attracting so much attention? Simply put, your job-hunting and career-building expertise constitute your only real job security in today's rapidly shifting workplace. In fact, the job hunter who lucks into a great first job quickly without doing her homework may eventually be less fortunate than she thinks. She'll be skipping a vital part of her education for success.

Here are seven main reasons why job-hunting and career-managing know-how, fine-tuned by experience, is an essential ingredient for success in the twenty-first century.

1. Job security is an illusion. Back in the forties, fifties, and sixties, when the U.S. economy was the strongest in the world and social change was slower, a company made a tacit agreement with anyone it hired to keep him or her on indefinitely. As long as you performed adequately, you could count on a job. But the day of the gold watch after forty years of faithful service is all but gone. The security you do have is not a pledge from your company; rather it is your own self-developed body of job-finding and career-building skills that you carry with you from company to company. Today it's not enough just to do a good job and count on your company to take notice; the smart employee also studies the company and the industry with an eye to career development. She not only builds skills and knowledge in areas that appeal to her; she also scans her organization for the growing departments, networks in her industry, and makes plans to leave if the situation in her division changes for the worse.

2. Company loyalty and worker loyalty are largely things of the past. Companies, even large ones, are fighting for their lives in a world of global competition, corporate buyouts, and ever-fluctuating economic conditions. If your company merges with another and your job is redundant, you may be let go no matter how valuable you have been to your division in the past. Cutbacks are commonplace. Company managers might want to take care of their employees but they can't afford to be sentimental.

And neither can employees. The response to the massive industry layoffs of the seventies and early eighties is that many wary employees often stay with a company long enough to beef up their resumes and then move on. Even people who love the organizations they work for and want to build their careers there keep a weather eye open for signs of distress, or for better opportunities elsewhere.

There's no doubt that the decline of company loyalty has heightened feelings of anxiety and uncertainty among employees, but there is a positive side to the situation. There is far less disgrace in being let go, in being unemployed, than in former years. People looking to hire readily understand that good people often find themselves out of jobs for all sorts of reasons that have nothing to do with their competence. And job hopping, as long as the hops are planned, is no longer considered the sign of instability that it once was. All the more reason to learn how to crack the job market, to uncover hidden jobs, and to present yourself as a strong, reliable candidate to someone who might want to hire you.

3. *Technology continues to change the workplace with lightning speed.* Here's a stunning prediction from the U.S. Department of Labor—by the year 2000, half the current work force will be in jobs not yet invented. At least once every decade, a major technological innovation causes enormous changes in the workplace: In the 1950s, it was television; in the 1960s and 1970s, it was the computer and the silicone chip. Who knows how many thousands of new jobs, not yet imagined, will be created after the turn of the century by the semiconductor and nuclear fusion? The other side of the coin is that many jobs that are important and pay well today will be obsolete tomorrow or will require very different skills.

What this means is that employees in the twenty-first century will be constantly scanning the job market, often way beyond their immediate industry, to see where they can take their transferable skills. They must be ready to update their job and life goals in light of new innovations, new possibilities. They must also be reeducating themselves throughout their working life. The recent phenomenon of holding down one job while educating oneself for another will be the rule rather than the exception. You can be sure that the job-hunting skills you'll gain in the process of finding the right first job will be practiced, expanded, and refined during the course of your working life.

4. *There will continue to be competition for the top jobs in every field.* In the 1970s, the combination of an economic recession and stepped-up worldwide competition caused American companies to scale themselves down, and they've never regained the heft that they lost. "Lean and mean" is still the standard. Organizations continue to want more work from fewer people and are quicker to eliminate redundant jobs and let unproductive people go. Workers can no longer afford to drift along with the tide, doing a good-enough job. Instead, smart career builders will continually be thinking of ways to make a greater contribution and to demonstrate their worth to their supervisors.

Again, the same economic trends that foster insecurity can also encourage a certain self-reliance. Because employers will be less willing to tolerate staff members who are unenthusiastic and barely productive, dissatisfied employees will be quicker to reassess their chosen company or career direction and look for a better fit. It will be far more difficult for employees to waste their working lives in jobs they dislike and are unsuited for just because of a steady paycheck.

5. *The world of work is wide open.* Only twenty or thirty years ago, people were very much bound and restricted in the kinds of jobs they could have. Professions and occupations were very much determined by what one's family did, what was appropriate according to certain social norms. For example, the professions (medicine, law, architecture) were dominated by upper middle class white men, predominantly Protestant. Tradition and social snobbery dictated the kinds of positions that were appropriate, and often kept people in jobs that did not reflect their abilities and interests.

Until about twenty years ago, sex and age also determined the kind of job you would hold. With few exceptions, professions, positions of leadership, and jobs entailing heavy financial responsibility were closed to women. And workers were very much locked into the unvarying life stages of education/work/retirement.

Now your choice of an occupation is much less hampered by social restrictions and taboos. This lack of boundaries and limitations in your career choice makes things at once more exciting and more difficult as you choose a career or look for a job. The lack of cues from the outside world as to which jobs are appropriate can leave you feeling at sea. But this sense of insecurity will motivate you to look inside yourself; to learn about your inner urges, talents, desires, and abilities; and to let them lead you in choosing your life's work. If you take up the challenge, the reward is likely to be a series of job and career choices more congruent with your unique nature, and therefore far more satisfying and self-expressive.

6. People today demand more from their jobs than money and security—they look for personal fulfillment. It used to be that except for the privileged few (artists or captains of industry, for example), people saw their jobs primarily as meal tickets. Jobs were something you needed for survival; if you didn't have to work, you were considered lucky. Men worked to support themselves and their families; young women worked as long a they had to, but most of them hoped to marry well enough to quit and raise a family.

Starting with the feminist movement of the early 1970s, women began to see jobs as a way of defining and expressing themselves, making an impact on the wider world beyond home and family. Today women and men both see their jobs as important, even vital, statements about who they are as people. Perhaps because what you do tends to be self-chosen, no longer a logical extension of your ethnic group or your social class, you're likely to regard your job as a carefully cultivated part of your self-image and a way to discover and express who you really are.

In addition, consciously or unconsciously, you're likely to seek from your job a large measure of personal fulfillment, whatever that term means to you—power and influence, fame or glamour, the ability to mobilize people for effective results, the desire to contribute to the quality of life and to the betterment of society and individuals, or the longing to create beauty in the world. If the career you've chosen doesn't match your inner yearnings and desires for self-expression, you, far more than your mother and father, will be motivated to leave your early choice behind and start over in another field, even though additional training may be required. Furthermore, a career that suits you just fine when you're twenty-five may no longer be as interesting when you're thirty-five or forty; in upcoming decades, working people will feel much freer to explore abilities and interests that arise in midlife or later.

7. *Many people will be seeking an easier blend of career/work life than in the past.* Although all-involving, high-pressured careers will probably continue to challenge the most competitive and financially ambitious young people, many others would prefer a life that more smoothly combines work, family, recreation, and the developing of individual talents and interests. Many rigid barriers that have defined and separated work life from personal life in the past are already breaking down, and the 1990s may see even more job sharing, part-time work, and work centered in the home. People will be blending work and home life more easily, or may hold down two jobs. The growth in the field of personal services (everything from management consultant to psychotherapist to masseuse to nutritionist) will encourage many individuals to build a clientele and to set up their own work schedules in a way that makes room for the demands and pleasures of their personal lives. People will continue to strive for a more satisfying mix of work, learning, and play—what Richard Bolles calls "the three boxes of life"—and when the ingredients in the equation change (a child is born or a company relocates), they'll reassess.

* * *

All this means that the shape of people's career lives over time will look a whole lot different than in the past. Career counselors used to use linear metaphors to describe careers; they'd talk about "your career path" or "climbing the ladder of success." Implicit was the idea that if you were diligent and followed the yellow brick road laid out by your company, your industry, or your profession long enough, you'd eventually reach your own particular Emerald City. Careers of the twenty-first century will look much less consistent, less predictable, less determined by factors exterior to the individual—the steps up a company's organization chart, for example. They will seem more amorphous, more exploratory, more reflective of the person's interior growth and unfolding. Instead of talking about climbing ladders, career coaches may soon suggest exploring landscapes of related fields. Activities that were formerly hobbies can become money-making propositions, latent interests can become full-time occupations, and certain areas, once explored, may lose their challenge and be replaced by others.

Exploring a landscape is far more exciting and interesting than treading a well-worn path, but it is also more challenging and unpredictable. Implicit in the process is losing your bearings, backtracking, walking for a long time only to reach a dead end, and checking out areas in great detail, only to find they weren't worth it. On the positive side, you'll be developing your expertise, flexibility, and self-presentation skills, and there's an excellent chance you'll find a unique opportunity that you would never have discovered had you not been willing to be a bit adventurous.

This description may make the process seem an aimless one, but it is not. In fact, the process has a definite structure that may be thought of as an ongoing and ever-changing spiral. Each time you make a career decision (or any change in your life) you may find it helpful to follow these steps:

1. *Self-Assessment*

Look at past experience; assess your values, priorities, interests, and skills; identify your definition of success.

2. *Exploring Options*

Read, research, create, and use your network; consider jobs, internships, volunteer work; evaluate further training.

3. *Conducting a Search*

Identify options to pursue; create a resume and cover letters; work on your interviewing style; evaluate offers; select your job.

4. *Using Your Job to Create Further Opportunities*

Strengthen skills; develop productive work habits and attitudes; discover routes to success in your field; build your reputation; showcase your abilities.

You'll go around this spiral again and again each time you make a career change or seek to restore a sense of work/learning/leisure balance to your life.

The *Smith College Job Guide* will take you through each step of the cycle to help make your career choice, your job selection, and your learning experience on your first job more self-aware and purposeful. Since the steps of the spiral are essentially the same whether you're just starting out or are far along in your career, you'll find this book is full of practical reminders and useful insights no matter what your age or stage.

You can consider it your road map as you explore the unfamiliar terrain of a new career field and your survival kit as you gear up for interviews, negotiate for salary, and identify and explore the opportunities for success once you've found that all-important first job.

For Further Reading

Birch, David. *Job Creation in America: How Our Smallest Companies Put the Most People to Work.* New York: Free Press, 1987.

Kanter, Rosabeth Moss. *When Giants Learn to Dance.* New York: Simon & Schuster, 1989.

Maccoby, Michael. *Why Work: Motivating and Leading the New Generation.* New York: Simon & Schuster, 1989.

Naisbett, John, and Patricia Aburdene. *Megatrends 2000.* New York: William Morrow & Company, 1990.

Peters, Thomas J., and Robert H. Waterman, Jr. *In Search of Excellence: Lessons from America's Best-Run Companies.* New York: Harper & Row, 1982.

Wendleton, Kate. *The Five O'Clock Club Guide to Changing Jobs.* New York: The Five O'Clock Club, 1987.

CHAPTER

2

Discovering Who You Are

Life would be infinitely easier—and infinitely more boring—if we could answer the question "Who am I?" just once, and have it be true forever. But human beings are mysterious creatures who continue to grow, expand, unfold throughout their lifetimes—if they allow themselves to do so.

Traditionally, identity crises were supposed to occur in adolescence and early adulthood, but recent studies in adult development have shown that "Who am I?" is a question that can yield fresh and surprising answers anytime in our lives. In fact, if our lives are to remain vital and meaningful, it is imperative that we periodically redefine ourselves. We may be pushed to do so by external changes—leaving high school or college, having children, getting divorced, experiencing a death in the family, coping with the empty nest, entering retirement. Or, we may be compelled by inner urges, feelings of discontent that come upon us for no apparent reason.

In a career context, the question "Who am I?" asks what our favored skills and abilities are, what engages our interest, what activities seem worthy of our effort for forty hours a week, where our most meaningful contribution might be. It's a question that almost every new high school and college graduate struggles with as she finds that first job and enters the workplace. It is a most important struggle, but it's only a start. Even the most diligent and introspective twenty-two-year-old will obtain only preliminary answers because she has only preliminary information. This is because who we are is revealed to us little by little, over time. We learn who we are by our surprise successes and false starts, our mistakes, our unexpected enthusiasms, our failures and how we handle them, feedback from others, job changes, and even those dry periods when we stick out a job without really knowing why. Thus the same inquiry process will yield much richer, more detailed, and more refined answers for older, experienced persons than for those in their twenties.

A recent college graduate, for example, might know she wants to work with people, but a thirty- or forty-year-old with years of working experience may be clearer on just how she wants to work with them. Does she want to manage them? Instruct them? Counsel them? Sell to them? Cut and style their hair? Also, the older job hunter who evaluates her work and life experience in retrospect will be able to identify threads of interest that weave through a number of jobs, as well as skills that reappear from job to job and are strengthened first in one way, then in another. These interests and skills could be called *inspired abilities.* They often appear when you are young, and they are an ongoing source of pleasure and accomplishment. You may choose to confine them to after-hours activities, but you may find yourself discontented if your main occupation does not include them, at least to some degree. Another interesting fact about inspired abilities: They're often hidden from us by their everyday obviousness. We're often so naturally good at them that we don't see them as anything special.

Discovering and Cultivating Your Inspired Abilities

But as your self-confidence grows, you'll learn to develop your inspired abilities and blend them into your work life in a way that makes your contribution unique. The course of putting these abilities to work in an unfolding career contains patterns that are typical for many people. Here are some of them:

1. Dreams and enthusiasms that are persistent in childhood almost always contain glimmers of potential inspired abilities. As a child, your interests were spontaneous and direct, untainted by social judgments, family agendas, or practical considerations such as the perceived limits of your intelligence or the need to support yourself. Reconnect with your childhood dreams to see your natural talents and interests in their purest form.
2. Family agendas and social expectations can be powerful distractions in locating and following your inspired abilities. If your parents have set a course for you, if they don't understand or respect your dreams, or they have rigid ideas about what's socially acceptable, you may need to struggle to discover your right livelihood.
3. Self-confidence is key in discovering and developing your inspired abilities. Whereas some young people are eager to go for the gold early, others need to hide and protect their cherished career dreams until they build their self-esteem and gain a bit in courage and maturity.
4. Jobs you dislike, or fail in, can teach you as much about your inspired abilities as jobs you love. The trouble is that they teach you in a rather backhanded way, and it takes some courage and confidence to learn their lessons. Being in the wrong job environment, having to do tasks you dislike, or being fired may all be disheartening experiences, but they can teach you valuable lessons about people and environments to stay away from, how to know when it's time to leave, what values and activities are important to you. Job unhappiness can

grind you down, depleting your confidence and energy, or it can be an occasion for reevaluation, deciding what piece of your current job you want to keep and what piece you want to trash—quickly!

5. Inspired abilities continue to ask you for care and attention, and through trial and error you can learn the best ways to work with them. Your most basic talents and interests have a way of pushing their way into your consciousness, even when you try to shove them aside. Once they have your attention, they press for complete development.

6. Inspired abilities can emerge through hobbies and volunteer work and later become a source of income. Perhaps your adolescent interest in human growth has led you to volunteer work with the Big Brothers. You may find that you're making a difference as a friend and counselor, and seek to develop this source of personal satisfaction further by learning formal counseling skills.

Connecting with Your Inspired Abilities

Now it's time for you to get to know yourself better—to identify your inspired abilities, to track how they've shown up in your life so far, and to get some hints of how they might be strengthened and developed in the future. On the following pages you will find eight exercises used by the counseling staff at the Smith College Career Development Office; they work well with every age and gender. They are designed to highlight your personality, your desires, your dreams, and your abilities in a number of different ways. Some of them will reconnect you with your childhood dreams or heighten your awareness of your family members' agendas for themselves and for you. Some will help you pinpoint inspired abilities through analysis of your favorite activities. Others will put you in touch with your desires and goals. The form of the exercises varies. Some resemble graphs that show patterns. Others are multiple-choice in nature; still others require short essays or drawings.

There's lots of opportunity in this section to increase and deepen your self-knowledge. To get the most out of these exercises, follow the suggestions below.

1. As you approach the exercises, remember that you're a complete person, not just a job holder or moneymaker. Forget for a while that you're looking for a way to support yourself and consider your life as a whole. What do you like to do with your family and friends? In your spare time? On vacation? Consider your intuition, your longings, your sky's-the-limit fantasies. Be creative and outrageous. Some of the exercises encourage a playful attitude. Indulge it!

2. Pick and choose among the exercises. You might want to do the Inspired Abilities Assessment first—it's basic and some of the other exercises refer to it—but you need not do the exercises in any special order. Some of the exercises may not appeal to you. Others may be irrelevant. Try to do at least five or six, so your abilities will be highlighted from different angles. Personal insights often come out of the interplay of various exercises.

3. Get these exercises out of your head and down on paper or onto a tape. It's a big temptation, especially when you don't have much time, to skim workbook material and do the learning activities mentally. But if you do this, you'll be missing most of their value. Ideas take on added meaning when they're written or spoken or shared. So clear a table, sit down, and start writing. Now may be a good time to begin a career journal to track your growth; such records can be incredibly valuable (more about them later). If you dislike writing, draw pictures instead, or ask a supportive friend or family member to interview you, and tape the results.

4. Take a right-brain (the nonlogical, nonlinear side that encourages creativity) approach to the exercises.

Memories and intuitive recall do not always happen on schedule. If you are doing an exercise and you draw a blank, or you can't remember, don't assume the answer's just not there. Hold the question in your mind for a few minutes and reflect. A memory or an association may bubble up from your unconscious. Be aware of any strong impressions that occur to you, even if you don't initially perceive them as related to the question. Write them down. Their relevance may become apparent to you later. After you've finished with the exercise and have gone on to other things, you may have a flash of insight or a memory, seemingly from nowhere. In fact, once you begin to do the exercises, you can count on memories and answers rising to conscious awareness when you're busy thinking about something else. This is your intuitive side working in its own time frame. If you can, take some time to jot down your thoughts, although these insights have a perverse way of flashing into our minds at the most inconvenient times for notetaking—while you're driving or in the shower, for example.

EXERCISE ONE
Reconnecting with the Childhood Dream

1. When you were a child, what did you imagine you would do when you grew up? Perhaps there's one pervasive image that comes to mind, or maybe you changed your mind a few times. If you fantasized about a number of activities and occupations, write down the most memorable ones and attach an approximate age to each. Don't overlook "impractical" dreams or sheer fantasies such as "aerial acrobat" or "orchestra conductor"—they can tell you much about your motivations, drives, and yearnings.

2. For each dream occupation, write down three memories from childhood that you associate with that occupation. If you chose acrobat, for example, you might remember practicing by swinging by your knees on the backyard jungle gym, or your father's discouraging you by telling you circus people aren't respectable. As each memory appears, immerse yourself in it and actually see it happening. As you write or record it, describe it in as much detail as possible. How old were you? Where were you? What did the setting look like? How did you feel? What people were involved? What did you actually say or do? If the memory seems vague at first, sit with your eyes closed and concentrate for a few moments; it may become clearer. Also, as you begin to write, more parts of the memory may come to mind.

3. Evaluate your exercise. What interests were reflected in your childhood dreams? What skills intrigued you? Are any of the same skills present in several dream occupations? How do your dream occupations coincide with the paying jobs you've held so far? What about your activities and interests outside work? Do any of your dreams have symbolic meanings for you? (Wanting to be a flying acrobat can symbolize a child's desire for freedom or excitement.) To what extent have you lived out the symbolic meaning? What is your mood when you think about these dreams? Excited? Energized? Nostalgic? Regretful?

EXERCISE TWO
Your Family Agenda

This is an important exercise. It's difficult to overstate how family agendas, openly stated or unconscious, influence our choice of careers. Your father may have designated you to live out the family dream. Your mother may want you to have a certain career that she really wanted but had no opportunity to pursue. Your family might be giving you a double message "Succeed—but don't surpass us."

- Diane loved everything about food preparation—selecting the food, cooking it, presenting it attractively. But she never considered making a career of it. Her father, a restaurateur, left the family when she was two, and was considered a ne'er-do-well. Besides, her wealthy and influential grandparents paid for her college education, and insisted that she find a secure, high-paying job. After several miserable years of pulling down a hefty salary in advertising, Diane cut loose and started her own catering business. She decided to do what she really loved, even if it meant displeasing the family power brokers and allying herself with the family black sheep.

- Patricia was the daughter of a woman minister who was not only a powerful person in her community but was also renowned nationwide for her books on religion and spirituality. Patricia always resented her mother's reputation as a loving and religious woman because she saw her as a rather neglectful mother who sought fame and influence at the expense of her family's well-being. Although Patricia was energetic and well-educated, she decided she wouldn't make the same mistake, that relationships would come first in her life. Until she was forty, she devoted herself exclusively to homemaking, vociferously taking issue with women who tried to have high-powered careers and families, too. When her children began to leave home, however, Patricia felt at loose ends. She began to see that in many ways she was like her mother—she enjoyed power, influence, making things happen. She returned to school for her MBA, worked in a management consulting firm for a few years, and recently began her own consulting business.

To get a bearing on your family dynamics concerning careers, do the following exercise as completely as you can. If possible, discuss the questions with your parents and siblings. A family dialogue may yield valuable insights and a new sense of closeness for everyone.

- Write down the names of any grandparents or ancestors whose occupations were the subject of family discussion. What was the family consensus on this person and his occupation? Was he/she glamorized? Disparaged?

- Are there one or more occupations that "run in your family"? List them below, and write down the names of the family members who have chosen those occupations. What are some of the points of view about these occupations shared by family members? Do family members who have *not* chosen these occupations feel left out?

Father (or Surrogate)	**Mother (or Surrogate)**
1. Father's career	Mother's career
2. Father's education and training (be specific)	Mother's education and training (be specific)
3. Father's major strengths	Mother's major strengths
4. Father's major weaknesses	Mother's major weaknesses
5. Father's major satisfactions about his life	Mother's major satisfactions about her life
6. Father's major regrets about his life	Mother's major regrets about her life
7. Father's "dreams" for himself	Mother's "dreams" for herself

8. Father's "dreams" for you	Mother's "dreams" for you

If you have adult brothers and sisters, you might write down their careers, education, strengths and weaknesses, major satisfactions and dissatisfactions, as well.

Now evaluate your results by answering the following questions:

- Where do you fit into the family picture?
- Are your inspired abilities ones your family can respect and support? Why or why not?
- Do your career interests fit the family pattern or run counter to it? Are they consonant with the values of your family, or will you have to separate more from your family?
- Are you choosing a career to "prove something"? What is it that you're trying to prove? To whom are you trying to prove it?
- Does your career choice represent some sort of dream or longing of one of your parents?

As you uncover your family's conscious and unconscious agenda for your career, you can begin to see whether you welcome this plan, resist it, or passively submit to it. Does your family's plan free you to be you, or burden you with undue responsibilities? If you discover that the career landscape your family has chosen is not one you would choose for yourself, you may need some support to go your own way. A well-chosen career counselor (see Chapter 3) or support group can help you affirm and fine-tune your abilities and support you in your chosen plan.

EXERCISE THREE
Inspired Abilities Assessment

The Inspired Abilities Assessment Inventory is a list of 107 different abilities in 14 categories (actually there are 93 abilities listed, with one in each category for you to fill in as you choose). Answer by putting a checkmark by any skills you have and enjoy *or* any skills that intrigue you and you'd like to develop. You don't have to be accomplished at something to check it.

If you are a number of years beyond college and have been working for a while, this exercise can give you an idea of where you might want to go next. Answer as follows: Put an *S* beside skills that you've learned well during your lifetime but which you dislike or feel neutral about. Put an *SI* next to skills which you have developed and which continue to be a source of pleasure and interest to you. Put an *I* beside skills that you don't have yet but you'd like to investigate or develop.

Again, don't limit your checks to skills you've used on your paying job—think about any skills you've employed in volunteer work, family management, or during times of relaxation and recreation.

Inspired Abilities Assessment

Leadership Skills

___ 1. Take initiative in developing relationships; move into a new situation on one's own; search for responsibility

___ 2. Work without supervision; "self-starter"

___ 3. Unwilling to accept the status quo; plan for, effect, initiate change; seize opportunity

___ 4. See a problem and act immediately to solve it; decisive in emergency

___ 5. Make a hard decision; take a risk

___ 6. Lead others; inspire, motivate; lead a group; chair an organization; delegate tasks

___ 7. Other leadership skills not listed above: ______
____

Management Skills: Developing, Planning, Organizing, Executing

___ 8. Plan; develop; plan on the basis of past experience; set goals systematically

___ 9. Establish priorities among competing tasks; set criteria; make policy

___ 10. Design projects; develop programs; plan and carry out well-run meetings

___ 11. Organize others; bring people together in a cooperative effort; build team; recognize and use others' skills; delegate

___ 12. Schedule; coordinate operations/details; arrange

___ 13. Direct others; supervise; administer; make sure things get done

___ 14. Review; make good use of feedback; evaluate performance of others

___ 15. Promote; sell a tangible item; sell an idea or a course of action; raise funds

___ 16. Recruit talent or leadership; motivate others; stimulate people to effective action

___ 17. Work with different kinds of people and bring them together

___ 18. Arbitrate/mediate between contending parties or groups; negotiate; crisis intervention

___ 19. Other management skills: ______________
____

Performing Skills

___ **20.** Get up before a group; respond to audience mood and ideas; perform; demonstrate; be poised in public

___ **21.** Address large or small group; speak/present well

___ **22.** Plan music, sing, dance; make people laugh; act; make media presentation, films

___ **23.** Play sports

___ **24.** Conduct/direct public affairs or ceremonies; conduct musical groups

___ **25.** Other performing skills: ____________________

____

Detail/Follow-Through Skills

___ **26.** Follow through; follow directions; get things done; bring projects in on time

___ **27.** Tackle tasks ahead of time; deliver on promises; be responsible

___ **28.** Handle variety of tasks and responsibilities simultaneously; work under stress and still improvise

___ **29.** Able to get materials, collect things, purchase, compile

___ **30.** Analyze data, organize, bring together in a coherent whole

___ **31.** Accurate memory for detail; retentive memory

___ **32.** Other follow-through skills: __________________

____

Numerical/Financial Skills

___ **33.** Compute rapidly in head or on paper; possess arithmetical calculating skills

___ **34.** Manage money; perform financial planning and management tasks; keep financial records
___ **35.** Execute economic research and analysis; do cost analysis
___ **36.** Develop a budget; plan; analyze; review; allocate scarce financial resources
___ **37.** Prepare reports; keep books; do accounting
___ **38.** Use numbers as a reasoning tool; possess sophisticated mathematical abilities; solve statistical problems
___ **39.** Use computers to calculate, analyze
___ **40.** Other numerical skills ______________________
____

Reading/Writing/Speaking/Communication Skills

___ **41.** Love reading; read rapidly, accurately
___ **42.** Proofread; edit; compose, compare
___ **43.** Communicate effectively; speak, think on one's feet
___ **44.** Define; explain concepts; interpret concepts
___ **45.** Translate; possess skills in foreign languages, linguistics; teach languages
___ **46.** Summarize; report accurately; write concisely
___ **47.** Describe; amuse; report; convince; promote; advertise
___ **48.** Other verbal skills ______________________
____

Instruction/Guiding/Educational Skills

___ **49.** Have a commitment to lifelong learning
___ **50.** Inform; explain, instruct; brief
___ **51.** Instill love of subject; convey enthusiasm; teach patiently; foster stimulating learning environment

___ **52.** Advise/help people in making decisions; encourage

___ **53.** Hear and answer questions perceptively; accept differing opinions; help others express their views

___ **54.** Counsel; put things in perspective; facilitate growth and development; clarify goals and values of others

___ **55.** Show others how to take advantage of resources; train

___ **56.** Facilitate groups; lead discussions

___ **57.** Other educational skills ____

Serving/Helping/Human Relationship Skills

___ **58.** Relate well to public, customers; render services; help and serve

___ **59.** Be sensitive to others; relate well to people; listen and convey awareness; show understanding, patience, fairness

___ **60.** Be empathic; be able to put oneself in someone else's shoes; talk easily with all kinds of people

___ **61.** Care for children, the elderly, or the handicapped

___ **62.** Administer a household; shape the atmosphere of a particular place; anticipate people's needs

___ **63.** Work well on a team; motivate fellow workers; treat others as equals; share credit with others

___ **64.** Take human failings into account; ignore undesirable qualities in others; deal patiently with difficult people

___ **65.** Nurse; provide care, treatment

___ **66.** Other human relationship skills ____

Intuitional and Innovative Skills

___ **67.** Be imaginative; develop and generate ideas, improvise

___ **68.** Be innovative; be creative; experiment with new approaches; be original

___ **69.** See relationships between apparently unrelated factors; integrate diverse elements into a coherent whole

___ **70.** Develop innovative program ideas; build on ideas of others

___ **71.** See commercial possibilities of abstract ideas or concepts; apply theory; create products

___ **72.** Visualize shapes; perceive patterns, structure, form

___ **73.** Possess spatial memory, memory for design, and color discrimination

___ **74.** Show foresight; instinctively gather resources even before the need for them becomes clear

___ **75.** Other intuitive skills ______________________
____

Artistic Skills

___ **76.** Show sensitivity to, and need for, beauty in the environment

___ **77.** Be expressive in body, voice, facial expressions, words

___ **78.** Imagine creatively; be skilled at symbol formation (words, pictures, concepts); write poetry; design, photograph; illustrate; draw; design fashion; decorate

___ **79.** Write; write plays; present theatrical productions

___ **80.** Possess musical knowledge and taste; perform; compose

___ **81.** Other artistic skills ______________________
____

Observational/Learning Skills

___ 82. Observe people, data, things
___ 83. Perceive; detect; discover; delight in new knowledge; learn quickly
___ 84. Be alert in observing human behavior; identify and assess potential of others
___ 85. Appraise; assess; accurately size up public mood; size up situations
___ 86. Other observational skills ____________________
____

Research/Investigating/Analyzing/Systematizing/ Evaluating Skills

___ 87. Recognize need for more information before decision can be made intelligently; clarify problems or situation
___ 88. Survey; interview; gather information from people by talking to them
___ 89. Collect information; assess needs; do academic research and writing
___ 90. Analyze; dissect
___ 91. Diagnose; organize; classify; identify elements, relationships, structures, organizing principles, cause-and-effect relationships
___ 92. Group; perceive common denominators; solve problems; determine, figure out
___ 93. Review; evaluate; screen; critique
___ 94. Other analytical skills ____________________
____

Machine or Manual Skills

___ 95. Design; build; construct; assemble; set up; install
___ 96. Handle; possess manual dexterity; possess finger dexterity (as in typing, etc.); perform handicrafts

___ 97. Do prevision work; use tools; operate machinery
___ 98. Fit; adjust; fix; repair
___ 99. Cook; perform household skills
___ 100. Other manual skills ______________________
____

Athletic, Outdoor, Traveling Skills

___ 101. Possess motor skills, physical coordination, and agility
___ 102. Be skilled at general sports or in a particular game
___ 103. Be skilled at swimming, skiing, backpacking; camping; outdoor survival; planning outdoor activities or travel
___ 104. Possess horticultural skills; cultivate; landscape
___ 105. Farm, ranch, work with animals
___ 106. Possess oceanic interests; handle boats; navigate
___ 107. Other athletic skills ______________________
____

After you've completed the inventory, leaf through it again and look for any patterns. Do your skills cluster under certain categories or are they scattered throughout the exercise? You might notice where your skills marked *S* or *SI* have been developed. On the job? In volunteer work? As outside interests?

If your *S* marks have mostly to do with your job, and your *SI* marks have to do with free-time activities, is there any way you can get more of your *SI*s into your paying job, or would you prefer to keep them where they are? What has kept you from further developing those skills you've marked *I*? Lack of confidence? No opportunity in your present career?

Keep these inventory results handy; you'll use them several more times in the following processes.

EXERCISE FOUR
Reliving Your Most Satisfying Accomplishments

In this exercise, you will recall five situations from your past in which you feel you accomplished something really worthwhile. These may have occurred at any time in your life. Be sure to choose situations that gave *you* real satisfaction, not just ones that earned you kudos from family, friends, and teachers.

- One young woman, at the age of eight, found an abandoned kitten—scrawny, sick, and so fearful that it scratched anyone who tried to help it. The girl took it to the vet and, following his directions, nursed it back to plump good health. Not surprisingly, this woman now works with animals in an ecology education project.

- A man tells of how he stood up to teachers and a school principal who had accused his friend of vandalism and persuaded them that the friend was innocent. The man is now a lobbyist in Washington, DC.

- A banker tells of how she set about to convince several graduate schools of business to admit her without a bachelor's degree—and two of them accepted her.

Work with one situation at a time. As with the childhood dream, close your eyes, allow the situation to become very real to you, then write a detailed narrative of one or two paragraphs. Describe what you actually did from beginning to end, what your feelings were along the way, and what family, teachers, and friends had to say about it (if anything).

After the description is complete, there are several ways you can work with it:

1. Go back through your Inspired Abilities Assessment list, and write the number of each activity that was in-

volved. When you complete the descriptions of your other accomplishments, you can compare numbers and see if the same abilities were involved in two or more accomplishments.

2. If the accomplishment involves working with people, complete Exercise Six, "How Do I Want to Work with People?" and list any numbers that apply. When you have completed all five accomplishments, compare the numbers listed for each to pinpoint your most fulfilling ways of working with others.

3. Ask a supportive friend or family member to pretend to be a news reporter interviewing you about your accomplishment. This person can ask you about the who, when, what, why, and how of your accomplishment, why it's important to you and others, and all sorts of television interview show questions. Put the results on audiotape.

4. Sum up in twenty-five words or less why this accomplishment meant so much to you.

Give yourself sufficient time to fully complete all instructions for all five accomplishments—several days or a week. And do push yourself to do all five. Two or three accomplishments may come to mind right away, and it's tempting to stop with them; however, if you dip deeper into the well of your memory, you may discover situations that you may have hidden away because you felt no one cared or because they didn't square with your conscious sense of who you are. These less accessible accomplishments may yield even more valuable and subtle insights than the obvious ones you dealt with first.

When you are finished, compare and contrast all five accomplishments. What inspired abilities run through all of them? Which accomplishments have elements of surprise?

EXERCISE FIVE
Favorite Activities Graph

This exercise is great if you don't like to write essays and your childhood memories are spotty. Just take a lined piece of paper, and along the left margin, jot down fifteen things you love to do in your life right now. Dig deep to get all fifteen, because again, the ones you reach for are often the ones that contain enlightening surprises.

Now make vertical columns across the paper, and fill in various ways you want to evaluate these activities. Here are some examples:

- How many days (weeks, months) since last done?
- Job-related or recreational?
- Expensive or cheap?
- Alone, with one other person, or with a group?
- Exciting or soothing?
- Risky or safe?
- Dealing with information, people, or things?
- Fast- or slow-paced?
- Physical, mental, emotional, or spiritual?
- Carefully planned or last-minute?

Look over your graph. What are the major groupings of your most favored activities? This simple chart can give much information not only about your preferred ways of spending time but also about your personality, your financial requirements, and the lifestyle you prefer.

EXERCISE SIX
How Do I Want to Work with People?

Part One

Rate each of these ways of working with others on a scale from *A* to *D* (*A* = best; *D* = don't like at all).

___ 1. Influence the attitudes/ideas of others
___ 2. Gather information through direct contact with people
___ 3. Help people with their personal problems
___ 4. Instruct others in various tasks or skills
___ 5. Confront others, present them with difficult decisions
___ 6. Supervise people in their work
___ 7. Manage the work of others, be responsible for their output, even though not in direct contact as a supervisor
___ 8. Investigate people by obtaining information about them
___ 9. Provide service to others
___ 10. Organize others, bring people together in cooperative efforts
___ 11. Mediate between contending parties
___ 12. Make decisions about other people
___ 13. Socialize with people and study their behavior
___ 14. Understand people and study their behavior
___ 15. Teach or advise people about something I know well

Part Two

Check any of the following statements that apply to you.

___ 1. I want to be part of a working team
___ 2. I want to have people seek out my help or service (come to me)
___ 3. I want to seek out other people (go to them)
___ 4. I want to see different people every work day
___ 5. I want to work with the same people for a long period of time
___ 6. I want a lot of contact with a small number of people
___ 7. I want brief (one-time) contacts with a large number of people

___ 8. I do not mind being interrupted by people, to be on call as their needs require

___ 9. I like to be able to regulate my own hours, decide when people will see me and when I can get away from them

___ 10. I want to get to know a group of people through regular contact (e.g., retail sales)

Exercises Seven and Eight below move beyond a discovery of your inspired abilities and begin to place your talents in a total context of your desired lifestyle, values, goals, and motivations. They help you answer the questions, "What is really important to me? How can I design my life to best meet my needs and those of my family? How would I like my job to fit into it all?"

EXERCISE SEVEN
Clarifying Your Values

Listed below are seventy-two alphabetically listed qualities or activities that people value. Take a sheet of paper and head three columns: Always Valued, Sometimes Valued, Never Valued. As you read through the list, copy each value under one of the three columns. Work rather quickly on this exercise; don't ponder. You want to discover what you value today; you may change your mind tomorrow.

1. Acquiring
2. Adventure
3. Authority
4. Autonomy
5. Beauty
6. Belonging
7. Challenge
8. Commitment
9. Competition
10. Contributing
11. Control
12. Cooperation
13. Creativity
14. Curiosity
15. Duty
16. Effectiveness
17. Excellence
18. Excitement
19. Exploring
20. Fairness
21. Family
22. Fast pace
23. Friendship
24. Gentleness
25. Growth
26. Health
27. Helping
28. High earnings
29. Honesty
30. Humor
31. Independence
32. Individuality
33. Influence

34. Intimacy
35. Knowledge
36. Leading
37. Location
38. Making decisions
39. Manipulating
40. Mastery
41. Moral fulfillment
42. Physical challenge
43. Potential
44. Power
45. Public contact
46. Quiet
47. Recognition
48. Risk
49. Security
50. Sharing
51. Social challenge
52. Spirituality
53. Stability
54. Status
55. Strength
56. Structure
57. Success
58. Supervising others
59. Time freedom
60. Tranquility
61. Trust
62. Understanding
63. Uniqueness
64. Variety
65. Wealth
66. Well-being
67. Winning
68. Work surroundings
69. Working alone
70. Working with others
71. Working on frontiers of knowledge
72. Working under pressure

Look at the items you have included in each column. Do they form any subclusters? For example, are there several having to do with how you relate to people or ideas or money? You might want to use different colored highlighters to mark related values. How many of your always-valued qualities or activities are in your life right now?

Date your list. When you get a job offer, return to it and make sure the job will make a positive contribution to your value system.

EXERCISE EIGHT
Create a Sky's-the-Limit Fantasy Day

You get to imagine your most outrageous dream in this exercise; you'll create a fantasy day, from waking to sleeping, in which *nothing is denied to you.* Here are just a few ideas of elements you might like to include:

- *Your ideal living environment.* Describe your dwelling in detail; then place it in a particular setting.
- *Valuable time spent doing the work you'd most like to do.* What does your workspace look like? What people

would you be working with and what is your relationship to them?
- *Recreational activities you'd most enjoy.*
- *The people you most love, relating to each other just as you'd like.*

Since nothing is denied you, remember:

- You can wish yourself endless money, so the job you have doesn't need to be lucrative.
- Space is collapsed, so you can travel instantaneously. You can design clothes in Paris in the morning and collect shells with your kids near the Great Barrier Reef in the afternoon.
- Time is collapsed. You can invite famous people from the past for tea and conversation. You can even add extra hours onto your day to include all important activities.

Now evaluate your fantasy day. Does it include your most cherished inspired abilities? Does it reflect your most valued qualities, which you discovered in Exercise Six? Is it consonant with your career style, which you looked into in Exercise Seven? If not, why not? If you brought any famous people into your fantasy scenario, why did you include them?

There's a serious reason for this marvelous flight of fancy. It is a truth widely observed that people are limited much more by lack of confidence and fear of failure than they are by the objective circumstances of their lives. Is there any reason why you can't achieve this dream (or a reasonable facsimile of it) in the future—if not all on one day, then different parts on different days or months or years? Save your description of your ideal day, or the part of it that means the most to you, in your journal and reread it occasionally. Hold it as a goal to shoot for. Dreams that seem totally unrealistic at one time in our lives can definitely materialize a few years down the road. Desires and yearnings, if taken seriously, have great power. Set yours in motion today.

Ten Truths About You

Now sum up what you've learned. Write down the ten most important insights you've gained about yourself from these exercises. (Push yourself to think of at least ten, but don't limit yourself to ten.) Write them each succinctly in twenty-five words or less; fewer words often mean more clarity. Put an *X* by those truths that you've always known and the exercises have confirmed. Put an *O* by those truths that have come as a surprise.

After completing these exercises, you probably have some new ideas about yourself, you see in a fresh light some truths you've always known, and you're beginning to envision the kind of job you might want and how it would fit into your preferred lifestyle. Now's the time to begin to explore the real world through reading, talking to people, and perhaps a short-term job or two that will test your interest in a particular field. This is called career research, and it is essential to your finding not just any job but the best job for you right now. You may be tempted to rush through this step and register with your nearest employment agency. Don't do it! You need to allow yourself a period of uncertainty, uncomfortable as it may be, to collect information and move gently toward a right and growth-full career move. The next step for you: a period of creative floundering.

For Further Reading

Bolles, Richard N. *The Three Boxes of Life and How to Get Out of Them: An Introduction to Life/Work Planning.* Berkeley: Ten Speed Press, 1980.

Bolles, Richard N. *What Color Is Your Parachute?* Berkeley: Ten Speed Press, 1991, updated annually.

Breidenbach, Monica E. *Career Development: Taking Charge of Your Career*. Englewood Cliffs: Prentice-Hall, 1989.

Crystal, John C., and Richard N. Bolles. *Where Do I Go from Here with My Life?* Berkeley: Ten Speed Press, 1980.

Figler, Howard. *The Complete Job-Search Handbook: All the Skills You Need to Get Any Job and Have a Good Time Doing It*. New York: Henry Holt and Company, 1988.

Sher, Barbara, with Annie Gottlieb. *Wishcraft: How to Get What You Really Want*. New York: Ballantine Books, 1979.

Sinetar, Marsha. *Do What You Love, the Money Will Follow: Discovering Your Right Livelihood*. New York: Dell, 1987.

PART TWO

EXPLORING OPTIONS

CHAPTER

3

The Art of Creative Floundering:

Getting Prepared for Your Job Search

Now it's time to place the self-assessment process in a larger perspective—that of your life stage, your life development, and your current circumstances. It would be ideal if you could conduct your career search in splendid isolation, removed from other considerations—and some lucky people do receive just the right opportunity at just the right time. Most people, however, find that they need to make important career decisions just at times when conflicts and changes are occurring in other areas of their lives as well.

Transitions—How to Recognize and Deal with Them

College graduation is one of the biggest developmental watersheds in anyone's life. Commencements are rituals that mark the end of childhood and the beginning of adult life with its new responsibilities. Your parents may make clear to you that it's time for you to start footing your own bills, and the bank will begin to expect repayment of your student loans. And most likely you'll be saying goodbye to the community in which you have lived for the last four years—the physical environment, the network of friends, the familiar adversaries. The genuine spirit of celebration and achievement at college graduation coexists with a sharp sense of loss, a feeling of being cut adrift. This is what makes graduation bittersweet.

Some young people arrive at graduation with a clear idea of what they want to do next. You might have wanted to be a doctor or a banker or an actress from the time you were in high school (or even earlier), and nothing you've learned in college has changed that. Or perhaps your college experience has highlighted certain interests and abilities; you've formulated your goal and you're fairly sure what steps you need to take to get there. If this is you, you might want to skip this chapter, and perhaps the next. You don't need to flounder or experiment, at least not at this point.

For other soon-to-be-graduates, well-meaning questions from friends and family, such as, "What are you doing next year?" or "Where will you be living?" or "Where will you be working?" can seem terrifying. You're soon to lose your identity as a college student and you don't yet know what the future holds. That sense of being anxious and disconnected can continue for many months. And it's just at this time that the world expects the college graduate to get motivated, set some goals, build a network, send out those resumes and launch a career! It may come as a relief to know that your upset is entirely to be expected. It might be a good idea to look at some characteristics of those unsettling transitional periods to get some perspective, so that the career decisions you finally make are as grounded and well-considered as possible.

Transition periods always contain both opportunities and losses. But often it's difficult to keep both aspects in mind at the same time. During so-called positive transitions, such as marriage or a college graduation, the opportunity element is stressed. College graduates are often bewildered by the sadness and disorientation they often feel a few months after commencement, when they're supposed to be enjoying the fruits of their success and energetically launching their careers. During other transitions, the sense of loss is emphasized. It's hard to see the opportunity in being fired or in going through a painful divorce; jobs and family connections are our most important outlets for love and work. They serve as organizing points for our day-to-day energy as well as our future goals and our unconscious yearnings. When they are disrupted in a major way, often there is a huge emptiness, a loss of self-definition and self-esteem, a frightening sense of "what now?" Yet beyond the emptiness there is a tremendous chance for change, for getting rid of aspects of your life that weren't working, for creating yourself afresh.

During a transition, you may feel great pressure from within to make a decision—any decision. Nature abhors a vacuum, and so does the human psyche. If you're passing through an empty spot in your life, very often your anxiety will rise, and you'll be irresistibly tempted to fill the void with good, solid stuff (activities, school, a job) that will give you an instant sense of purpose. If you've suddenly lost your label ("University of Michigan sociology major" or the "Eleanor" half of "Eleanor-and-Harry"), you may find yourself in a rush to pin "IBM trainee" or "first-year law student" on your lapel. But if you haven't taken the time to reconnect with your inspired abilities, to look around a bit in a thoughtful, unhurried way, and see what your best options are, you might find yourself moving full-speed in the wrong direction, becoming more and more invested (but unhappy) in a choice that was impulsive and poorly thought out.

During transitions, other people may pressure you to make a decision. People in transition tend to make their friends and family nervous, especially if the latter are uncomfortable with uncertainty themselves. Parents can press a new college graduate to hurry up and get a job so that they'll be reassured she can finally support herself, so that the family will appear successful, or so that they have proof positive that their child's $80,000 education has paid off. People who are living with someone in the middle of a career change may get impatient if their partner can't make up his mind or won't move quickly enough. Overeager to settle things, they may want to shout "Don't just stand there; do something!"

In a transition, external circumstances may push you toward a premature decision. If your college friends succumb to senior panic and become competitive about their job searches, you may be drawn into the general stampede. You may feel justifiably flattered if a prestigious graduate school accepts you or a well-respected company makes you a job offer; delighted that you're wanted, you may forget to ask yourself if this is what *you* want. Most urgent are pressing financial needs—if you've lost your job or you've recently been divorced, for example—that may compel you to take a job quickly without much prior consideration.

The most productive way to navigate the riffles and rapids of a transition period is to give yourself time. Resist all that internal and external pressure to settle things quickly, to find yourself a secure spot before you're really ready. Give yourself a chance to experience your uncertainty, to flounder. You might actually take out a calendar and label the next six months, the next year, or even the next two years as floundering time. Floundering, in this case, does not mean wallowing in helpless confusion; rather, it means experimenting, sampling, approaching your career decisions provisionally. It means giving yourself permission to be unsure of your career course for awhile as you try on different hats. It means making short-term, temporary decisions rather than long-term, lasting ones. It means taking the time to explore and get your bearings. In other words, feel free to flounder, but do it with awareness and creativity.

Decisions, Decisions!

After the flurry and excitement of graduation is over, you'll probably begin to feel waist-deep in a number of major decisions, of which your career choice may hardly be the most immediate. If you were living at home during college, do you want to continue living there? If you were living on campus, do you want to move home or go somewhere else? Then there's the status of your important relationships to consider. Are you involved in a romance and if so, what does he or she want to do next? What opinions does he or she have about what *you* do next? Do you need money right away and how much? All this is in addition to that overwhelming matter of what to do now that you've grown up.

When you're in this state of flux adopt a strategy of one day at a time and first things first. Separate out the things that have to be decided right now from those that can wait. Try to avoid setting up situations where you'll be overstressed and undersupported. For example, think twice about moving by yourself to a city you don't know and entering a high-powered management training program. Unless you're really clear about your career direction right now, it's best to give yourself some time before entering a fast-track, competitive job. Find ways to test your career interest (see Chapter 4) before making a major time-and-energy-consuming commitment. Feel free to give yourself a year, or even more, to be sure that this is the track you want to follow.

If college itself was stressful and you tend to be overserious, you may want to take some time to have fun. Invent an adventure for yourself: Travel, take a vacation, get a low-level job at a resort area or in an exciting city overseas. Side-stepping the fast track in this way can refresh your mind and body, and enable you to gain some perspective and consider your options in a relaxed setting.

Suppose you've always wanted to live in Seattle or Santa Fe, or the most important person in your life right now has just landed a great job there. You might want to take time to settle into your new city and get the feel of it before you make a major job commitment. A great way to learn the city layout and to get an overview of the kinds of organizations found there would be to sign on with a temporary agency, and ask for assignments of a week to two weeks (more about temp work in Chapter 4). Or better yet, give your city a test run the summer before you graduate.

Whether you're exploring a new community or staying at home, consider taking courses in typing, word processing, or computer literacy, if you haven't already done so. They'll look good on your resume and they're really bottom-line skills in many occupations these days. Even if having your own secretary is one of your career goals, there will be those days when you need to handle your own paperwork. Like a good college record, these basic skills will always be with you and you can use them between jobs while you're exploring new interests.

What About Graduate School?

Graduate school requires a major commitment of money, time, and energy. Many, many college students choose it for all the wrong reasons, and as a result, lose self-esteem, struggle against themselves, and eventually either fail out or burn out. Here are three common, but wrong reasons for going to graduate school:

1. You think a graduate degree will make you more marketable. It may or it may not—but if this is the main reason you're deciding on graduate school, you're missing the point. You need to go back once more and reconnect with your inspired abilities. The rush to become "marketable" in a career that's "hot" in the 1990s is certainly appealing to many new graduates, but ten years later they may well find that they've spent much money

and time getting marketable in a field that doesn't suit them. And few people remain marketable for long in a career they dislike or have no talent for.

2. You're getting pressured from your family, friends, teachers. You may hear a chorus of voices saying "We know you'll be a wonderful doctor (lawyer, psychologist, business person, engineer). Training takes time. Get started right away, before you have other commitments." If you feel annoyed and resistant to pressure like this, pay attention to your inner voice. To sustain and succeed in a graduate program, the desire must come from within *you*, and your family and friends do you no good service to hurry you along. If pressure from others is strong, what you may need, instead of graduate school, is support in breaking out of your family's preset agenda for you, so you can explore your own interests, talents, and desires more freely.

3. You don't know what else to do. If this is the case, what you need is floundering time, not graduate school.

The one and only good reason to go to graduate school: You're fascinated by your subject and you're hungry to learn all you can about it. If you're not hungry to learn anything right now, that's fine. Your interest in the law, for example, may well grow after a year or two or three of experimentation. Take some courses; work as a paralegal. If the law excites you and you can taste the possibilities for yourself after law school, that's when you should think about applying.

And While You're Floundering . . .

Get a Support Group in Place

When it comes to figuring out what you want to do, forget those all-American adages about going it alone and handling it by yourself. You'll be far more able to overcome any uncertainty, confusion, and discouragement that comes your way if you develop your own free consultants' network and cheering section. Your "group" doesn't have to meet regularly. They don't even have to know one another. They should be people who, like you, are excited about your search and are willing to give you moral support and/or practical advice when you need it.

Fill in the rectangles below *in pencil* with names of people whom you usually count on to support you:

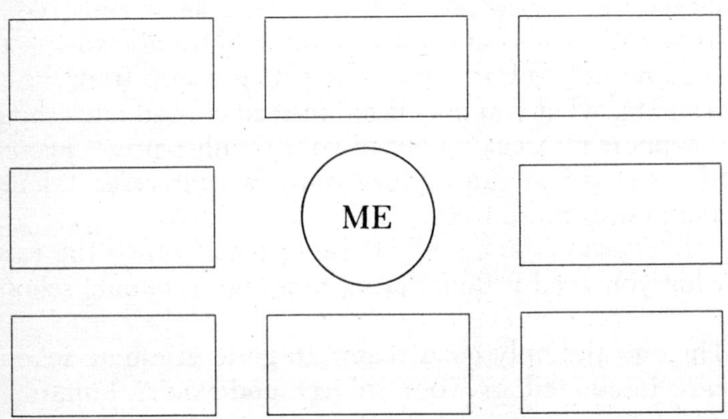

Now look at each name again. Will these people and/or groups really encourage you to grow and change? Or will they give you mixed messages, expect you to measure up to their standards, or perhaps fear that if you change, you'll leave them behind? Bear in mind that as you launch your career you may be shedding an image of yourself that your family and friends are invested in. Or you may be breaking a family or cultural taboo, or escaping the confinement of outdated values and negative thinking. If a so-called supporter constantly tries to talk you out of making changes, or sabotages your efforts the minute they begin to succeed, or is always full of warnings about the worst that can happen, erase him or her from your support list and actively search out a replacement. Here are some good places to look for new supporters:

- Career-changing clinics
- College clubs
- Churches or synagogues
- Classes, lectures, workshops
- Therapy groups or twelve-step programs
- Exercise or sport clubs
- Neighborhood associations
- Volunteer organizations

In choosing supporters, look for good listeners who bypass clichés and combine a positive attitude with a healthy dash of realism. Steer clear of people who are burnt out, who are protecting their turf, who constantly talk about how wonderful *they* are and how easily *they* did it, or who constantly harp on the negatives. It's good, although not strictly necessary, to seek out people who are struggling with the same issues as you, so that you can support them in return. If you're really enterprising, you could even start a specialized support group in your home or local church. Get the word out with a notice on a community bulletin board, a classified ad in a pennysaver or community newspaper, the church bulletin, or by word of mouth.

Take Courses on an Informal Basis

A great boon of the 1980s has been the tremendous growth in opportunities for adult learning—everything from community colleges and learning centers, to special scholarship offerings for middle-aged people at major universities, to tuition-free education for senior citizens. During your floundering period, search out some informal courses (no grades, no tests, no pressure) at a community learning center, and use them for career exploration. They can be actual career courses that teach you how to research a career field, how to find your strengths and weaknesses, and so on. Or they may be skill courses in which you'll learn, for example, how to use a certain computer language. Or you may even take a course that will increase your exposure to a field you might be interested in, such as antiques or advertising.

Courses at a local learning center will be much less expensive than at a university, and usually you can just sign up, with no time-consuming applications. Because they're nonacademic and practical, they'll be more easygoing and fun.

If you opt for a job-hunting clinic, you'll be informing yourself about the career-counseling resources in your community, and meeting people who are also in the job search and might be great for your support system. If you take a course in order to explore a new field, you'll be testing your compatibility with the field. (Are these my kind of people? Are the values, interests, and concerns expressed here ones I can get excited about?) The instructor may be a good link to other people, information, or even job opportunities.

Seek Out Role Models

Role models are as necessary for growing adults as they are for growing children. If someone else has started medical school in middle age or has founded an at-home business while caring for small children, so can you. Have friends introduce you to their friends in the fields you're exploring (more about formal networking and approaching people for information interviews in Chapter 5). If you're trying to get started in a new community, search out people just a little older who have gotten a bit of a foothold. Read biographies of people who have been successful in the career areas you're considering. Actually, most biographies are inspirational tales of people who found creative ways around insurmountable obstacles and snatched victory from the jaws of defeat. Reading the life story of anyone you admire will do wonders for a sagging morale.

The Intelligent Shopper's Guide to Career Expertise

Do not hesitate to hire an expert to help you through the floundering period if your support group is small, if you remain stubbornly stuck and indecisive after a reasonable length of time, of if you just feel more confident and directed with an expert on your side. Your sense of the problem will determine what sort of help you'll want. If creative blocks or fear of success or need to separate from your family are adversely affecting your career growth, you might opt for psychotherapy, individual and/or group. For people who need know-how in the nuts and bolts of information gathering, resume writing, and interviewing, a career counselor may help them focus their research and job hunt. Actually, the best-qualified career counselors will do a little (or a lot) of all of the above. But there are more than a few who will do little except take your money. Here are some tips for picking your way through all the alleged "career services" on the market and finding the people who can really help you.

Start with Your College Career Office

If you're a recent college graduate, you may be quite familiar with your college job placement or career development office, or you may not have used its services at all. The good news is that your college's career services are still available to you, even after you've graduated. Be sure to reacquaint yourself with them.

College career and placement services vary widely in size, scope, and quality, of course. Some contain wonderful and complete career libraries; others are bare-bones. Some are free or charge nominal fees for their services; others are expensive. At any rate, a quick survey of what your college offers may be worth your while for a number of reasons. Most important, your college may provide you, as an alum, with assessment and counseling for less money than a career counselor you might pick out of the phone book. The Smith College Career Development Office provides alumnae with in-person counseling sessions with a trained staff member for a small fee; phone appointments are free (the caller pays the toll). At the very least, your college could recommend a career counselor or two in your area or could supply you with names of alums in your community who might be willing to talk to you about their job experiences. Here are some services college career development offices may offer:

- A career reference library
- Aptitude and interest testing as well as interpretation
- One-on-one career counseling or referrals to career counselors where you live
- Lists of job openings
- Seminars and workshops, either on campus or in your community through your college club
- Articles about career trends written by staffers and published in your alumnae magazine
- Computer searches and printouts of all alumnae in your area in a particular field who have said they'd be willing to talk with other alums about their jobs
- Reciprocal services with a college career office at a university near you

If you live in a college or university town, call their career office, even if you didn't attend the school. Sometimes colleges make their career libraries, or even their counseling services, available to the public in the town where they're located. This is more likely to be the case if the community is a small one.

The Proper Place of Vocational "Testing"

One of the things you might be tempted to do if you're feeling unclear about your direction but pressed to get on with your job search is to opt for a battery of vocational tests. After all, spending $1000 on a whole bunch of different assessments will surely point you to some definite career, right? Not necessarily. Testing may be useful—or it may be exactly what you *don't* need. At any rate, you need to approach it with realistic expectations. Here are some things to think about before spending your savings on vocational tests.

Even the most seemingly comprehensive test system will give you only indications, hints, and partial answers. The very word "test" implies a black-and-white conclusion, a judgment, a final answer, and if you approach vocational testing looking for definite and complete answers about what you "should" be doing, you may be misled rather than helped. Unfortunately, the expensive battery of tests reinforces the mistaken notion that by the time you're finished with so many hours of tests, you should have discovered a life goal and taken your first step toward it. The term vocational "tests" is a misnomer—they'd be more accurately referred to as indicators or assessors or measurements.

Vocational tests are far from the objective indicators they're purported to be. Many tests are only as good as your mood on the day you take them. Others are old-fashioned and strongly male normed. In addition, it is in the nature of tests to put you in pigeonholes and categories. This may be fine for some people, but for others this kind of categorizing may be just the opposite of what they need. If you're trying to shed some old ideas about yourself, a test result that seems to confirm "the old you" may be disheartening.

Testing without counseling and interpretation is at best useless and at worst harmful. All those pages of printouts and raw scores will be confusing and misleading unless you can discuss the results at length with a knowledgeable and sensitive career counselor (more about selecting a career counselor later on in this chapter). A human being can do what a test sheet and a computer can't—factor in your personal, family, and socioeconomic background, your past work experience, your desires and dreams. Instead of starting with the tests, it may be better to get a connection going with a counselor who you feel really understands your personal situation and will suggest what, if any, tests would be most useful for you. Some counselors have their own assessors or indicators that they've created for their own clients, and which they consider more incisive than the standardized ones.

You might not be the type of person who warms up to the testing process. Perhaps you don't like seeing data sheets that are supposed to describe you. Or you would rather do your assessment by yourself at this point, rather than having a counselor or a testing service employee present you with a lot of rather self-revealing material.

If you decide to take one or more standardized assessors, shop around for reasonable fees and all-inclusive counseling. Your college career development office may offer a testing-plus-counseling package you can afford, so check with them first. If a commercial testing center is asking for a lot of money, research the center carefully. Make a list of the kinds of tests and what they measure, and try to get an independent evaluation. How much counseling will you receive afterward? Ask for references, and make sure you'll be getting what you pay for.

What to Look for in a Career Counselor

A good career counselor can be one of the most valuable members of your support group. She can give you relevant tests and help you interpret them; she can hook you up with resources in your community; she can get you focused, keep you researching, and help you sort out information. She can reveal potentials you never knew you had and suggest shortcuts to realizing them. But bad career counseling—and there's a lot of it—will give you little more than a slimmer wallet. Even in the twenty-five states that license career counselors, it's still up to you to separate the qualified and ethical career coaches from those who prey on your insecurities and charge huge fees but don't deliver much. Depending on where you live and the counselor's credentials, $50 to $100 an hour is fair. A $3,000 package, paid up front, is exorbitant.

Watch out for aggressive, prefab sales pitches filled with promises—particularly tempting if you're unemployed—such as "We'll do your resume, coach you on calls and interviews, provide at least three executive contacts, and get you a job within three months at a 20 percent higher salary." Reputable counselors never make such guarantees; they know a well-thought-out job search can take a long time.

Steer clear of organizations that won't say anything over the phone but require you come to their offices to discuss fees and programs; once you're there, they may pressure you into signing a contract for pricey services. Also avoid employment agencies that pose as "career advisers" and try to force-fit you into slots in their clients' companies, and resume services that promise advice but lack the know-how to counsel wisely.

One thing a good career counselor can give you that books can't is step-by-step, individualized coaching plus follow-up. On a first appointment, for example, a counselor would encourage you to describe your career goals or your current discontent, while listening for patterns that reveal your personality, aspirations, and the way you deal with work, authority figures, or coworkers. The counselor may notice that a self-described "people person" really loves research best, or that a terrific fund-raiser is miserable because the environment is wrong. Experience-honed instincts, though, are just the tip of the counseling iceberg. Your coach may offer specialized know-how such as:

1. Insider's knowledge of the local job market. In many cities, counselors are in touch with local business people and know which industries and companies are financially healthy, which are growing, which are cutting back. Some consultants actually employ labor-market specialists who can supply clients, for an hourly fee, with a written report on the need for, say, advertising salespeople in the San Francisco area.

2. Negotiating unusual arrangements with your employer. Counselors well versed in the latest labor-market trends can coach you on negotiating a better deal for maternity leave or for working fewer or irregular hours.

3. Individualized interpretations of aptitude and interests tests. If you're unsure of what you want or a current job feels very wrong, coaches often offer standardized tests for personality types, interests, and aptitudes. These indicators point up whether you'd shine in management or thrive in creative work; whether you crave structure or chafe under "stupid rules," whether you think with a mathematician's precision or a poet's flair. Good counselors won't hand back raw test results without tying them in to your specific situation.

4. Focus and encouragement during your search. Studying careers to find the ones you might enjoy may be the most daunting part of a job hunt: poring over books and articles, asking strangers for information, going on interviews, and hitting dead ends can be frustrating. A counselor can focus your search so that you can find pertinent information in days instead of weeks.

Shopping for a Career Counselor

Begin by gathering referrals from friends and people you trust. The best recommendation, of course, is from a satisfied client whose needs are similar to yours. If that effort doesn't turn up any good names, send for the free Catalyst Career Development Resources brochure, which lists selected career services nationwide (send a self-addressed, stamped envelope to Catalyst, 250 Park Avenue South, New York, New York 10003). Or check the Yellow Pages under Career & Vocational Counseling. Another good source may be a local college's career development office; it might have a cross-country referral network. Career experts often hold job seminars at adult learning centers and community colleges; participants can get an idea of the counselor's personality and approach for the cost of an evening.

Once you've got some good possibilities, make a list of questions (Are you licensed? Do you give tests? How long have you been in business? What's your basic approach?) and information you want to get across about yourself. If you're just starting out or haven't yet found a satisfying job fit, you may want to spring for aptitude testing. Make sure counselors include personalized follow-through, not just a list of scores. If you've narrowed your search to two or three fields but need help gathering information, ask the counselor how he has helped clients in your situation.

When making preliminary phone calls, compare services, prices, and packages. Be sure to speak to the person who will actually counsel you (not just a salesperson). Make certain that you feel comfortable, not pressured. A counselor should ask questions about your needs and offer insightful comments. Many counseling agencies offer a short, free information session. This gives prospective clients and counselors the opportunity to sound each other out and test personal chemistry. Be sure to ask about this possibility when you call; if the counselor says that this is not part of her policy, be sure that she will answer enough questions over the phone to give you a sense of who she is and what her services are.

Credentials. Although good career consultants aren't

necessarily psychotherapists, someone with a Ph.D. in psychology or a master's in social work (M.S.W.) is obviously better qualified to handle personality assessments or help with "people skills." Experts with these degrees tend to charge more, but your health-insurance plan might cover psychologically oriented counseling. Equally qualified consultants might have a master's degree or doctorate in education (M.Ed. or Ed.D.) or have started out as teachers or guidance counselors, with strengths in teaching new skills and attitudes. Some coaches have an M.B.A. and/or extensive business experience in personnel, management consulting, or executive search. They often know the realities of business—what kinds of people are promoted, how to influence decision-makers, how to position yourself. A counselor who combines all these disciplines is a real find.

Assessing fees. Some consultants prefer to deal with clients on an individual basis, charging by the session, pay-as-you-go; standardized tests may cost extra. For example, a counselor may charge $150 per two-hour session, with the expectation that within four or five sessions, you'll have a solid body of information and self-knowledge to continue on your own. It's advisable to get a time estimate from any counselor who charges by the hour. A good question: "How many sessions do most of your clients feel they need to get the help they're looking for?" Also check your counselor's telephone policy; is she willing to give you a quick tip on a salary negotiation or a job interview over the phone at no charge, the way doctors do with their patients? Some counselors encourage this; others don't.

Then there's the group or workshop approach to career counseling. Many counselors offer a series of classes in packages ranging from about $40 (for a half-day workshop) to as much as $8,000 (services this expensive do most of their business with corporations). The trick here is to find packages that are flexible enough to meet your needs. Many career counselors that offer package workshops have a range of services and fees: You might take a three-hour group workshop for $40 (including self-assessment, career overview, and how to decide on a career change) or a twelve-hour workshop (including testing, information gathering, how to conduct a job campaign, negotiation skills, and access to the firm's library) with unlimited one-on-one follow-up for $1500. With services costing more than $1000, be sure you've checked the counselor's reputation and have a written contract outlining specifically what's included. You may be able to start with a low-cost workshop and upgrade to a more expensive one if you like the counselor's approach and feel you need more.

Forming a working partnership. In evaluating the help you're getting, it's useful to know that working with a career counselor doesn't exempt you from the extensive research and legwork necessary for you to choose the best career course. Counselors often talk about how clients arrive with an expectation that somehow the counselor will do it all for them; a more helpful approach would be to look to form a partnership with your counselor. Expect to do about two hours of "homework" for each hour in session. This may include journal keeping to pinpoint inner motivation and goals, library research and reading, contacting people for information by letter or telephone.

Since career counselors are not placement agencies, don't expect them immediately to link you up with people who can offer you a job. Many reputable counselors don't offer contacts at all, feeling that to do so may short-circuit your own learning, building, and networking efforts.

Learning to think differently about your career is like changing your image of yourself; it takes some courage to open your mind, absorb and evaluate your counselor's suggestions, and implement the ones that seem right to you. A professional can get you started, but it's up to you to muster the assertiveness and motivation to take the process all the way.

Self-Assessment and Job Search via Computer

You can also take advantage of computer technology to aid you in each phase of your job search, from PC programs for self-assessment and resume writing to databases that link you electronically with job openings. This area is sure to grow as people invent more varied electronic shortcuts to career information. Here are some examples of the different sorts of programs being offered now.

Discover is a program available at many colleges and university career centers and also at public libraries with career divisions. Discover can provide you with extensive information on 450 occupations. It also provides information on over five thousand schools—two- and four-year colleges, technical schools, and graduate schools. It can also inform you about financial aid, military programs, and help bolster your job search skills. You can use Discover as a source of information only, or you can create your own user record. If you choose to interact with the computer, it can help you through a step-by-step process of career decision making, gain more knowledge about your abilities, interests, and values, find occupations or schools that match your personal characteristics. To use Discover, you usually make an appointment for computer time and use it for several sessions. You can store your information under your Social Security number and retrieve it again for up to six months.

If you have your own personal computer and are a little computer literate, you might look at Career Navigator, a comprehensive, computer-based job search program. It consists of four discs and an easy-to-follow manual which will take you from self-assessment all the way to salary negotiation. It administers assessment tests and interprets your answers. It identifies your skills. It gives you instructions for networking and coaches you to prepare for interviews. It guides you in writing letters and resumes. And it stores all your input for future reference. If you prefer to work in peace and quiet on your own rather than with another person, it's like having an electronic career counselor. You can purchase Career Navigator to use on your IBM-compatible PC by telephoning 1-800-345-5627. The cost for college students is $95.

Your college career development center can participate in several programs that can deliver your job qualifications to actual employers. KiNexus, a job candidate information service developed by the College Placement Council and Information Kinetics, is being used at six hundred college career centers around the country. You supply extensive information about yourself, your skills and experience, and the kind of position you're looking for (full-time, part-time, summer job, internship) either on a disc or on a written form. Your college career office electronically transmits this information to a database that's available to many employers. The system allows the subscribing organizations to scan the database to find the kinds of students they're looking for. KiNexus is virtually free to you and your college—the employers pay for the information.

There are two hundred college career services on the supplying end and two hundred employers on the receiving end of Connexion, an electronic career/graduate school network from Peterson's, the company that publishes Peterson's career guides. All you need to do is to fill out a form and give it to your college career office, which then mails it to Peterson's for inclusion in the Connexion database. You can use Connexion to search for graduate schools, summer jobs, internships, and full-time, postgraduation employment. If your college career office doesn't offer Connexion, you may call 1-800-EDU-DATA for registration forms. Both KiNexus and Connexion are available to older alumnae and career changers as well as new graduates.

Joblink is an employment information system that is now providing current job listings electronically to sixty major western U.S. universities. Students and alumni can check the Joblink system for possible job openings via computer at any college career office tied to the system. All they have to do is to enter certain criteria into the computer, such as occupation and location desired, employer size, industry, and experience level. The job openings can be printed out from the computer to be included in binders for the career development office or to be announced in bulletins written and sent to off-campus alumni. Check your career development office to see how many and which of these services they subscribe to. Their big benefit is that the services are virtually free to the colleges and students using them.

For Further Reading

Bernard, Susan, and Gretchen Thompson. *The Job Search Strategy for College Grads: The 10-Step Plan for Career Success.* Boston: Bob Adams, Inc., 1984.

Snelling, Robert O., Sr. *The Right Job: How to Get the Job That's Right for You.* New York: Penguin Books, 1987.

CHAPTER 4

Mini-Jobs That Test the Current

For some of you, the self-assessment process may be like a wonderful "aha!" that confirms what you've always known about yourself or that puts you quickly in touch with the career areas you wish to research. For others of you, however, self-assessment generates more questions than answers. Even as you're becoming clearer about your strengths and weaknesses, your skills and values, you still find yourself in the fog when you try to imagine what actual, real-life job would suit you. This is because most jobs are essentially a mystery, except to the people doing them. How do accountants, market researchers, and fund-raisers really spend their time, and how would it feel to us if we did the same? To get a sense of how hidden and private jobs really are, ask yourself if you have a clear picture of what your father, mother, or partner does each day. Chances are you have only the most general notion of how even the people you're closest to spend their time at work.

To make matters more complicated, the same basic job can be done in an enormous variety of settings. You may want to do accounting, for example, but do you want to do it for a brokerage firm, a ski resort, a department store, a university, or a religious organization? The surroundings, the pace, the values, the people, the atmosphere will be entirely different in each.

Of the three ways to do career research—reading, talking to people, and gaining hands-on experience—only the last, actual time doing a job, gives you the rich, multifaceted experience of immersing yourself in a particular work environment and seeing how the activities and skills there fit with your inspired abilities.

Fortunately, there are ways to test the current in a particular career field or work environment, to get on-the-spot experience, without making the one- or two-year commitment of a full-time job. The most popular opportunities are summer jobs, internships, temporary work, and volunteer work. Because these positions are relatively low level, are temporary or part time, are done for little or no pay, and are usually relegated to young people or beginners, they're often considered throwaway jobs, ways to kill time or earn some pocket money in between semesters. (Prize internships, often hotly competed for, are the exception.)

Actually, the flexible, temporary nature of these mini-jobs makes them full of hidden opportunities. Some or all of them can give you the chance to:

- Sample a work environment or a number of work environments
- Learn or brush up on important work skills and people skills
- Meet and work with people who can give you perspective on a career field
- Gain college credits while working
- Make contacts with people who might know of full-time jobs
- Work with people who can get to know your work and recommend you for a permanent job or graduate school
- Explore a new city or a different part of the country for a limited time, without commitment

- Support yourself while you search for a full-time job
- Test a new career field while continuing to work full time at your current job
- Show what you can do for a company that might later offer you a full-time job

Because these jobs require less commitment than a full-time position and are usually of limited duration, they provide great opportunities for experimentation. If the mini-job experience is a good one, you'll have plenty of positive examples to cite on your resume and some people you can use as references. If the temporary job did not go so well, nothing much is lost; in fact, much can be gained from a less than ideal job experience if you spend some time on after-the-game analysis—figuring out what went wrong and why.

Getting the Most from Your Mini-Job

Actually, the comparison of a part-time job to a scientific experiment is really quite an apt one. You'll learn a great deal from even an average summer job if you plan in advance, set goals and objectives for your experiment, monitor your experience as it develops, and evaluate it when you've finished.

Set It Up Early

There's no need to panic or give up if the summer's upon you and you still don't have a job or internship; many good internships remain unfilled and people often discover excellent opportunities at the last minute. Bear in mind, though, that if you can plan in advance, some of the best career experience occurs before you're even offered a job. Targeting the jobs you'd like most, preparing resumes slanted toward those jobs, writing cover letters, and interviewing—all this is great warmup for your first full-time job campaign, but with much less pressure.

To get your pick of the most tempting summer jobs and internships, begin your detective work in the late winter or early spring. (Prime time for submitting internship applications is between December and March for the following summer, but feel free to apply up to the last minute.) Here are twelve effective ways to start job or internship hunting:

1. Go to your college career office, let the staff know you're looking, and get to know their resources and how to use them.

2. Ask your friends, their parents, your parents, and their friends (more on networking in Chapter 5).

3. Type a classified ad and post it on a bulletin board in your dormitory or any centrally located college bulletin board, on your father's or mother's office bulletin board, on your church bulletin board, on your neighborhood bulletin boards.

4. Print your classified ad in the college newspaper or the local pennysaver press.

5. At your public library, college library, or college career office, check out whichever directories and reference books the librarian recommends. There are many of them and they're constantly being updated. Good places to start: the books listed in this chapter's bibliography and the appendices at the end of this book (more on job research in Chapter 5 and Chapter 6).

6. Check the "Career" or "Employment" or "Reference" shelves of your local bookstore for any books on summer jobs or internships.

If you're looking for a job or internship in a specific city:

7. Check out directories of employers in the geographical area, such as *The California Job Bank*.

8. Get your hands on a telephone book (the Yellow

Pages) in the city that interests you for a good overview of the organizations in that area.

9. Scan the articles and "want ads" in newspapers and local magazines of the city of your choice for names and addresses of possible employers.

10. Telephone the chamber of commerce in the city where you would like to work. They have names and addresses of area businesses and nonprofit organizations, as well as information on the services or products each provides and the number of people each employs.

If you especially want an internship:

11. Look at directories of companies offering entry-level training programs. Organizations that hire new graduates may look favorably on interns. Most of these publications give contact names and addresses.

12. Check your bookstore or library for specific books that list internships; see this chapter's reading list.

Be Clear What You'd Like to Get Out of Your Mini-Job

At the same time you're conducting your search and seeing what's out there, clarify what you'd like to get out of your summer or part-time position in addition to money. You may have general or specific, few or many objectives, depending on your age, how long you've worked, and what your work experience has been to date. If you're a college student and this is the first time you're using a summer job to test for a future career or lifestyle, some objectives might be:

- To work for a small business (a bank, an advertising agency, a real estate agency, a public relations firm) and see how it is run

- To see what it's like living and working in San Francisco (New York, Miami, Chicago)
- To work for an environmental or nature center, perhaps one that is doing some experimental research
- To hang around a summer theater or a city symphony at its summer home
- To see if your love of children would actually translate into a career with children—in other words, would you like to work with a lot of children all the time?

In thinking about what you'd like to learn from your part-time or temporary experience, consider that there are three elements to work—content, process, and meaning.

Content of a job is the individual tasks, what you actually do. You might, for example, want to learn more about running a restaurant, including preparing and serving food.

Process refers to how and where the job is done and under what circumstances. Preparing and serving chicken and ribs at a loud and fast-moving country-and-western restaurant is an entirely different experience from preparing and serving nouvelle cuisine at a quiet museum garden restaurant near splashing fountains. Process includes atmosphere, pace, kinds of people involved, aesthetics, and many other variables.

Meaning refers to the *raison d'etre* for the job. The meaning of a country-and-western restaurant may be to give people a lively time and good chow. For an elegant restaurant, it may be to give people good food and a quiet, tasteful aesthetic experience. For some people it's important that their jobs have some sort of larger meaning, that the jobs and the organization stand for something they believe in. To others, it's more important that the job be challenging and fun.

After you've listed your objectives, evaluate them with a realistic eye. Most of these temporary, trial jobs require a fair amount of scut work, but some jobs permit you to be close to the action and some don't. It does make a difference whether you get to watch the actors rehearse while you sweep the theater, or whether you're glued to a busy switchboard and find that all you've done all summer is to say "Manick, Cross and Lowly, Inc. How may I help you?"

Some jobs for young people (camp counseling, teaching children) do allow for variety, interaction, and a fair amount of responsibility. In others, such as office work for a law firm or a bank, your actual duties may be routine. The primary bonus of such jobs is that you do get to sample a particular work environment and see how you feel about the pace, the people who work there, the values that are implied by what goes on around you.

When you interview for your job, figure out what sorts of opportunities you'll be given by asking specifically what your job duties would be. If you're eager to have a particular kind of experience that might be a little beyond the province of a beginner, ask tactfully: "Do you think I would have an opportunity to try my hand at article writing?" If the answer you receive is vague, don't push. Evaluate the job on its merits. If you decide to take it, you can look around for opportunities after you begin. Bear in mind that supervisors have most likely done their fair share of gofer work, and won't look favorably on young people who think they're too good to start at the bottom. See if your college career office can help you square your personal goals with the kinds of opportunities you can reasonably expect. Or find out who had the job last year, if you can, and call him or her for an appraisal.

Monitor Your Job as You Go Along

A good way to do this is to start a career journal. If kept faithfully (or even sporadically) over the years, it can be a key tool in career building. Your journal is your ongoing log of how the job was for you. A couple of paragraphs two or three times a week would probably provide an excellent record. Things to note down: actual tasks that you do each day, your differing moods about the job (Are you stimulated? Bored? Energized? Angry? When and why?), activities you like, activities you hate, feedback and interactions with your boss and colleagues, any praise or criticism you receive.

You'll be amazed how helpful your career journal will be when it comes time to write a resume and and your memories of summers past have grown dim.

Evaluate Your Experience

After the job is over, give yourself a couple of months to gain perspective, then read over your career journal. It can be better than a standardized interest or personality indicator in showing what you're good at doing, what fires you up, and what you loathe. You might want to take it to your college career office or a career counselor and ask for their opinion of what your reaction to this particular job says about you. It may give you and them valuable insights into what you should and shouldn't be doing when you start to work full time.

Which kind of mini-work experience is best for you depends on your current age and status, whether you're a college student or a career changer, where you live, what your personal and financial circumstances are. Here's a breakdown of the most common part-time/temporary work experiences useful for career sampling, how to find them, and how to make best use of them:

Summer and Part-Time Jobs

Most young people have had summer or part-time jobs since high school. Because these positions tend to be low-level, require relatively simple skills, and have little to do with what the high school or college student will eventually be doing, these beginner jobs are often taken for granted. What can a future teacher learn from busing tables, or a future banker from working in a boutique? The answer: a lot! It's easy to sleepwalk through a routine beginner's job, but if you remain awake and aware, your summer or part-time experience can reveal many new insights into your inspired abilities (what turns you on, what environment energizes you, what people you like to work with, and how). Here are four categories of ordinary low-skill jobs—the kind thousands of young people find each summer. If you have one of them now (or have had in the past), here's what you can discover.

Restaurant work (waiting tables, hosting, busing, bartending) gives you an opportunity to learn:

- In what way you prefer to work with people. Do you like constantly reaching out and making contact with people you will never see again? Are hard-to-please customers a challenge or a strain? Do customers respond quickly to you? Do you get good tips compared to your colleagues? Do you care whether customers like you? If you thrive on this sort of brief, social interaction, you may be ideal for certain sorts of service work—selling, resort work, leisure-time activities. If you find the social relating of restaurant work exhausting and unsatisfying, you may prefer to work with facts or ideas, or to develop deeper connections with people in which substantive information is exchanged.
- What kinds of people you like to work with. Are you particularly solicitous to old people or to children? Do you enjoy waiting on groups of men discussing business over lunch? Do you love waiting on families? Are you particularly bothered by fussy snobs? People who throw their money around? Loud, tactless people? Do you notice table manners? The answer will give you valuable clues to the kinds of people you want, and don't want, in your work environment.
- How you like dealing with the unexpected. What's

your reaction to the Saturday-night crowd? Do you enjoy the challenge of taking care of ten busy tables at once, keeping everyone happy? Do you thrive in situations that threaten to get out of control? Or do you prefer low-key, controlled situations where you have time to think and plan what needs to be done?

- Whether you enjoy working as a team. Are you a good manager of time and people? Do you like supervising and training others?
- Whether you enjoy being physically active. Do you feel most alive when you're bustling around, running from place to place, or would you rather sit still when you're working?
- Whether aesthetics are important to you. Does it matter that you're working in a beautifully appointed restaurant, presenting food beautifully arranged and prepared, or don't you care? How important is the ambience where you work?

Working with children (camp counselor, lifeguard, babysitter) gives you an opportunity to learn:

- Whether you enjoy working with children and how you work best with them. (If you want to be a teacher, it's a good idea to have these kinds of jobs on your resume.) Is the best part teaching the children (giving them instruction and seeing their swimming or pottery-making skills develop); relating to them (consoling Bobby after he struck out); or managing them (getting every single camper out of the tents in sixty seconds on fire-drill night)?
- Whether you like solving logistical problems (involving things and people). Was it a disaster when the sky opened up and the hot dog buns got soaked—or was it kind of fun? Do you like the challenge of figuring out what to do when things go wrong? If not, you may prefer solving problems with ideas or words.
- How you feel about the out-of-doors. Were gorgeous

sunsets and sweet air worth sleeping on the hard ground when the air mattress collapsed and someone lost the insect repellent, or did you long for a luxury hotel?

- How you feel about dependence. Did you like it or loathe it when fifteen small campers crawled all over you and relied on you for answers?

Retail sales (clerking in a large or small store) gives you an opportunity to learn:

- What kind of business person you are. Did you increase sales volume? Design displays that brought in customers?
- Where you are about business values. Do you like figuring out better ways to sell products or services and make a profit? Do you get a high from a big sale? How do you feel about selling someone something expensive when you're not sure they need it or can afford it?
- Whether you enjoy or detest the orderliness involved with keeping records and handling money. Did your register always come out to the penny and were your sales slips always in order at the end of the day? Did you take pleasure when they were? Or does money and paperwork confuse and irritate you?
- What part of business interests you most. Suppose you're working in a small stationery store. Do you most enjoy (a) making the sale; (b) giving people information about what they might buy, educating them, figuring out their needs, and giving them options; (c) keeping the store going—making sure the shelves are stocked, getting in touch with manufacturers about orders; or (d) training and managing others in the business?

Office work (receptionist, clerk, secretary, assistant) gives you an opportunity to learn:

- How to use organizational, secretarial, and detail skills to complete various projects.
- Your favored way of working with people. Do you like working alone, with one other person, in a small group, in a large group?
- Your preferred stress level. Do routine tasks soothe you or bore you? Do you find office crises and last-minute problems energizing or anxiety producing?
- Your optimum level of physical activity. Does sitting at a desk for long periods of time make you restless or do you enjoy work that's mentally challenging but physically quiet?
- What values are important to you. What does your office stand for? Is the meaning of your work important or unimportant to you?

Internships

"Internship" is a grab-bag word that encompasses many different work–study arrangements that companies, governments, and communities make with students and other people who wish to participate in this learning experience. Some internships are full time for a summer; others are part time during the school year. Some are arranged through college career offices, faculty advisers, or various academic departments, and allow students to earn college credit; others do not. Internships can be negotiated by students themselves, who agree to work for little or no pay in order to get firsthand experience in a specific career (often a creative and/or competitive one, such as television or filmmaking).

What all internships should do is provide that extra measure of on-the-job experience that will add a practical dimension to your college coursework and give you an edge when you go after a full-time job in your field. Internships can also give you a chance to see how the theoretical information you're amassing in your college courses applies to real-life situations. Although the internship has been around for years, it is an option that became immensely popular among the practical, career-oriented students of the 1980s. According to the National Society for Internships and Experiential Education in Raleigh, North Carolina, 20 percent of undergraduate college students are taking part in internships during the academic year, up from just 3 to 4 percent a decade ago.

Colleges, companies, and interns themselves all find some value in these work-for-learning arrangements. Students or career changers get to test what a real job would be like in a field of their choice. If you don't like your internship, you can redirect your focus. If you enjoy the work, you'll have pertinent experience for your resume, a chance to make important contacts in the field, and perhaps a shot at a job offer. Although some companies feel that internships serve the student more than the business, others relish the chance to dip into the pool of possible employees ahead of time, to pretest new talent without making a long-term commitment. Lesser benefits for businesses: Students fill in for regular employees on vacation and will spread the good word about the organization if they find their summer slots worthwhile and challenging.

Pay for internships ranges from zero to considerable; some blue-chip companies and high-tech firms offer interns nearly as much as their new full-time employees. Because of the intense competition for choice spots, students often need to start their search for an internship several months before they're ready to begin (more lead time is advisable if you're going after a blue-chip company).

To be sure your internship is worth the pay differential, make certain the organization is offering you a real opportunity to observe, learn, and participate, not just a job as a file clerk or errand runner. If you will be receiving college credit, work closely with your career office or student adviser to design a program that best fits your own needs and those of the employer. Find out all you can about the organization you'll be working for. What specifically will you be expected to do there? How will you be evaluated for credit? Be sure the total number of hours you'll be working adds up to the number you'll need for credit (this seems obvious, but misunderstandings among colleges, students, and companies do happen). On your in-person interview with the company, make sure you meet and talk with the actual person who will be instructing and evaluating you. Does he seem eager to have an intern, or is he taking you on reluctantly, by a supervisor's request? Has he had good experiences with interns in the past? You might have a struggle getting a good evaluation from someone who's sour on the whole internship idea. To get a true picture, talk to students who have had internships at that organization in previous years.

After you have been offered the internship, but before you've actually started, it's a good idea to work with your college placement office or adviser to write up a specific three-way agreement, or "learning contract" (see sample) to present to the company where you'll be interning. Ask them to look it over, be sure it's realistic, make whatever changes they think are necessary, and then sign it. A learning contract, worked out thoughtfully in advance and agreed to by everyone involved, should forestall any misunderstandings that could ruin your learning experience—and your semester. Use the contract to make any special interests known to the person who is hiring you. You might, for example, ask to spend a few days in each department to obtain an integrated picture of what goes on in the organization.

Sample Learning Contract

Name: ________________ **Social Security No.:** __________
Campus address: _____________________ **Tel:** _______
Home address: _______________________ **Tel:** _______
Address while on internship ____________________
Telephone while on internship ___________________

• **Job Description:** Describe in as much detail as possible your role and responsibilities while on your internship. List duties, projects to be completed, deadlines, and so on, if relevant.

• **Supervision:** Describe in as much detail as you can the supervision to be provided. Include what kind of instruction, assistance, consultation, and so forth, you will receive, and from whom you will expect to get it.

• **Evaluation:** Note when, how, and by whom your work performance will be evaluated.

• **Learning Objectives:** List what you intend to learn through this experience. Include the specific internship goals you established.

• **Learning Activities on the Job:** Describe how your internship activities will enable you to meet your learning objectives. Include whatever projects, research, report writing, seminars, interviews, and so on, you will do while working, relating them to what you intend to learn.

• **Relationship to Academic Work:** Specify how you can apply what you've learned in the classroom to the internship.

• **Agreement:** This contract may be terminated or amended by intern or internship supervisor at any time upon written notice, which is received and agreed to by the other party.

Intern's Signature ____________________ **Date** ________
Supervisor's Signature _________________ **Date** ________
Adviser's Signature ___________________ **Date** ________

Even if your job yields token pay, behave as professionally as if your position were permanent. Be on time and dress appropriately. Observe, learn, and be discreet; don't get involved in office politics. Bear in mind that temporary people are much resented if they pass on gossip. You'll also be resented if you try to change or upset the status quo. Even if you think people are being ridiculously inefficient or wrongheaded, keep your thoughts to yourself and try to figure out the real reasons why things are not working better; if you do, you'll learn much about how organizations work. Keep personal phone calls, photocopying, and other office privilege to an absolute minimum, no matter what other employees do. Concentrate on being helpful and friendly. Get to know your officemates; have lunch with them, find out what they do. Because you're just starting out, no one will expect you to know a great deal. This is your chance to ask as many questions as you like. Take full advantage of it.

Temporary Work

Another very useful way to sample different work environments and perhaps get yourself in front of people who would hire you full time is through temporary work. Temping has some terrific advantages. It can help pay the bills while you wait for the full-time job you really want. It can give you a summer "working tour" of a city where you may want to relocate after graduation. You can fit informational interviews, job interviews, or unpaid, part-time internships in between two- or three-day-a-week temp assignments. Finally, if you ask your temporary service to focus your jobs on a particular field, you can make contacts and sharpen appropriate skills as you search for the right spot.

Temp agencies have traditionally filled slots for receptionists, secretaries, bookkeepers, word processors, research assistants and paralegals, and banking and brokerage aides. Today, temp work has taken on a wider dimension and specialized temp agencies now fill highly skilled and professional positions for lawyers, accountants, managers, and computer and human services personnel. If you are a beginner, the better you are at standard office skills—typing, shorthand, word processing, and computer literacy—the more you'll be paid, so if you decide you want to go the temp route, you might want to take an office skills course beforehand. Some temp agencies will train you, but only after you've worked awhile for them—usually the equivalent of about six months full time.

Since the quality of temp services (and the amount they'll pay you) varies from city to city, do some research before you register. Read a month's worth of Sunday papers from your chosen city, and check want ads for temp services with many offerings in your preferred field. Your college career office may have suggestions about such services, too.

Telephone the most promising agencies. Ask if they have many clients in your area of interest, and whether you may limit your assignments to that group. Does this service offer a group health plan, as many do, if you sign on for, say, a minimum of three months? Are there training opportunities? If the service seems responsive, make an appointment to register and have your skills evaluated. You might want to register at two or three agencies to make sure you'll get steady work; as time goes on, you might find that one is more reliable and easier to work with than the others, or you may continue to take assignments from all of them.

If you're hunting for a full-time job while you're temping, don't make the mistake of relying solely on contacts made through temporary work to lead you to it. Occasionally an employer will offer a temporary worker permanent employment, but not often enough that you should count on it. In fact, to protect client companies from being besieged by job seekers, temp services will probably ask you to sign an agreement *not* to seek a regular spot from companies where you temp. Technically, you must wait for an employer to approach you, so if you spot an opening while temping, use discretion and good judgment to avoid jeopardizing your agreement. You might ask circumspect questions about openings ("What skills are involved? What are the job's requirements?") to signal your interest without actually stating that you want to apply. When your temp assignment ends, indicate interest without violating your contract by saying "I've enjoyed working here and would be glad to return at any time."

Temp agencies also ask workers not to use their clients' names on resumes or give them as references, because they don't want their clients bothered, and because they want to keep their clients' names confidential. However, if temporary workers want to list the service as the reference, most services will pass on evaluations from clients to possible employers. If you have a potentially good reference from a prestigious client, you might request permission from your temp service to ask for a direct recommendation. A good gambit for researching a particular company or getting your foot in the door is to ask the company's personnel department what temp agency they use, then go to that agency and ask to be assigned to that company.

One of the trickier aspects of temporary work is to decide what length assignments to take—they can be as short as one or two days and as long as several months. Be aware of the tradeoffs. Short stints fit more easily around your job campaign, but one or two days won't be adequate for making contacts or truly demonstrating your skills. Long-term assignments may boost your visibility and references, but you'll see a limited number of firms. Also, you may get stuck in a back room where you can't really observe the company or meet the people. Ask your temp agency whether they'll allow you to quit if you dislike a job, and if they'll be willing to arrange time off for you if you have a job interview.

Another caveat: Be sure your temp work doesn't sidetrack you from career goals. If you're not clear what you're really looking for in a full-time job, you may be overly quick to take a job that is offered to you by an employer for whom you've been temping. The fact that the company is pleasant, or you like the people, or you're flattered to be hired may persuade you to take something that's not exactly what you were looking for. Then after a few months you may realize that this isn't the position that you want, and you've lost time.

Volunteer Work

Volunteering shares many of the benefits of interning and temp work: It can be done for a limited period, it can be fitted around a full-time job, it can help you make contacts and add substance to your resume. Furthermore, the willingness to do unpaid work for a cause you believe in makes a powerful statement about you that potential employers are likely to notice and respect. In many parts of the country, there's a growing sense among organizations that volunteerism is good for the community and should be encouraged. In fact, as many as five hundred blue-chip companies actually have volunteer offices to encourage their employees to participate, and some organizations offer released time from work for volunteer activities. If you work for one of these companies and are considering a career change, this opportunity might help you take a giant step in your new direction. One thing is certain: There is no lack of volunteer jobs and the learning possibilities are endless.

Most people volunteer because they want to lend a hand for a worthy cause or because they want to meet people who have similar values. But your volunteering can give you career credentials as well. What you need to do is to survey possible volunteer jobs with an eye to what you want from the opportunity, not just what you'll be giving.

The best way to get a bird's-eye survey of the volunteer opportunities in your area—there are more than you can imagine—is to contact your local United Way. The people there can put you in touch with your community's services to find you a volunteer job. You're in luck if your community has a volunteer center; these clearinghouses match volunteers with jobs, usually with the help of a computer database. There are almost four hundred centers nationwide; they can be found in all major cities. Look in the white pages of your telephone book under "Volunteer Center," "Volunteer Bureau," or "Voluntary Action Center."

At most of these centers, you'll make an appointment to go in and fill out a detailed form. Your interviewer—a volunteer, of course—will explain the opportunities, ask you what you want from your job, and help you zero in on the positions most interesting to you. When considerations such as your schedule, your geographic preference, your education, skills, and interests are all tabulated, the computer comes up with four or five carefully matched suggestions. If you're vague about exactly what you want from your volunteer experience, a skilled interviewer can help highlight your abilities and interests and direct you, much as a career counselor would. It's best, of course, if you have a general idea about areas to explore, but allow yourself some flexibility to recognize and consider intriguing alternatives.

If you do want to go for one of the jobs suggested, the volunteer center may make the contact for you; that way you're a screened candidate, not an unknown person making a cold call. All of this advice-plus-matching is free to you.

If you prefer to approach a not-for-profit agency on your own, keep your tone professional by submitting a resume with a cover letter, then following up with a phone call in about ten days. Keep in mind that organizations that use volunteers are often underfunded and understaffed, and their volunteer coordinators are usually part-time volunteers themselves. Therefore, don't be offended if it takes them awhile to return phone calls and schedule interviews. They do need your help, so gently persevere with follow-up phone calls until they notice you. Volunteering in general will demand you be self-motivated. There isn't always adequate staff for careful supervision and direction, so you'll have to see what needs to be done and take the initiative to do it.

On your volunteer interview, be sure you make clear what you want from the experience, always bearing in mind that beginners get beginning work and the most exciting and prestigious tasks are given to volunteers with seniority, as is true on any staff. Just because you're donating your time doesn't mean you won't have to prove yourself.

Assess your volunteer coordinator or direct supervisor as you would any boss. If there doesn't seem to be a personality fit, it might be better to offer your services elsewhere. Look around at the other volunteers as well. Are they your kind of people? What's the emotional climate and temperature where you'll be working? If it's not to your liking, somewhere else will be.

Five Ways to Increase the Value of Your Mini-Job Experience

1. *Ask for feedback.* Request an appointment with your supervisor every month or so to discuss how you're doing. Ask for both positive and negative reactions to your job performance: The affirmation that you do certain tasks well or are learning quickly will give you a confidence boost, and negative comments will get you used to hearing and assimilating criticism and making corrections. Hearing about the downside of your performance is never easy, but learning to take criticism of your work and evaluate it objectively is a prime criterion for success in any field.

2. *Interview the people around you about what they do, especially those people whom you admire or whose jobs interest you.* Just say something simple like, "Your job seems so interesting to me. Would you mind explaining to

me exactly what you do?" People always like to help newcomers and talk about themselves, so you won't have any trouble getting information. Your curiosity will be noticed, and since you're there only on a temporary basis, people may be more forthcoming and less threatened than if you were a full-time employee.

3. *If things get slow, look for ways to make yourself useful.* Go to the person whose job interests you the most and volunteer an afternoon of assistance (with your supervisor's permission). If you sit around twiddling your thumbs till business picks up, you'll lose the opportunity to prove you're a self-starter.

4. *Reach out to other people around you—but in the context of getting the job done.* Beginning workers usually make one of the following errors: focusing totally on the job task and ignoring other people, or socializing at the expense of the job. The best solution is to do both at once. Offer to pitch in and help if a colleague has a difficult task. Get to know people as you work with them. You're sure to be rated, formally or informally, on how you get along with others.

5. *Start a contact file and keep it for the rest of your life, updating it as you go.* A contact file is simply a box of 3 x 5 or 5 x 8 cards, each devoted to a person you've worked with whom you want to remember. File them alphabetically by the person's name or the name of the company, or by year. On each card, write the name (check for correct spelling), title, address, and telephone number of anyone who has been important to you in the career area. This might include your supervisor, a higher-up for whom you did a special project, someone in a beginning spot who helped train you and show you the ropes. On the card jot down how you happened to meet this person, what you did for him, any words of praise or advice he gave. Later on when you need a recommendation, an informational

interview, a lead for a full-time job, you'll have all the data you need to write a gracious letter ("Dear Dr. Vane, You may remember that in the summer of 1989 I helped you with Project *X*"), or to call your pal ("What's her name? Oh, yes—Cynthia . . .") in the production department and tell her you're looking for a job.

6. *Before you leave your temporary work, be sure to ask for any recommendations and to collect work samples.* They'll be much harder to round up once you've moved on.

For Further Reading

Bauer, Betsy. *Getting Work Experience.* New York: Dell, 1985.

Eisenberg, Gerson G. *Learning Vacations*, 6th ed. Princeton: Peterson's Guides, 1989.

Fry, Ronald W., ed. *Internships.* Hawthorne, N.J.: The Career Press, 1990.
Volume 1: Advertising, Marketing, Public Relations, and Sales
Volume 2: Newspaper, Magazine, and Book Publishing
Volume 3: Accounting, Banking, Brokerage, Finance, and Insurance
Volume 4: The Travel and Hospitality Industries

Jobst, Katherine, ed. *Internships: 38,000 On-the-Job Training Opportunities for College Students and Adults*, Cincinnati: Writer's Digest Books, updated annually.

PART THREE

Conducting a Search

CHAPTER

5

Basic How-To's of Career Research

People often approach their job hunt with a general idea about what they have to offer ("I'm a good communicator who likes a fast pace") and a general idea about what a particular field is like ("Advertising seems like an exciting, glamorous area for a good communicator"). Then they take the first job they can get with an advertising agency and end up unhappy. Why? Because they haven't taken the time to research the field, the company, and the job in enough detail to see how well it suits their unique personality, goals, values, and abilities.

Time spent collecting information *before you even begin a job search* is key in finding the spot that will offer you the richest possibilities for growth. But it's easy to convince yourself to bypass this most important process. There are a number of reasons for this. The main one is that when people want a job, they usually want one quickly. They may have pressing financial needs. They may feel insecure until they locate a source of income. They may have an idea that successful, marketable people get jobs fast, and people who remain unemployed for months probably aren't as desirable as employees. Think of the people you know who got jobs right after graduation or within two weeks of job hunting. Although they're usually considered especially talented or very fortunate, they may have been searching in a field that hires large groups of people at a certain time of year. Nevertheless, if your friends are hired quickly, this may increase the pressure you feel—from within and without—to get your resume in front of people who have jobs available and can hire you right now. The process recommended in this book suggests a different allocation of your time and energy, which leads to a far better job fit, a more growth-producing career start. And because it stresses the building of a supportive group of people who have talked with you and who know what you're looking for, you'll be able to tap that hidden job market, that great majority of all available jobs that are never advertised and that are filled through word of mouth and personal recommendation.

The surprising thing is that this more efficient and educational process takes no more time than the less effective but more traditional send-out-a-hundred-resumes-and-cover-letters approach. Job campaigns usually take from six weeks to eighteen months. The two diagrams below assume a campaign will take a year; they show the more efficient and the less efficient allocation of that time.

Begin job search; Send out mass mailing	Waiting time; a few interviews	Finally take a job because you can't wait any longer
Day 1	6 months	1 Year

Research, informational interviews	Decide on area	Make contacts; send out resumes; many interviews	Select the best job offered
Day 1	6 months		1 Year

Another reason the career research process is often abbreviated or skipped over is that it tends to be time consuming and anxiety producing. It may involve library visits, reading, note taking, telephone calls, evaluating material, sending away for information by mail, writing individual letters and waiting for replies, arranging interviews. It can also be confusing: Where do you start? It can lead you down blind alleys: You've spent three months learning everything you can about advertising, only to discover you'd loathe the field. And the research process contains many of the same discouraging moments you experience when you're job hunting; you assert yourself to meet someone who you're sure will be full of information, only to find she doesn't have a lot of time, or doesn't know a lot, or couldn't care less about you.

However, if you're willing to dive in and do your homework, and stick with it, thorough career research will yield you four big bonuses:

1. Specific, detailed information about jobs, companies, people. What are the many things people actually do in the field you're exploring, and how would your skills fit in? How does Organization *X* differ from Organizations *Y* and Z, and which would be better for you? What are the concerns, values that drive the people and organizations in this field? Mastering this information—or at least knowing enough to ask the right questions—takes time, but it will be crucial to your success on job interviews.

2. Two-way exposure. Information interviewing gives you the opportunity to visit and evaluate work sites and talk to the people who are doing the jobs you might want. And they get to meet you, give you feedback about the usefulness of your skills and talents in their industry, and perhaps pass you on to other knowledgeable people. Furthermore, you get a morale boost each time you get a new piece of information or meet an interesting new person.

Exploring fields, companies, environments is like doing field anthropology, and you'll find that ultimately no contact is wasted.

3. Experience in how to get along in the working world. Career research, like job hunting, will help you develop valuable skills you'll use on the job. The very process of networking, presenting yourself to strangers who might help you, accepting positive and negative feedback, packaging your skills and ideas attractively, and dealing with all kinds of people are wonderful warmups for job interviews as well as powerful training for holding your own and promoting yourself in the day-to-day work environment once you have the job you want. Furthermore, you'll be starting to master these skills on informational interviews with "easy," friendly people who are friends of friends, and who will already be favorably disposed toward you.

4. Enthusiasm and a feeling of finding your spot. As you collect information and get closer to the organizations and jobs that are right for you, you'll find your enthusiasm, curiosity, and energy increasing. You'll find you generate good questions and retain information easily. You begin to feel you've found your world, the people and work situations that interest you. And you'll bring this combination of knowledge and excitement to job interviews, greatly increasing the chance that you'll be hired.

Actually, career research needn't be all drudgery. It can be fun if you give yourself the time you need and approach it in a fairly systematic way. And common sense dictates that you start with a broad survey of possible fields and jobs, then narrow the focus as you compare possibilities and eliminate options.

It's not the purpose of this book to give a complete rundown of the many career fields out there—that would be an impossibly large task—or even to talk about "the hot careers of the nineties." Careers that are hot one day can be stone-cold the next, and anyway, the only hot careers for you are the ones that really excite you and draw you in.

It is useful, however, to have an overview of the work world—a place to begin, a way to see how your abilities and interests would mesh with the jobs available.

Fields and Functions—An Organized Way to Think About Careers

Here are a few oversimplified but helpful generalizations about the business world that may provide some clues to finding your niche.

Generally, any organization that pays people to work for it is selling or promoting a product, a service, an idea, or a combination of these. This is just as true of nonprofit organizations as it is of profit-making ones. Products are usually concrete and tangible—cars or snack foods or trips to Bermuda. Service organizations do something for their "customers," such as provide them with an education (schools and universities), or give them a chance to improve their physical health (medical group practices, health clubs, spas). Religious institutions, organizations that protect the environment, and political parties promote ideas.

The term "career field" refers to the kind of product, service, or idea that's being promoted. Examples are travel, insurance, banking, aerospace, health care, public relations, real estate, theater, consumer protection, and so forth.

"Functions," on the other hand, cut perpendicularly across all fields. In other words, the activities in any organization, regardless of field, are divided roughly into nine functions. They are sales, marketing, creative, production, finance, management, policy and planning, human resources, and support. All of these functions are necessary in some form or another for a business to create and sell its product, service, or idea. Of course, in the real world these functions are not so clear-cut and do overlap, but for now, let's consider each one separately.

Sales

Very simply, salespeople are responsible for getting the public to buy the product. They must find and contact customers personally, convince them to buy their product instead of a competitor's, complete sales contracts with customers, and follow up to make sure that the company keeps its end of the bargain and that the satisfied customer will continue to buy. Owners of car dealerships, food company reps who take orders at local supermarkets, and the admissions department of a college or university are all salespeople. The nonprofit version of salespeople are fundraisers—the telephone reps who try to sell you memberships to the local art museum or public television.

Marketing

The marketing function serves as a backup to the salespeople. Marketers define the look of the product and how it is presented, decide what people the product should be pitched to, and make sure the product becomes known to the public. Marketing may include demographic research: Which people are most likely to buy the product? How old are they? Where do they live? What is their educational level? Their socioeconomic group? Is the possible customer base growing or shrinking? Why? How many potential customers are there, and how can we reach them?

Marketers also concern themselves with product image. How should the product be packaged in order to appeal to the target market? How should the product be priced? Marketing people work with creative designers and advertising agencies so that the product's appearance is congruent with the way it's packaged, priced, and presented to the public. They arrange with public relations agencies for promotion of the product.

Creative

The creative function can involve artists, writers, musicians, architects, designers, chemists, and design engineers of all sorts. Creative people design the products—from pump dispensers for toothpaste to suspension bridges to laptop computers to a new formula for a pain-reliever to an effective program for teaching adolescents about birth control. Creative people work closely with marketers and production people.

Production

The production people do everything that needs to be done to make the product. Production includes people on the assembly line, their managers, people who buy raw materials and machines for the factory, and the people who package the product and deliver it to the retail stores. In a service industry, the production people are those who deliver the service—the aerobics instructors at a health club, the counselors at an alcoholism treatment center.

Finance

The finance people handle the money. They collect it, borrow it, lend it, and disburse it. They bill for services, keep the books, pay the creditors, and cut checks for salaries and wages, and they keep their eye on budgets and the bottom line. They are the bookkeepers, the comptrollers, the treasurers, the people in the accounting office.

Management

These are the executives who run the company, determining its goals and direction and then structuring the organization to make sure these goals are met. They make the most important decisions, and others in the company are answerable to them. Management includes presidents, chief executive officers, vice presidents, and department managers.

Policy and Planning

These people serve as advisers to management on key issues such as corporate strategy, research, development of new products or services, legal policy, or social responsibility and consumer advocacy.

Human Resources

The human resources people concern themselves with the kind of staff the organization has. They're in charge of finding the best people to hire, supporting and training them, and making it worthwhile for them to stay around. They also help deal with layoffs, firing, and other people problems as they arise. Career development, on-staff training and education, the employee assistance program, and the personnel department are all part of the human resources function.

Support

The support function keeps the business running smoothly and backs up every other department. Support people include office managers, secretaries, the people in the typing pool and the mail room. Traditionally, beginners have started as support people, and still do in many fields.

Here are some further useful observations about fields and functions:

1. *Fields and functions are often confused.* For example, are "advertising" and "accounting" functions or are they fields? The answer is either, depending on the context. For a company that sells a product called mousetraps, advertising is part of the marketing function and accounting is part of the financial function. However, advertising agencies actually sell a product called advertising, and accounting firms sell a product called accounting. Thus, these adjectives refer to the field. And advertising agencies and accounting firms each have the same functions in their organization as any other organization. They must sell, market, create, produce, finance, and so forth.

2. *The larger the organization you work for, the more you'll specialize in one particular function.* It might be your job as a member of your company's personnel department to interview new candidates for job vacancies—one small part of the human resources function. Or you may obtain bids from four-color printers to print a coffee table book of photographs—a small part of a publisher's production function. In small businesses, on the other hand, you may perform multiple functions. A freelance jewelry maker, for example, must purchase his supplies, design and produce his jewelry, decide where to sell it, and keep careful track of his income and expenses. The most successful entrepreneurs enjoy wearing all the different hats, or can hire one or two people to take over the functions that they dislike or are not so good at.

3. *Many jobs—in fact, most jobs—are admixtures of various functions.* There are many support-type functions in any job, whether in the creative department or sales or

marketing—you may need to type your own letters, make out your schedule, and replenish your own supplies. Also, you'll probably be called upon to do some selling, even if it's only to convince your boss to do something more efficiently. No matter what functional department you're in, once you reach a certain level, you'll be concerned with making up a budget and living within it; thus, you must think about finance.

Some jobs, such as teaching school, contain a bit of every function. Teachers "sell" education by making their lessons interesting to their students and convincing parents and the community at large that their programs are worthwhile. They market education by clueing in to how their students think, taking their age group into consideration, and "pitching" the product directly to them. Teachers certainly have a say in the creative design of their product, and they must also manage—keep discipline, determine grades, correct papers, make sure the children have the proper work materials. And if a teacher is head of her department, she must also concern herself with the allocation of funds.

4. *A good way to begin to narrow your career search is to think not only about what field you'd like to work in, but also what function you'd prefer.* Do you like the competitive challenge of selling? The research involved in marketing? Would you prefer to design products or solve management problems or work with numbers? Go back to your inspired abilities list for clues.

5. *A good way to analyze any job you're considering (regardless of the functional area you're theoretically interviewing for) is to look at a job description and see what percentage of the job includes selling, finance, managerial, creative, and so on.* One young woman was very excited about her new job with the internal communications office of a major corporation. Because she was told she'd get to write and edit the employees' company newspaper, she was sure her job was largely creative. But after she began

working, she discovered that the newsletter, which came out bimonthly, was only about 25 percent of her job. The rest of the time she typed internal memos and wrote letters for her boss—basically support tasks. Needless to say, her initial enthusiasm soon waned.

By the way, it's important to know that many beginning jobs, regardless of their functional area, contain a lot of support tasks. Beginners commonly learn about their field by answering phones, writing letters, and so forth for their bosses or for themselves. It's a strange contradiction of the working world that the better newcomers perform these support tasks, the better their chance for promotion, even if what they'll do after they're promoted has little to do with what they did before. In other words, in order to shed the support parts of your job, you often have to prove to higher-ups that you can master them. It's part of the tradition of paying your dues.

The Research Process

Now the detective work begins! As you explore possible career landscapes, you'll find yourself engaged in two main activities—reading and talking with people. The two activities feed each other: As you read, you'll think of more kinds of people you'll want to talk to, and the people you interview can also suggest further reading.

Setting Yourself Up to Succeed

As we've said before, if you're researching career possibilities and then moving into a job hunt, you'll have some stress-filled times ahead. A certain amount of nervousness comes with the territory. But you needn't be overwhelmed by it if you plan your activities in a sensible way and make a point of taking care of yourself. Here are some tips for arranging your life in as stress-free a way as possible.

Plan for your finances. What are your financial realities and what are your options for the next months? Can you live with your parents or with relatives rent-free or with minimal rent until you've completed the job-search process? If you want to move to another town and job hunt there, do you have somewhere to stay? If not, can you postpone the move until you're really ready to look for a job? Make a budget for the next three to six months, with built-in time for reconsideration and revision. The thing not to do here is to talk yourself into taking the first full-time job that's offered just because you're strapped for money. Far better to take a temporary or seasonal job or do part-time work to support yourself. One recent college grad picked cucumbers for a couple of summers while interning for free at a local cable TV station. She had never done any sort of farm work before, and she remembers those mornings in the dew-soaked cucumber fields as intensely enjoyable. Besides, the experience she gathered as an unpaid intern eventually enabled her to find a job in a competitive field.

Plan your time so as to conserve your energy and to allow the learning process to occur. With the help of a calendar, break your information search into manageable tasks with space around them for evaluation, rest, and recreation. Two mornings a week at the library is enough. One interview and two phone calls a day is enough. Writing four or five individualized letters (door-openers, thank-yous, whatever) a week is enough. Get a sense of your own saturation point; when your head is spinning with opinions, advice, or information, take a break. Change your type of activity—stop letter writing, for example, and go over reading material instead. Or quit for the day. Pinpoint activities, such as meditation, exercise, seeing friends, that provide a change of pace and help you unwind and reward yourself with them. Overscheduling yourself may make you feel efficient at first, but you won't be absorbing what you learn and you may be setting yourself up for an early burn-out.

If procrastination is your problem—some people can avoid making career-forwarding phone calls for weeks—work closely with a calendar, and block out specific times for specific activities (Call Mr. Brown Monday at 11:15; scan San Francisco newspapers at library, Wednesday from 3:00 to 4:40). Promise yourself a reward once the tasks are done—a dinner out or a Woody Allen movie. Join a support group and use the peer pressure to get you off dead center. Or get a friend to call you in the morning and urge you along. If you break the wall of inertia and manage to get started each day, your natural momentum will carry you through.

Go with your own learning style. Figure out how you learn best, and then seek out situations and experiences that will help you. Here are some typical learning styles:

1. **Working alone.** Some people absorb material best when they're by themselves. They learn by reading, writing, keeping records, and thinking things through by themselves. If you're one of those people, what you probably need most is a peaceful, quiet place to work.
2. **Consulting one-to-one.** If you learn best by tossing ideas around with another person, you might do well to work with a career counselor. He can steer you through the research process, giving you feedback as you go. If you tend to be a procrastinator, your career counselor can keep you on track with regular "homework" assignments, and support you in anxiety-producing situations.
3. **Working in a group.** If you prefer to learn by listening and sharing in a group, check with local career counselors, career centers, and community colleges for classes, support groups, workshops, and so on. Career groups and seminars can serve many purposes: They can help you break into a new community, expand your contacts, find you supportive people who can play buddy to

you during your job search, and help you make new friends. Also check your college alumnae association or career development office for career nights in your town or for week-long career workshops on campus. Three days of intensive brainstorming with other people in a situation similar to yours can give you momentum that can last for months.

4. Learning by doing. People who learn best by active participation might want to take workshops that emphasize role playing. You'd be able to practice your interviewing skills in a group or even be videotaped for later review.

Getting Into the Material

The most valuable and thorough career research begins with a broad exploration of a number of possibilities, then narrows and intensifies when you discover the specific areas or environments that most intrigue you. When you're ready to switch from information collecting to job hunting, you may even find yourself concentrating on two or three organizations within your chosen field.

As implied earlier, career research is most difficult at the beginning. You're trying to put together a puzzle, but as yet you have only a few pieces. Your early reading and first informational interviews may leave you more confused than ever. You may decide upon a course of action, get excited about it, and then run into some people who tell you it's the worst thing you can do. The more anxiety you're able to tolerate as you amass conflicting advice and information, the more likely you'll discover an area that's really right and true. Stick with it. You'll find that as more of the pieces fall in place, your research will take a particular direction, you'll abandon some avenues that prove less interesting than you thought, and you'll find yourself naturally more engaged and focused in those areas that energize you.

If the research task seems daunting and you're stymied about where to begin, there are several approaches you can take. You can start your research by:

Learning more about fields or functions that interest you. This is the traditional way—to learn more about what accountants do or the different kinds of jobs in hospital administration.

Searching by environment. Do you have a strong visual image of where you'd like to work—a resort with palm trees or a warm, friendly place where you can go to work in casual clothes? Do you have certain values (nonhierarchical decision making, consumer awareness) that you want to be sure are shared by the company you work with? Then first look for organizations within your community that meet these criteria, and find out all you can about them. Next step: See what beginning jobs they offer. Would any of them help you develop skills you've identified in your inspired abilities assessment?

For example, Lee knew she wanted to work in an easygoing environment where people dressed casually and related informally. She preferred being part of a small organization or department to working for a big company, and she needed to be near nature, even if she only got to look out at the trees through her office window. As for her skills, Lee had strong artistic skills and loved photography. She was also interested in educating or counseling people—adults and children—but not in a classroom setting. In time, Lee had identified four organizations in her community that could meet her environment criteria and that offered beginning jobs that could develop her inspired abilities: a small company that made educational videos for sale to schools; a hospital well known for its program for chronically ill children; a travel organization developing a program of walking tours in Europe; a zoo that gave guided tours to school groups.

Following a particular interest. Suppose you've always been concerned about the problem of waste disposal and the environment. Start by learning about where the situation stands today. As you do your research, certain job possibilities will become evident.

Looking to develop a certain skill. You might want to learn more about how to help people manage their money, or how to create a certain kind of computer data base, or how to work with elderly people. Many organizations in many fields can offer opportunities to develop these skills.

Choosing a lifestyle. You might decide that you must be in a city—no small towns or suburbs for you. Or you must have the summer off. Or you must have a commute that's less than a half an hour, or a job that you can leave at 5 o'clock. These preferences are powerful indicators of the kinds of jobs that will make you happiest and in which you will perform best.

As you collect facts, figures, data and details, don't forget to check regularly with your intuitive side. When all is said and done, your natural feelings about a field and a job will be your best guide.

Exploring Possibilities

Reading

Libraries. Your first step is to find a good library, preferably one with a separate career research section. Your public library might be all you'll need. Or see if you may use a main library or a career development library at a local college. It might be worth a trip (or at least a phone call) to your own college if it has an extensive career library. Other places to check: YM/YWCAs or career resource centers (look in the Yellow Pages under "Career and Vocational Counseling" or a similar listing). If you choose to work with a career counselor, she might have a library you can use.

Make friends with your local librarians and ask for their help if you need it. They might be able to guide you to books and other resources you hadn't thought of. The library you choose to work from will be the starting point of many of the research avenues suggested below.

Newspapers. If you already live in the town where you plan to be job hunting, scan the paper regularly for news that may be of interest in your field. Look for feature articles in the general or business section on companies being acquired, agencies expanding or cutting back, people being promoted, new projects being funded. Clip and file these articles; underline the names of important people (they may be future contacts). Also check general advertisements and, of course, the want ads for other clues to who's hiring, who's launching a new product, and so on. Check the book review section for new books that might be of interest; there are many books about careers and the work world these days.

If you're planning to move to a new locale, see if you can subscribe to the newspapers there or look for them at your library.

If you plan a business career, familiarize yourself with *The Wall Street Journal* and the business section of *The New York Times;* most libraries will have them on hand.

Magazines. Valuable information on people, organizations, and opportunities in a given locale can be found in city and regional magazines *(New York* magazine, *Texas Magazine).* Almost all large American cities have their own magazines these days. If you plan to move, subscribe to the magazine that covers your new region.

For business news, the classics are *Forbes, Fortune,* and *Business Week.* And in this era of specialized publications, many fields have popular and professional magazines, both of which may be valuable. If you're interested in clinical psychology or counseling, for example, you might look at both *Psychology Today* (pitched to the general public) and *Family Therapy Networker* (intended for the practicing family therapist). To learn more about photography, you might glance at *Popular Photography* and also at *Photo District News.* If banking's your field, check out *Money* and *The American Banker.* It's from the magazines and newspapers published for the professional that you'll get the best insights into the day-to-day life of people in the field—their rewards, problems, values, and concerns. You'll also learn the latest gossip (which companies and people are on the rise, which are not) and the jargon, the buzzwords, that will signal to others in the field that you've done your homework.

For individual articles on specific subjects, check the *Reader's Guide to Periodical Literature* and other periodical indexes.

Books. There are thousands of books available on every phase of job-search strategy, from resumes to retirement. Also, for every field or area you want to explore, there will be many volumes to dip into. A good book to use at the beginning when you're trying to make sense of it all is *Where to Start Career Planning: Essential Resource Guide for Career Planning and Job Hunting,* seventh edition (Career Center, Cornell University, 1989–1991). Basically a bibliography, this book gives extended lists of books on various fields, plus books on career planning. Another equally useful book for career researchers interested in the public sector or nonprofit organizations is *The Fourth of July Resource Guide for the Promotion of Careers in Public, Community and International Service* (by Devon Smith, Middle Atlantic Placement Association, 1987). As you track down various books on job hunting in specific fields, don't bypass their introductions or forewords. The authors often talk about how they came to write the book and in doing so, acknowledge the books, ideas, and people that inspired and helped them. These personal statements not only provide you with examples of how creative people get things done and how tiny ideas blossom into successful projects, but they also provide you with books to read and names of people whom you might want to write to for advice. Biographies of leaders in particular fields will give you an excellent behind-the-scenes preview of what life as a detective, forest ranger, or fashion designer would really be like. Ask your librarian for biographies of people who work in the areas you want to explore.

Some publishers have excellent series on various career fields and functions. If the ones at your library are incomplete or out of date, note the publisher's address and write for a recent catalog. Also, your local bookstores are good sources; they may have more recent books than your library.

Professional and trade associations. Each profession has at least one, and you can find them listed in the *Encyclopedia of Associations/National Organizations* in the library. Write or call and request free information on training and careers, plus any information on professional journals or newsletters they may publish. You may also telephone the national office of the association and see if there is a local chapter (the local telephone book should tell you, too). Then phone the local chapter and ask whether newcomers or interested people may attend their meetings. Ask about their membership qualifications; some have stringent criteria, others don't.

Newletters. There has been a tremendous proliferation in recent years of special-interest newsletters on every conceivable subject. They're a great source of specialized information and news tidbits found nowhere else. Skim the *Newsletter Yearbook Directory*, the *Oxbridge Directory of Newsletters*, or the *National Directory of Investment Newsletters* (all available at many libraries) to see whether some may be of interest to you. Specialized newsletters often have a high subscription rate, but their publishers will sometimes send potential subscribers a few free copies for inspection.

Telephone books. If you're moving to another city, it would be very helpful to have that town's White Pages and Yellow Pages. Call information for the area and ask for the customer service or business office of the phone company. Then call to find out how to order the phone books. If your new city is large, its telephone book may be on file at your library.

Social service directories. These are usually published by the United Way; they give you a rundown of social service organizations in the community you're interested in.

Chambers of commerce. Another way to explore a new community is to call its chamber of commerce. It will likely have a members' directory as well as information on business growth, local organizations, and housing, most of which will be free.

Individual organizations. If you wish to check out individual employers at this early date, call the company's headquarters and ask for their public relations office. Say you want to know more about their organization and ask for an annual report and any promotional brochures, sales catalogues, press kits, and so forth that they can send you.

Informational Interviews

After you've spent a fair amount of time at the library, reading and gathering together relevant information, you'll find that two or three fields or job areas are increasingly attractive to you. Now's the time to start networking—talking to people who work in those fields, or whose jobs or companies you'd like to learn more about. You'll probably want to have done some reading before you begin your informational interviews for a couple of reasons. First of all, it takes *your* time to set up and conduct informational interviews, and you're asking people to give you *their* time. Therefore, you'll want to have narrowed your focus somewhat. If you've done your reading, you will have eliminated certain career areas or kinds of positions that weren't as appealing as you thought they'd be, and you'll be ready to look more deeply into those that have engaged you. Second, reading will give you enough background so that you'll seem fairly informed, and your questions will be more to the point.

Informational interviews fall into a number of different categories. Peer interviews are talks with people who have the same level jobs that you'd be looking for or who are just a few years ahead of you. Peer interviews are usually informal and easy to arrange, and they're great for finding out what it's like to start out at a particular company, what beginning jobs in a certain field are like, and what skills you need to get them. Informational interviews with busier, more experienced people are sometimes more formal and can be more difficult to arrange. Interviews can also be described as "warm" or "cold." In "warm" interviews, you'll be talking with someone whom you have some connection with already, someone who'll be willing to give you the benefit of his advice because you're a friend of a friend. An interview with a friend of your father or the mother of your roommate is a warm interview: These people already know you or at least know of you. "Cold" interviews are those with strangers or people with whom you have only a distant connection. Interviewing for information takes a subtle combination of self-assertion and genuine consideration, and you may well feel shy at first about contacting people and asking them for their time. The best tactic is to start "warm," with people who are less intimidating to you.

Information Seeking versus Job Seeking

As you begin to make your contacts, be very clear that you're seeking information at this point, and not a job. This is an important distinction because, since informational interviewing became the rage in the 1970s, many people have (unwittingly or on purpose) abused the system. They have contacted people asking for information about the industry ("I'm eager to learn about what you do"), but once on the premises, have put their contacts on the spot about jobs. In some cases, they have even besieged them with phone calls after the interview. This leads the information givers, who, after all, are doing the information seekers a favor, to feel exploited and taken advantage of; they may be glad to give newcomers information, but they have not agreed to be ongoing suppliers of news about jobs openings or to promote the inquirer's job candidacy.

It's easy to see how these misunderstandings occur. Your contact mentions during the interview that some departments at the company may be expanding and with all good intentions, you ask, "Do you think I might be suitable for one of those positions?" You've crossed the fine line between information seeker and job hunter, and you're putting pressure on your contact to evaluate your candidacy. Instead, you might say "What kinds of employees will be needed?" The difference is a subtle one, and you need to be sensitive to the distinction, or you may hamper the growth of your network and contact system. The best way to avoid falling into this trap is to give yourself a sincerity check before you set up the interview. Do you *genuinely and sincerely* want information from this person, or are you really scouting for available jobs? Be honest! If it's a job you're after, one of two things is going on: Either you're jumping the gun and going after a job before you have enough information to know if it's what you want or you have all the information you need, and it's time to change your tactics (see Chapter 6). In any case, it's best to give the matter a little more thought. If you switch tactics in the middle of the interview, even though you don't mean to, you can appear to have approached your contact under false pretenses, which is exploitive—and unethical.

Paradoxically, if you stay in your role as information seeker and manage to favorably impress the contact, she may give you names of more people to talk with and may eventually choose to be your advocate. An appropriate stance to take in a general information-gathering interview is—and you might even use these words in your introductory letter or phone call—"I'm not yet ready to look for a job; I'm in the information-gathering stage." There is more in the etiquette section of this chapter about how your presentation can confirm this stance, and what to do if your contact directly asks you if you're interested in a job.

Finding Contacts

When you first begin thinking about people you could approach for informational interviewing, you may draw a blank. You may not have a list of interior decorators or company travel managers or commodities traders right at your fingertips. However, you'll be amazed, once you start asking around among your family, friends, and acquaintances, how many of them will say "My husband has a friend . . ." or "My college roommate might be just the one . . ." Then you're on your way. If you're at a party or socializing with people at the P.T.A., don't hesitate to ask people you get a good feeling about whether they know of anyone in the fields you're exploring who might be willing to talk with you. Here are some places to network for contacts:

- College career development offices
- College clubs or other social clubs
- Classes, seminars, or workshops

- Therapy or support groups
- Places of worship

These are some people who might be willing to help you:

- Classmates from high school or college
- Spouses or partners of your friends
- Parents of your friends
- Neighbors or neighborhood businesses (your local travel agent, boutique manager, or real estate agent, for example)
- Teachers, professors, or any professional people whom you work or associate with regularly (your accountant, lawyer, doctor, librarian, clergyperson)
- Your career counselor

Another way to make a contact is to write to someone you've read about in a newspaper or magazine. If the paper announces Mr. Brown's promotion or mentions that he's just received an award, you might want to write him, mentioning the newspaper notice. Offer your congratulations, say you're considering a career in his field, and ask if you could speak with him briefly about his career. Approaching a stranger in this way takes nerve, but even important people are flattered by genuine expressions of admiration and enjoy assisting newcomers to the field. Be aware, though, that people who receive major publicity, such as notice in national magazines or big-city newspapers, may be besieged by information gatherers or job seekers. If you receive a curt "no" to your request, this is probably why. You may have better luck with someone you read about in a small-town newspaper.

Setting Up the Interview

Once friends and acquaintances start giving you names, get some organization system in place to store the information. (Later on, when things get complicated, you'll be glad you did.) One way to organize is to keep a supply of 5×7 index cards handy, and start a new card for each contact. A notebook or an entry in your personal computer may suit you better. If a friend or acquaintance gives you a contact name, try to get at least some of the following information right away:

1. The exact connection between your acquaintance and your potential contact. How is this person related to your friend? When did this person last work with your friend's husband?
2. The exact spelling of her name. If your friend doesn't know, call the organization your contact works for, tell the receptionist you want to write Ms. Frantz a letter, and ask for the exact spelling of the name. The correct spelling of a difficult name makes a powerful impression.
3. Her exact title, if possible, or at least her position in the organization. Is this a support-staff person or a decision maker?
4. What is this person like, and how is it best to approach her? Is she breezy or starchy? Would she prefer a letter or a phone call? (Usually phone calls are appropriate for peer interviews, and letters for interviews with more experienced people.) Would your friend/acquaintance be willing to call her and ask if she'd be available to speak with you? (This is almost always a good idea, unless your friend and her potential contact live very far away from one another.)

For the peer interview. To arrange peer interviews, a phone call is fine. Introduce yourself and mention the name of your contact ("I mentioned to Susan Brown, who lives down the street from me, that I'm trying to find out everything I can about entry-level jobs in media sales, and she felt you'd be just the one to talk to.") Briefly mention some salient details about your background by way of providing context, but keep it low key; since this is not a job interview, you don't have to sell your job skills. Then ask if you could drop by her office some day for half an hour or so and speak with her. Depending on her schedule and how the interview goes, you might ask her for a brief tour of the premises: Your intuitive response to the place where she works can give you worlds of information about whether this company or this field will suit you.

For higher-level people. If a friend or acquaintance has given you the name of a relatively high-level person, who might be in the position to hire you or to influence someone else to do so, think about whether you'd like to wait to make the contact until you've done all your research and are ready to move from informational interviews to exploratory (job-seeking) interviews. You don't want to play your trump cards too soon in the process. On the other hand, higher-ups can give you a perspective on the industry that beginning people don't have.

If you decide what you want is an information-gathering session, it's best to do some research on this person's company first (see Chapter 6). You want to avoid taking her time to ask questions that could have been answered by her secretary, a member of the personnel department, an annual report, or a company brochure. Then write this person a gracious letter requesting an interview. Even though you may feel you speak more effectively than you write, it's best to use brief letters throughout this whole process to open the way to communication. A cold phone call can catch a busy person at an inconvenient time, and since this person has never heard from you before, you might get a brusque response. If you experience some shyness and hesitancy in your job search—and almost everyone does—a brushoff is hardly a boost to your self-esteem.

A letter, on the other hand, can be reserved for a free moment when the person has time to read, reread, and think about the information presented, making him more likely to be receptive to your follow-up call. And, because you've taken the care to write him, he may respect your seriousness and invite you to his office, rather than giving you a quickie session over the phone. Also, letters give you more control. You get to make the points about yourself that you wish to, without being thrown off by the flow of conversation. Lastly, the very discipline of writing sharpens your awareness of your goals, your skills, and what exactly you want from this particular session.

The letter should be short (two or three short paragraphs). Begin with your contact's name (first paragraph); then briefly state your relevant background and some positive reasons why you're considering his field. End with a paragraph requesting an interview. "I'd be very grateful if I could have half an hour or so of your time. May I give you a call next week to ask if I might set up an appointment?" Then do so. Be warned: Busy people may want to save time by talking to you over the phone. Lightly press for an office meeting, but if they demur, be gracious about it. Most people won't be able to talk to you at the very moment you call, so ask to make a phone appointment a few days hence. Then you'll have the time to prepare.

Interview Smarts and Etiquette

It's been said before in this chapter but it bears repeating: Informational interviews are not the same as job interviews. You'll want to take a different approach to the person you're talking to. For one thing, *you're* doing the interviewing, the information gathering, so come prepared with a list of good questions. (You might want to type them and leave space between them to jot down answers.) The answers you get from your contact are almost sure to generate other questions not on your list. So ask follow-up questions instead of automatically running down your list. It shows you're listening and that you're flexible. Try not to spend the whole time taking notes, however; eye contact is important. Here are some questions you might consider asking at an informational interview:

- What kind of background, training, special programs, or other learning experiences does one need to enter the field? to advance and be successful?
- Tell me what you do. What tasks take most of your time? How many hours do you work each week? What are your working conditions (pay scale, hours, surroundings, pressure, pace)? How does your position relate to the rest of the organization?
- How did you get into this field and into this position? Are there other ways? How does one advance? Is there competition?
- What special character and personality traits should one have to consider such a career field?
- How do your education and experience relate to what you are doing now?
- What kind of lifestyle choices have you had to make and how do you feel about these decisions? Are you expected to travel? To take work home at night? To dress or speak in a particular way?
- What kind of status, power, and money can one expect at the various levels within the field? Are there other rewards and incentives to consider? What do you find meaningful in your work? What are the frustrations?
- What choices are there within this field and to what types of other organizations can one move? What might I read to better understand the field?
- What professional journals, books, newspapers, or publications do people in your field generally read? Are any professional associations particularly influential?

Use follow-up questions to encourage your interviewee to be specific so you can get as close as possible to the nature of the job. For example, if he says "This work is tiring and exhilarating at the same time," you might ask

"What is a typical day like for you?" or "What is it about your work that keys you up the most?" or "What sorts of specific projects are you working on now?"

Something else to bear in mind: It's not appropriate on an informational interview to sell your skills or showcase your abilities, as you'd do in a job interview. You want to impress your contact favorably, of course, but in a low-key way. You may share information about yourself if it seems to fit in or if you're asked, but it's best not to go on and on. You're not in a competitive situation. Also you'll want to seem a mature, hireable person, so assume a professional manner and stay focused, even if your contact has a breezy, informal manner. This might be more difficult to do in a peer interview, when you might find yourself so "in sync" with your interviewee that you slip into a social mode.

Even if the person you're interviewing throws out some tantalizing leads about job openings, such as, "We may get more funding in the fall" or "Our assistant may be moving to another department," don't press for more information without clear signals of her interest in you. Do not hand her a resume unless she asks for one. You might say, "Would it be appropriate to follow up on that after my research is complete? Whom should I contact?" That way you'll stay in your information-collecting role, and you'll come across as a thoughtful, confident person who wants to do her homework.

Before you leave, *be sure to ask your contact for the names of any other people that it might be useful for you to talk with.* Ask if you may use your interviewee's name when you contact them. This is a most important request, for it expands your information network. Be sure to get the correct spelling and titles of any names and any other information she gives you (see page 117).

Also, take special note of how you left this person. Did she say, "Be sure to let me know what you decide" or "Feel free to call me if you need more information" or "When you start your job campaign, be sure to let me know"? You shouldn't presume that you can continue to phone your interviewee for advice or job leads after the interview without an invitation from her. But comments like this are signals that she was favorably impressed by you, and she's giving you permission to contact her again. If you feel her warmth and interest, you might even ask, "Would it be all right for me to telephone you if I have a specific question?" Or "Would it be all right for me to telephone you for one more piece of advice?" This will be very important when your job hunting starts in earnest.

The Work Site—Take a Good Look

If you're lucky enough to meet this person at her office, be sure to make the most of it. Carefully observing the environment can give you an excellent idea of whether this is the kind of company or field that's right for you. Of course you don't want to snoop around the office taking notes, but read this list over the night before you go, and think about it as you sit in the reception room, walk through the halls, or are given a tour by your interviewee.

Physical Environment

- How did you get to the work site? Car? Public transportation? Is public transportation available? If you drove, was it easy to park?
- In what sort of neighborhood is the work site located?
- Are the people working in an open space or in private offices?
- Are their workspaces decorated? Individually or uniformly? Are there windows? What kind of lighting?
- What is the noise level? The source of noise?
- How is the air quality (stuffy, smoky, air-conditioned)?

- What types of equipment do you see? Is is up-to-date? Who uses what equipment?
- Does the physical environment seem one you could be in for eight to twelve hours a day, five days a week, fifty weeks each year? Is there a place to relax?

People and Atmosphere

- How are people dressed (formally, informally, and so forth)? Does there seem to be a "uniform"?
- Are there more women? Men? What's the age range of the employees? Is there ethnic uniformity or an ethnic mixture?
- How do the staff members address one another? Interact with one another? Does there seem to be a sense of hierarchy?
- Do you have any sense of the stress level? Are people's faces happy, tense?
- How were you treated when you arrived? By whom?
- Did your first impression change after you spoke with staff members?
- Does it feel as though people enjoy working there? Are they enthusiastic? Did they make you share their enthusiasm?
- Were staff members comfortable talking with you, ready to share ideas and impressions, or did they seem to feel restricted in what they could say about the work site?
- How did the conversation flow? Was it interrupted by telephone calls or other employees? Did you have to ask all the questions, or did it become a real interchange of information?
- What have been sources of pleasure or aggravation in your previous situations? How did those situations seem to be handled at the particular work site?

Following Up

It's hard to overestimate the importance of follow-up because it keeps your name and the impression you have made in front of the people you have spoken with. If done with sincerity and enthusiasm, it can land you a job a couple of months down the road. Here are the three main steps in effective follow-up:

1. Record your impressions immediately in some sort of organized form. Don't assume you'll remember what happened; you won't. As you begin to have more and more interviews, the information will be lost or mixed up if you don't write it down. You might use your 5 × 7 index card with the name of your contact to jot down your main information and observations. You may also want to put down the names of the contacts she gave you, so you'll keep track of how you met various people. Automatically date every entry you make on the card—the date of your interview, follow-up note, and so on. Then you'll have a record of just when and how often you touched base with this person. Write down her parting words to you as a cue to how you can follow up. Also make note if you have felt a special rapport with one of your interviewees. You can build on mutual good feelings by keeping in touch by mail.

2. Write a thank-you note within forty-eight hours. Thank-you notes demonstrate your courtesy and ongoing interest, and also keep your name in front of your contact. Your note need only be two or three paragraphs long. You can use the first paragraph to express your warmest thanks, the second to mention which ideas and information were most valuable to you and why, and the third to restate the invitation of your interviewee (if there was one) to keep in touch. For example, you could say: "I much appreciate your invitation to contact you again, and will do so when I narrow my focus and begin my job campaign." If you have written or called one of

the names this contact gave you, you might mention it. "I was especially eager to meet your former colleague Suzanne King, and she was most cordial when we spoke on the phone. I have an interview with her on Wednesday."

3. When the time comes to renew this contact, it's probably best to send a letter. Phone calls are often intrusive and people can feel put on the spot. The attitude to have in network building is: Don't push, don't rush. You'll seem more calm and confident, less frantic, if you use a light touch.

Evaluating Your Informational Interviews

Although some of the people you talk with may be very inspirational, full of encouraging stories and love for their careers, other interviews may be real downers. Even successful people can be protective of their turf, jealous of newcomers, or accustomed to shedding gloom. They can tell you how the economic downtrends are harming their field or how heavy the competition is or how arduous is the life of a banker or a restaurant owner or an architect. Many people take a complaining attitude about their jobs, although their friends know they're devoted to their careers. Also, you may have a particular negative reaction to someone you speak with. You might think: "Well, I thought I wanted to be a hotel manager, but I don't like this person. I would never want to be like him!" For these reasons, it's smart to talk to a minimum of three people in each career field before you write off a particular area of interest. The more people you talk with, the more you balance the particular personalities and biases of individuals and begin to see themes and trends emerge. If several people say the industry is in trouble, then it's more than one person's rainy-day opinion. Even if negative people are highly placed and full of facts and information, keep your contacts with them to a minimum. Instead, cultivate enthusiastic, supportive people in your network. People like this generate their own energy and can pull you along in their wake if you form an alliance with them.

For Further Reading

Cohen, Steve, and Paulo de Oliveira. *Getting to the Right Job: A Guide for College Graduates.* New York: Workman Publishing, 1987.

Salzman, Marian L., and Diedre A. Sullivan. *Inside Management Training: The Career Guide to Training Programs for College Graduates.* New York: New American Library, 1985.

CHAPTER

— 6 —

The Hand-Crafted Job Search

Somewhere in this information-collecting process (maybe later rather than sooner), you'll wake up one morning with a rather clear idea of what you'd really enjoy doing. You may have narrowed down to an environment where you'll get to develop certain skills that interest you. Or you may feel very much attracted to a particular field (travel, child welfare) and be willing to try several types of jobs within that area. This new clarity means that you've reached a critical point in your information gathering. You're willing to let certain old ideas go, at least for the present, and focus more narrowly on a particular goal. A certain area of concentration seems clearer, more real, more attractive to you. When this happens, you're ready (or almost ready) to begin a job campaign.

First, see if you can answer the following questions about your chosen area:

1. Is your field growing? Stable? Declining?
2. Are the kind of jobs you want plentiful? Scarce?
3. Are these jobs highly sought after? Is the competition intense?

4. Is there a geographic factor in your job hunt? If so, what are the geographic centers of your field?

5. What specific organizations or companies within your field would you like to learn more about? Which are the ones with good reputations?

6. Is further education necessary (now or later) in order for you to get the job you want?

7. How do your experience and skills stack up against others who want the kind of job that you would want? If there's a gap between your experience and the requirements of your desired job, how can you fill it?

8. How well connected are you in your field? Do you have friends, family members, other contacts there already?

9. Given your own strengths and weaknesses, plus the current situation in your field, what are the best strategies for a job hunt?

If you still feel foggy and vague about some of these questions, don't be concerned. The landscape will become clearer in the course of your job campaign. Yes, it's finally time to begin actively seeking a job. How do you do it? By reading and talking with people, just as before, but in a much more focused and strategic way. Your purpose is now to:

1. Get exploratory interviews—face-to-face conversations with people who can hire you or who know people who can. Like informational interviews, exploratory interviews serve the double purpose of netting you important information and increasing your visibility, this time with people who might actually be able to hire you, if not at this moment, then sometime in the future.

2. Get job interviews—meetings in which both you and your interviewer understand that you're applying for a particular position.

Here are some things you'll want to do to shift from

information gathering to a more focused job search. You can do them in any order you like, whenever they seem appropriate.

Prepare Your "Success Stories"

This exercise is similar to Exercise Four (Reliving Your Most Satisfying Accomplishments) in Chapter 2, but it is focused on experiences you have had on summer jobs, internships, volunteer work, and campus activities. Your "success stories" will show potential employers the kind of person you are, how you use your skills to solve problems, and your understanding of basic business goals. They can be recycled endlessly: You may slip them into door-opening letters, adapt them for your resume, and use them on interviews to show your stuff.

It helps to know that most employers understand that new graduates don't have all that much experience. What they're looking for is potential—intelligence and positive energy. In 1987, Howard-Sloan, a New York City–based executive search firm, identified four qualities all employers seek: initiative, motivation, the ability to work on a team, and the willingness to get the job done regardless of the time it takes. Other vital skills: the ability to communicate and write well or to do computation, self-confidence, integrity, and a sense of responsibility.

Bearing this in mind, see if you can think of at least five instances where you demonstrated these qualities while doing a job. Then create a "success story" from each one by explaining the problem or situation you confronted, telling how you handled it, and stating the results. Consider how the following success-story excerpts highlight these key attributes:

From a young woman who had a summer job at a catering service:

The party ran long and the other waiters wanted to leave, but I persuaded most of them to stay and make sure the client's kitchen was spotless before going home.

Message: "I'm not a clockwatcher; I don't quit until the job is done. I'm a leader in a group situation, but I'm also a team player who's willing to do whatever work the job requires."

From a young woman who interned with an environmental research organization:

Although she didn't say so, I knew my boss was worried about letting me collect the research data by myself, so I gave her daily updates on my findings, and took the opportunity to demonstrate that I understood the collection methods.

Message: "I know instinctively what people need. My communication skills are good, and I keep supervisors informed of what I'm doing."

The "results" of your stories should demonstrate, whenever possible, that you made or saved money or time for your organization. These are the bottom-line goals of every business, and they're on every interviewer's mind. Here's a case in point from a woman who had a summer job at a boutique:

When the store hired me, I felt its display windows weren't as inviting as they could be. After a few weeks, I asked my boss if I could try redesigning them. She liked my displays so much that she asked me to create new ones every week that summer.

A good kudo, but what were the results? Did any customers comment on the windows? Did the displayed merchandise sell exceptionally well? Did sales increase, and if so, by how much? Use statistics, numbers, dollar figures, but only if they help your case. See how this success story is strengthened by the use of numbers:

When I took over the presidency of my college ski club in my sophomore year, it was loosely organized and had about seventy-five members. By focused advertising and specific opportunities for signups at activities fairs on campus, I raised the membership to two hundred within the next year. This increase in membership allowed me to successfully request a larger share of student activity funds from the college, and by my senior year, the club was offering excellent bargain ski weekends to its membership.

Be careful, though, not to take full credit for profits or income, or you'll seem presumptuous. The woman who did the window display, for example, could say something like: "My window displays contributed to a 4 percent increase in sales."

Write out your stories. Make them as lively, punchy, and brief as possible (four or five sentences is adequate). Figure out which ones are the strongest and which demonstrate skills most pertinent to the field you've chosen. Use bits and pieces of these stories on interviews, in letters, wherever it fits naturally into the job search process.

Warm Up Old Contacts

Pull out your files and go through the names of all the people you talked with when you were collecting information. Which of them were in the field you've actually chosen? Which were in allied fields? Which were friendly and encouraging? Which are working for companies that you've targeted—or that you'd like to learn more about? Now's the time to let them know the decision you've made and see if you can enlist their help without bothering them or making them feel obligated.

Letters or Phone Calls?

Make judicious and courteous use of both. For example, you might telephone those friendly peers you talked with and tell them your news. Here's a possible opener:

> *Hello, Laura? This is Susan Queue. We spoke back in October about careers in library work. You gave me so many good tips back then that I wanted to let you know that I'm now actively seeking a job in the field. I'd love to explore possibilities at Memorial Library, and I wondered if I could ask you how I should proceed? What do you think my next step might be?*

Here are some ways Laura might answer you, and some suggested responses on your part to keep the ball rolling. (Be sure to word them in your own way.) And also keep an ear open to the warmth and energy of her response, to gauge just how far she's willing to go for you.

Laura's Answer 1: *Well, I think you need to talk to more people around here.*

Your Response: *Any ideas?* [Most likely, she'll give you names, and you'll want to know as much as possible about these people in order to approach them in the most appropriate way (see page 117). Ask if you might use her name in the letter you write.]

Laura's Answer 2: *Gee, I don't know of any jobs right now.*

Your Response: *Well, I'm really looking to build a network in this field over the next months and also to collect as much information as I can. Is there anyone there whom it might be helpful for me to know?*

Laura's Answer 3: *Well, you could send your resume to Mr. Hargis . . ."*

Your Response: *Mr. Hargis. What exactly is his position? May I use your name in my cover letter? Can you tell me a little about him so I can write as relevant a cover letter as possible?*

Laura's Answer 4: *Well, I think there's an entry-level spot opening up in the department next door.*

Your Response: *Sounds interesting. Do you have a moment right now to tell me what you know about it? Or would it be better if we talk later?*

Your purpose here is to find out as much about this job as possible from an insider's point of view, so you'll be able to both write a convincing application letter emphasizing your most pertinent experience and skills, as well as get a sense of the history of the job and what it offers for the future. (Look ahead to page 143 for good questions to ask.)

So by reconnecting with one of your warmer and more encouraging peer interviewers by telephone, you will most likely add one or more names of people to talk with to your list, and perhaps even come away with a job lead.

For busier, higher-level people you've spoken with, a letter is less intrusive and yet gets your name on their desk again. If this person is in the field you have chosen, write and say you've decided to enter his field, tell him that you're excited about your decision. Remind him of any insights he gave you that guided your choice. There are a number of ways you could end this letter, depending on your relationship thus far. Here are some possibilities:

Since your organization is so highly regarded in the consumer advocacy field, it's one of the three I've targeted to study in depth. I've read extensively about your organization and I would be delighted to speak with anyone there who you think might have more insights for me. Could I call you next week to see if you have any further suggestions for me?

Or:

Since your insights and suggestions were among the most on-target and helpful that I received, I wonder if I could call you sometime in the future for one more piece of advice.

Or:

Enclosed is my newest resume, which highlights many of

the skills you emphasized. I would welcome your reaction to it. Would you mind if I give you a call to find out what you think?

What you have done here is to update these people who were encouraging to you in the past about your career plans, indicate some ways they could continue to be helpful to you, and prepare them for a phone call from you.

Similarly, you might want to contact friendly people you spoke with earlier whose field or function you are *not* choosing to pursue, but whose career area is in some way related to yours. For example, you might want to keep in touch with:

1. A person whose company you'd like to work for.
2. A person who might hear of a job opening in your area (public relations people, for example, may hear of job openings in publishing).
3. A person who might someday be your client or supplier.

Again, your letter can be focused around your excitement about your chosen career direction. But the wording of this type of letter is trickier because you'll have to explain why you chose another field and not theirs. As you compose your letter, try to think of some insights this person gave you that pointed you in your current direction. Be positive, not negative.

Negative: *After we talked I decided that there was too much traveling in your branch of sales for me.*

Better: *Your observation that I seemed to enjoy activity and interaction led me to search for the kind of job where I'd be moving around and meeting people rather than concentrating at a desk.*

Again, your concluding paragraph depends on how you'd like your relationship with this person to proceed. You might ask if you might call for one more piece of advice, or say you wonder if there are any people in his organization you could speak with, or you might enclose a resume and ask him to pass it on to anyone who might be interested.

Research Your Target Organizations

Suppose Laura gives Susan three names of people to speak with at Memorial Library.

Or suppose Susan wants to write a cover letter to Mr. Hargis that will set her apart from other applicants.

Or suppose Susan has been especially intrigued by three or four organizations that offer the kinds of opportunities she wants.

The time has come for her to study these organizations in depth. As she does so, she'll get more and more of a sense of which organizations would offer her the strongest beginning. In addition, she'll be able to write informed door-opening letters and speak knowledgeably about the company's current strengths and challenges on interviews, and will be able to pinpoint where she can best fit in. And her knowledge will increase her sense of confidence on interviews.

Here is an outline to guide you as you gather information about specific organizations.

Organization X—What You Need to Know

The Big Picture

The organization's purpose or mission

- What business(es) is it in?

- What services or products does it provide, or what ideas does it advocate?
- Who are its customers or clients?
- With what other organizations is it affiliated?
- Is it a subsidiary of another company? Does it have subsidiaries?
- What values drive this organization?

The size and structure of the organization

- How many people does it employ?
- Does it have one location? Or is it regional, national, multinational?
- Is it privately owned? Publicly held? A nonprofit organization? If the latter, what is its source of funding?
- When was it founded and how has it grown? Have there been any recent structural changes, and what do they mean?

The organization's financial health

- What were the organization's profits last year? How do they compare to previous years? Is the organization growing? Declining? Holding steady? Why?
- If it is a not-for-profit organization, is it well endowed? Able to raise funds? Struggling financially? Why?

The organization's reputation

- How is this organization regarded? By the community and its citizens? In the industry? By its employees? By its competitors?
- Is it notable in the field? Is it a leader in some way? Does it have a corner on some market? Does it excel in some area?

Trends and issues in the industry, and how this organization fits in

- Is this organization part of a growth industry?
- How does it use its resources?
- What has been written about it in magazines and newspapers? Has it been a part of a news story? If so, what has the impact been?

Environmental factors affecting this organization

- What laws or governmental regulations affect this industry and this organization?
- Does this organization have the natural resources it needs? Does it use its supplies and handle its wastes in a manner that is environmentally sound? Which environmental laws affect it now? Which may be a factor in the future?
- What scientific or technological changes now, or will in the future, have an impact on the industry and this organization?
- What national or international political situations may affect this organization?
- Who are the organization's foreign and domestic competitors? What is their relative strength?
- What social or lifestyle trends may affect the organization's workers? Its consumers? Its clients?

The Small Picture (the division, branch office, department, job you're looking at)

Relationship to the parent company

- How does this part of the company fit into the big picture? Is it part of a support function?
- How much of the company's success depends on this part of the company?

Types of jobs in this division or department

- What are the responsibilities, lifestyles, working conditions, morale of the people who work here?
- What types of people work here? What is their experiential and educational background? Their outlook?

Best Information Sources

Material from Libraries

Unless you're a library expert and/or a business school graduate, digging around in business directories trying to make sense of their entries can be frustrating and confusing. Of course, a lot depends on the quality of the library you use and the kind of help you get from the librarians. It might be worth your while if you live in a town with modest library resources to find out the best career library in a nearby large city, and make special plans to visit it. You might even be able to call the library in advance and ask which days are the least crowded with the best chance for uninterrupted help. The following information and the annotated bibliographies in Appendices A and B in the back of the book should demystify things just a bit.

Here are some hints before you start:

1. Publicly owned companies will be easier to research than private companies, since the former are required by law to make information known to the general public.
2. It's easier to get information on an umbrella corporation than on its individual subsidiaries. And, of course, the smaller and more regional the company, the less chance it will be listed in the large library directories. You may need to use other research strategies.

3. Nonprofits have their own directories and resources (see Appendix B).

4. Dates are important when doing this research. Note the date of every directory or other publication you use, and record it in your notes and on your photocopies. The CEO of Paws 'n' Claws Pet Food Company listed in the 1985 directory may not be the same now.

Reference books by type. Here are some categories of reference books helpful when researching organizations and some general ideas how they may help you. For specific examples and recommendations, see Appendix A.

1. Business information bibliographies. These are books that list business information books, articles, and printed material.

2. Directories listing companies (both publicly owned and privately held). These directories give such information as: corporation names, addresses, and telephone numbers; types of products; divisions; annual sales volume; total number of employees; names of the corporation's bank, legal firm, and accounting firm; names of the top executives. They may have several listings—alphabetical, geographical, and product-type. Read the introductions to see the kinds of companies that are included and the kind of information given.

3. Directories listing only privately held companies.

4. Directories of subsidiaries. Some examples are *Who Owns Whom* (D&B), and *America's Corporate Families and International Affiliates* (D&B).

5. Directories of foreign-owned companies and multinational corporations.

6. Directories with specialized kinds of information about companies. These directories may include biographies of a company's top executives or in-depth information about a company's history.

7. Directories of business organizations and professional associations.

8. Directories of special interest to job hunters.

9. Indexes of business journals and papers. These will lead you to articles on companies, industries, trends, mergers, and so forth. Look under the name of the company or industry being researched.

10. Guides to industry trends, analyses of industries, rankings, forecasts.

Materials from the Organizations Themselves

Promotional literature. Whether they're public, privately held, or nonprofit, almost every organization has a public relations department. The smallest organizations may have a single employee assigned to give information to the public; the largest companies may have an entire staff or may hire an outside agency. All you need to do is call the organization, ask for the public relations office, and say you want to know more about the company. You'll be sure to get lots of promotional literature, including press releases, press kits, memos, public announcements, brochures, and flyers. You may even be put on the organization's mailing list. All this literature is a gold mine of information about the organization's doings—its staff, its activities, its plans for the future. Even the look of the material will give you a sense of the company—whether it's warm or cool, elegant or down-home.

Annual reports. Annual reports are required by law from all publicly owned companies. They give a review of the company's history and financial performance during the preceding year, and will also include news on acquisitions, subsidiaries, and plans for future expansion—great for job leads. You can have an annual report sent to you if you call the company's public relations department, personnel department, or legal department. Also your public library may keep copies of annual reports or 10-K reports (these are similar). Try to get your hands on an annual report before any interview with a publicly owned company. It will help you think of relevant questions to ask, and a mention of it during an interview or in a door-opening letter will show you've done your homework.

Company newsletter or house organ. Many organizations publish periodical newsletters for their employees, to inform them about doings in all parts of the company and to boost team spirit. These publications will give you a sense of the "family feeling" of a company and are an excellent way to get the lowdown on what departments are newsworthy, what staff members are receiving gold stars. The personal profiles that abound in these newsletters can give you a good sense of the kinds of people who work for the company, and may even provide you with some points of contact: If a staff member is interested in long-distance bicycling, for example, and so are you, you have an excellent excuse to write to him. For a partial list of in-company newsletters, check *Working Press of the Nation*, Volume 5: Internal Publications Directory, or the *Gale Directory of Newsletters*.

Other Assorted Publications

Trade magazines, professional journals, and industry newsletters. These publications are great for tracking trends and also the performance of specific companies. Look for them in your library or write directly to the publishers.

Word of Mouth—Networking Your Way Around a Company

Collecting General Information. To get information about "the small picture" (local office or division) or about a small, local organization, nothing beats word of mouth from actual employees. You may get the best information about a small- or medium-size local organization from people lower on the organizational totem pole (beginners like yourself or those with only a few years' experience). Higher-ups may feel it necessary to serve as spokespersons for their organization and may not be as free to be candid with you. Here are some questions for peers who work for a particular company:

1. How is this organization (branch, division) doing financially?
2. How does this financial well-being (or lack of it) affect the day-by-day mood? Is everyone working harder? Is the mood tenser? Are people excited? Overwhelmed? Downhearted?
3. Which parts of the company are best to work for? Why? Who are the best supervisors? What makes them good?
4. Who holds the formal power in this organization? The informal power? Which people are most influential and why?
5. What are the challenges the company is struggling with at the moment? In what way do they reflect the challenges in the industry? The situation in the community?
6. What written or unwritten expectations come down from management about how people should behave at work and how they should do their jobs? Are these expectations rigid or flexible?
7. What is the pace of work? The level of expectation? The amount of tension and competition at this company?
8. Are there any political struggles that I should know about? How do they affect employee morale? How might their outcome affect the future of the organization?

If there are several people whom you've spoken with, compare and contrast their responses. Arrange with one of them to take you on a site visit. You'll find your knowledge of the company broadening and deepening as you see it from different perspectives.

Scoping Out a Particular Job. Should a specific job become available, you'll want to call one or several of your contacts to see what they can tell you about the history and future of this opening and the kinds of people you'd be working with. The answers to the following questions will greatly increase the quality of your door-opening letter, or if you're in the door already, the background information you'll bring to an interview.

1. Who held the position before? What were that person's strengths and weaknesses? How will his or her legacy be a factor in this search?
2. If the position is a new one, why is it being created? To meet whose needs? Which people have a vested interest in how the search goes?
3. To whom would I report? What is the power structure for this unit, and how does it relate to the organization as a whole? What is the history of the relationship between this office and the organization?
4. Is there an "inside candidate" for the job? How could I best position myself to be a more viable candidate than that person?
5. What new organizational goals or needs will this position be expected to serve? What new skills or qualities are needed to accomplish those goals?
6. What facts or factors would make this a good place to work right now? What would not make it a good place to be?
7. What is the management style of the person or persons to whom I would report? What is the general style of the office?

Consider all this information very carefully. A few negative elements in the picture need not be enough to turn you away from the job opportunity. On the other hand, especially when you're beginning your career, you want to choose a spot where you have a good chance for success. No matter how badly you need a job or how much you want to work for a particular organization, you're setting yourself up for unhappiness if you enter a toxic environment thinking, "Oh, well, it doesn't really matter; I can handle it." If the reports don't bode well, pass this opportunity by. Have faith that a better position will soon come your way.

Set Up Exploratory Interviews with New People in the Field

Suppose you get a promising name from a friend or from a company newsletter or from a peer interview at a company you'd like to work for. This person might be able to hire you or influence someone to hire you at some time, although there may not be any jobs at the moment. What you need to do is to write a door-opening letter so that this person will give you an exploratory interview.

Exploratory interviews are actually a more focused kind of informational interview. You still want career information, but of a more specific kind. Instead of asking about a field, you'll want to know about a company or a department: what people do there, how and when they are hired, what qualities and skills are most valued, and whether you would fit in.

As in informational interviews, you're seeking to learn more about whether this company would be right for you; you're not asking for a job. Again, do a sincerity check. If you've done enough homework to know that this company is worth exploring, or something about this person and his job has intrigued you, more information *is* what you want, and your genuine interest will come across in your letter.

Effective Door-Opening Letters

Good door-opening letters run under a page in length. It's best not to include a resume with this kind of letter because you're seeking information rather than a job, and it's usually best if people meet you before they see your resume.

The outline below is a suggested format; needless to say, you can combine the elements in other ways and double up on paragraphs—whatever you feel is appropriate.

Paragraph 1: Mention how you got the name of the person you're writing to, and also say why you're writing. Try to strike a personal note without getting overly familiar.

> **Example:** *Shortly after I decided on a career in marketing and merchandising of educational toys, I saw the short profile of you and your company, Pooh Bear Toys, in our college alumnae magazine. I was intrigued to read that your company began to make a profit only three years after startup, and I thought you might be a perfect person to ask how to approach my job search in the toy industry.*

Paragraphs 2 and 3: In the next one or two paragraphs you want to show your knowledge of the company and industry trends, and then indicate how your background and skills might be of value. Pull together the homework you've done on the company and the industry, and search your "success stories" for the ones that most strongly display your relevant skills.

> **Example:** *I received my B.A. in June, with a major in child psychology. In the nursery school observations I did for my courses, I saw toddlers playing with both the Sandbox and the Dinosaur lines of toys. I observed firsthand how children learn differently depending on the toy—Sandbox encourages creativity, whereas Dinosaur toys help youngsters coordinate thought and movement. I understand that Pooh Bear specializes in toys and educational software for children ages six to ten, and I would be interested in learning how much of the knowledge I have of young children's toys would be transferable to the older age group.*

Paragraph 4: Sum up by briefly mentioning some other topics you'd like to discuss about the organization, the field, and how you'd fit in.

Example 1: *I'd also like very much to find out more about Pooh Bear Toys—whether you're expanding, what your hiring plans might be, and whether my background and skills would be of value to your organization.*

Example 2: *I'd be most grateful for any insights you could give me into the toy industry, especially how I could best approach the job search and present my skills in the most marketable way.*

Paragraph 5: Keep the ball in your court by saying when you will call for an appointment; don't wait for the person to respond to you. You might, however, give your phone number so that she can call you if she wishes. If you are looking for a job in a faraway city, it might be good to schedule a visit of a few days to a week; then inform the person you write to of when you will be in town. That gives her an incentive to see you when she can. If you say "I'll be glad to visit Chicago anytime you are available," she may feel undue pressure to make the trip worthwhile for you.

Example 1: *I would like to call you the week of March 22 to see what time would be best to set up an appointment. Should you wish to contact me, my number, days and evenings, is 804-555-1212.*

Example 2: *I will be visiting Chicago the week of April 16 and would be delighted if I could see you at that time. I will call you next week to see if an appointment can be arranged.*

The Interview

The same basic approach that's best for informational interviewing also pertains to the exploratory interview. Come prepared with a list of questions (you are still the interviewer), don't overstay your welcome (half an hour is plenty), and don't impose upon the person who's granted you this favor and jeopardize a budding professional relationship by asking directly about jobs. (Reread the material on the informational interview in Chapter 5.)

A good tack to take—one that may net you plenty of useful information—is to ask the person to take a look at your resume and give you feedback. What are its strengths and weaknesses in terms of beginning jobs in his industry? Ask if you could present your skills in a stronger way. Is there any important skill that employers are looking for that is absent from your resume? Before you leave, don't forget to ask about your interviewee's suggestions for other people in the company or industry whom you should speak with. Follow up with a thank-you note.

If an Exploratory Interview Becomes a Job Interview

Once in a while you may be surprised when, on an informational or an exploratory interview, the person you're speaking with suddenly tells you of a current job opening and asks if you'd be interested in being considered. Or the person might offer to take you down the hall to speak to Mrs. Brown whose assistant is leaving next week. Since you've trained yourself *not* to ask about jobs on these interviews, the situation may throw you for a loop. As you consider what you want to do, stall for time by asking your contact as much about the job as he can tell you. Take notes. You may decide you're not properly prepared at the moment to segue into a job interview, so you can always say: "It sounds like a really interesting job, but your suggestion takes me a bit by surprise. Perhaps I ought to wait before I meet Mrs. Brown. Could you give me her phone number? I'd like to think it over and maybe make an appointment next week." Or, you could opt for meeting Mrs. Brown, just to say hello, get more information about the position, and make an appointment for a bona fide interview. Tune into your gut reaction and go with it, if you can. You might want to capture the energy of the moment, and talk with Mrs. Brown right away. On the other hand, you don't want to blow a good possibility by allowing yourself to be pushed into an interview you're unprepared for. On each exploratory you arrange, you might give some thought beforehand to strategies you could use if a real job possibility suddenly pops up. If the job *doesn't* sound like something you'd want, you may not want to cool off your contact by saying so directly. In this case stall by asking for more time, and when you get home, call your support network for advice.

What About Direct Mail?

During the course of your job hunt, someone, a friend of your parents, for example, will say to you "Are you getting your resumes out?" Probably this person is referring to the direct-mail approach—sending out a resume and a cover letter to a large number of companies with the hope that at least one of them has a job that would suit your skills. There are a number of reasons why this is still a popular strategy for a job campaign. First, it feels as if you're blanketing the market. You believe that there's sure to be a job for you in one of those two hundred companies. Also the process of preparing your resume, your cover letters, and getting names of companies and people to write to seems like a productive endeavor. You feel busy. Also, if you're rather shy and underconfident, as are many new graduates approaching the world of work, it is far less stressful to do a mailing and wait for replies than to approach a chosen contact and present yourself in person.

Despite the seeming advantages of this approach, direct-mail campaigns are usually ineffective and ultimately discouraging, especially for new graduates. Here's why.

1. A new graduate is selling her potential, not her experience. Resumes are summaries of experience, and unless you have had a particularly unusual background, there won't be all that much on your resume to distinguish you from other college graduates. The kind of personal letter described above, that's targeted toward a special person at a special company, is a much more flexible and effective way to present your potential—your enthusiasm, intelligence, problem-solving skills, and eagerness to learn—than a resume. And if you've done your contact-building homework, you'll be writing to someone who has a reason to take a special interest.

2. Resumes that are sent in cold have a dim future. People who hire other people get dozens of resumes a year. If you send your resume to someone who has no idea who you are, most likely he will glance briefly at it and send it to the personnel department. The personnel staff will look it over and, since they are often trained to spot problems in people's resumes, they may quickly screen you out as a potential candidate.

3. The period of time during which you'll be noticed and considered is very short. Although it seems that the direct-mail approach gets your resume in front of many people, it does so for only a few days. There may be just the right job available at the time your resume arrives in the mail, but if there is not, your material will be hidden in some file. The system does not allow you to make a "warm" contact whom you may reapproach a month or two months later, and who will remember you when a job opens up.

4. Direct mail is usually a one-way communication. Although direct mail gets out information about you, there is usually no feedback, no way for you to collect information, get to know individual companies, departments, and people, and to generate new contacts. It is a one-shot strategy, not a flexible one that allows for process and growth.

5. The results from this sort of direct-mail campaign

are usually discouraging. Direct-mail marketers will tell you that a 1 or 2 percent expression of interest is good and a 4 percent return is excellent. That means that you'll be doing well if you get four or five bites for the two hundred letters you have sent out—and it's very possible you'll get no response at all, even if you are in truth a very viable job candidate. Such a low response, especially after so much effort, can be very damaging to your self-confidence.

Nevertheless, you may have some good reasons for using this approach: You may have a highly unusual background or you may have ready access to a mailing list. Or your networking sources may be temporarily dry, and you want to try a different tack. Whatever the case, direct mail is best used as an adjunct to a more personal approach. It is not a strategy on which to depend or to focus your efforts.

However, there are times when sending a resume plus cover letter may serve you just fine. Those are times when you have heard of a definite job opening and you want to apply.

What About Employment Agencies?

Private employment agencies (there are probably between eight thousand and ten thousand in the United States) are used by companies to find applicants for available job slots. Agencies that specialize in a certain industry—accounting, banking, data processing, engineering, for example—usually prefer applicants with experience. But many agencies place secretarial and clerical help, and some even specialize in college graduates. If you are interested in a field where higher-level people traditionally begin their careers as secretaries and administrative assistants—this is sometimes true in competitive "glamour" fields, such as public relations, advertising, and television—you may want to look into employment agencies as an additional resource.

If you've been researching and networking for a while and you're a bit burnt out, an employment agency may be particularly tempting because they have something you may not have yet been able to locate on your own—real job openings. Furthermore, as you go to register, you may find a nice, encouraging employment counselor who will give you advice on your field and even redo your resume—all for free. But before you deliver your job search into the hands of this person who seems all-knowing, it's a good idea to understand how employment agencies work so that you can use them to *your* advantage instead of vice versa. (The description below applies only to employment agencies, not to executive search firms or head hunters. Executive search firms are not described here because they are used almost exclusively for managers and other highly experienced people.)

Employment agencies are hired by (but are not usually under contract to) companies who want them to fill their job vacancies as quickly as possible. The agencies work on a contingency basis; that is, they do not get paid until they actually fill a job. In addition, they may be competing with other agencies to fill the same spot. What this means is that most agencies don't have the time or motivation to find the right job for you; they're far more interested in convincing you to take the jobs they have available right now. If they get you an interview and an offer is made, they may put considerable pressure on you to accept it. Unscrupulous employment counselors might tell you, for example, that the kind of job you really want is unrealistic for you, that the market in your chosen field is impossibly tight, that considering your qualifications you're lucky to get an offer at all. In other words, beware of any "job counseling" offered by employment agencies: It can be manipulative, deflating to the self-esteem, and downright incorrect.

Employment agencies also sell applicants to the companies almost entirely on the basis of their resumes. They'll look over your resume and match you to the most obvious job, whether or not it's what you're looking for. Since they want to fill the requirements of their client companies, they may not be willing to take a chance on you and send you on an interview that may be of interest to you if your resume doesn't exactly match the job requirements. Furthermore, if you do get a job through an agency and they negotiate a salary for you, you might not get as much money as you would have gotten on your own. Although the agency naturally wants as much commission as possible, it also want to please its client companies and generate more business by getting you as cheaply as possible.

All this having been said, there are reputable employment agencies out there and as long as you have a strong ego and know just what you want, there's no harm in working with them. If they get you interviews, you can practice your skills, get your name around, and make new contacts. Just be sure that you know exactly what you want beforehand. Don't settle for anything less on the advice of any employment agency, and don't take any job unless you're sure it's right for you.

Here's how to find a reliable agency and work with it:

1. Use your network to find agencies that your friends or contacts trust. Try to get the names of specific counselors within the agency: The dedication and sensitivity of counselors can vary widely within a particular organization. One way to get yourself some names is to call the personnel departments of the companies you're interested in and ask them for recommendations.

2. Check your comfort level as you visit agencies and speak with their staff. If the offices are shabby, if the counselors are insensitive to your needs or require you accept their agenda, feel free to leave.

3. Before you register with any agency, make sure you read the contract carefully and understand its implications. Don't sign any sort of contract that requires you

work with that agency exclusively. If signals get crossed, you may end up paying a fee for a job you get yourself. Who pays the agency fee if you're placed is most important: It should be your new employer, not you. (Fees are usually 10 percent of the annual salary, and $1,500 on a $15,000 job is a chunk of money to a new college grad.) If you've answered an agency ad that says "fee paid," don't take it for granted that the company pays—ask. If the agency does find you a job, find out what happens if you don't like the job and want to leave after a few weeks. Is there any length of time you must stay in order not to be responsible for the fee? Get clear answers in writing.

4. Discuss with your counselor exactly how the agency handles resumes. Does it show them to individual employers who have already indicated a suitable job opening, or does it send them out *en masse* to many companies? If they do go in for mass mailings, you may want to consider whether you want your resume floating around in organizations unknown to you.

No matter how professional an agency is or how "in sync" you feel with it, never turn your job campaign over to them or allow them to be your only source of job leads. As with the direct-mail strategy, your use of an employment agency should be only an addition to a much larger job-search effort instigated and managed by you personally.

For Further Reading

Fowler, Elizabeth M. *The New York Times Career Planner: A Guide to Choosing the Perfect Job from the 101 Best Career Opportunities of Tomorrow*. New York: Random House, 1987.

Leape, Martha P., and Susan M. Vacca. *The Harvard Guide to Careers*. Cambridge: Harvard University Press, 1987.

Levering, Robert, Milton Moskowitz, and Michael Katz. *The 100 Best Companies to Work for in America.* New York: New American Library, 1984.

Salzman, Martin L. *Wanted: Liberal Arts Graduates.* New York: Doubleday, 1987.

CHAPTER

7

Winning Resumes, Intriguing Cover Letters

Your resume is your sales piece, your prime marketing tool, your personal press release. It needs to be your best statement about yourself as potential employee, your most effective representative in an employer's office. As you write your resume, you'll be bringing together, concisely and on paper, the two main types of information that you've been collecting in your career research. On one hand you'll be sorting through your own skills, interests, achievements, and abilities—all of what you've learned about yourself in the self-assessment process—to see what it is that you have to offer, what you *want* to offer. On the other hand, you'll be distilling the results of your reading, information, and exploratory interviews, studies about field and function, to see just what kinds of staff members employers are looking for in your chosen area.

The result: a resume that highlights your education and selected experience in ways that are most attractive to the people you want to hire you. Put another way, your resume translates past achievement into statements of what you can do for a potential employer in the future. An effective resume should contain brief but sufficient information to tell a prospective employer:

- Who you are
- What kind of work you would like
- What you know
- What you have done or learned
- What you can do
- What you *could* do or learn

And a good resume performs two more very important functions:

1. It captures something of your personal energy and unique achievements.
2. It carefully considers the audience—the employer who will be reading the resume—and focuses only on those skills most important to him or her.

That's a lot to fit on one piece of paper, so each word must be chosen carefully.

Actually, when discussing resumes it would be more accurate to use the plural, because if you're to use your resume most effectively, you'll want to be always rearranging, changing it, adding to and subtracting from it. For example, you'll probably write a resume at the very beginning of your career exploration process, long before you're ready for actual job interviews, just to update it from your summer job-search days, and to have something to show should a dream job opportunity unexpectedly arrive. But you'll almost certainly want to change it as you refine your self-assessment, collect information about various fields, and generally crystallize your career focus. During your exploratory interviews, you'll want to ask for feedback from the people you're talking to, and then incorporate their suggestions. When you get to the point where you're going on hot job interviews, you'll be constantly refocusing your resume, taking out some skills and experiences and substituting others, depending on the particular job, company, and department where the position is available.

Because your resume is a flexible, changeable document, it's best not to write a "final form" and get five hundred copies printed. Especially if you're searching in two or three fields, it's a good idea to write two or three versions of your resume with different job descriptions and skills emphasized, and make fifteen copies of each. Or better yet, if you have access to a computer, you can refocus your resume for each job opening you hear about, print it out as needed, and save all the versions on a disc.

This chapter will guide you in writing resumes that represent you most effectively. It includes exercises that will help you unearth your marketable skills, suggestions on the various parts of the resume (what to include and what to leave out), and advice on appearance and layout. Last are tips on how to write cover letters that expand and complement the resume material.

Before You Write: A Ten-Step Focusing Exercise

Writing the main body of your resume—the part that talks about your experience, your skills, and the results you've obtained—is largely a matter of selection, distillation, and focusing. If you're feeling confused about what to include or not to include and how to target the material properly, here's a ten-step exercise to help you clarify your experiences. You'll need a pencil and paper, your self-assessment exercises, and your "success stories" from Chapter 6. (If you haven't done the "success stories" exercise before, you might want to do it now—it can be tremendously helpful for resumes, cover letters, and job interviews.) And get out your career journal, if you have kept one. It will really pay off now.

1. Make a list of school and job activities and accom-

plishments. It might help (although it's certainly not necessary) to make it chronological: you could start with, say, your junior year in high school and list any high school offices and committee memberships. Then think about your summer job between your junior and senior year, your senior year activities, the summer after your senior year, and so forth. Include jobs, internships, volunteer work, activities, hobbies, and interests.

2. Identify the most meaningful and persuasive experiences, and break each into tasks. Describe all the various parts of your job or activity. Take all the time you need and be as lengthy as you want. Leave room to fill in more tasks under each activity in case you remember them later.

3. Look at the tasks and list the skills and qualities you used, learned, or developed. For example, a waitressing experience requires teamwork, organization, money management, time management, and people skills. A legal assistant must have excellent communication skills to write and present information. Turn to your inspired abilities assessment (pages 25 to 32) for lists of skills. Here's an example of how to break a job down.

Ad Sales Representative, Summer Pennysaver Paper

Task	*Skill*
Went to local merchants to persuade them to advertise; presented them with options and page rates	Convincing others; inspiring trust; persuasive reasoning; gave information; answered questions; helped merchants clarify advertising goals
Sent ad copy to the typesetter; proofread copy; worked with layout people to assure proper placement on page	Detail oriented; good with words; good follow-through; working to deadline; working well with others

Collected money from advertisers; kept accounts up to date	Good with figures; organized with money details; trustworthy; tactful; remembers to follow up

4. List, for each activity, the kinds of results, accomplishments, examples of leadership that employers are looking for. Here are some of the most important.

Made or raised money	Functioned effectively in a crisis
Saved money	Headed up a successful project, start to finish
Saved time	Made maximum use of a limited budget
Brought in new customers	Thought of a creative idea that was successfully implemented
Increased sales, club memberships, donations	Demonstrated responsibility for the safety of others
Persuaded people to work effectively together	
Caught a costly error	
Handled a large amount of money	
Averted a crisis	

5. List basic general skills that you have developed and practiced during your college years. These are abilities and qualities that can be used across the board in many situations: written and oral communications, research and analysis, leadership, independence, teamwork, international living, language experience, and computer proficiency. Then there are personal qualities that show maturity, such as patience, creative abilities, people skills, ability to do several things at once.

You may have done something unique and unusual that doesn't fit into the job task category, such as pay every cent of your own college tuition, or work for the same employer for four summers with increased responsibilities each time. Such accomplishments show discipline, determination, and follow-through—qualities greatly valued by employers. Go back to your lists of tasks, and add these skills where they apply.

6. Go back to the research you have done on your chosen field(s), and see what sorts of tasks and skills are most important in entry-level jobs. Then compare them with your list of proven tasks and skills. Which of your skills are transferable and which are not?

7. Go over your skills list and note those skills you enjoyed the most and those you enjoyed the least. If in a particular experience, you liked 10 percent of the work and disliked the rest, you may wish to focus on those particular skills that you enjoyed, and deemphasize the others.

8. Now look at everything you've listed, and begin to prioritize. Mark, perhaps with different colored markers, which two or three experiences you want to highlight or describe on a resume, which you'd like to simply list, and which you'd like to omit.

9. Write a brief description of each item you've decided to feature, using short verb phrases (see the list of action verbs on the following pages). Make your phrases as vigorous, lively, and specific as you can. The energy of these phrases will determine whether or not a recruiter will finish your resume or put it aside.

Less Convincing: *Led weekly overnight hikes at Camp Chattahoochie.*

Strong: *Planned for and headed up one seven-mile overnight hike weekly. Supervised pitching tents, making campfire, preparing food. Responsible for safety of fifteen ten-year-olds each hike.*

Less Convincing: *Visited local merchants to get them to advertise in pennysaver paper.*

Strong: *Persuaded twelve new merchants to advertise in pennysaver paper; increased the ad base by 3 percent.*

Less Convincing: *Waited tables at Mathilde's fine French restaurant.*

Strong: *Handled waiting station of six tables with three to* *four seatings each evening. Persuaded waitresses in my section to sub for one another to speed up service.*

Notice how the use of numbers, specific examples, and results (underlined in the examples above), sharpened each example and gave it a take-charge tone. After you've written each of your verb phrases, you might go over the list of action verbs to see whether another verb might be stronger and more accurate.

List of Action Verbs

accelerated
accomplished
achieved
adapted
adjusted
administered
aided
allocated
amplified
analyzed
answered
applied
appointed
approved
arbitrated
arranged
assisted
assumed
attained
augmented
awarded
began
broadened
brought
built
calculated
catalogued
chaired
compared
compiled
completed
communicated
conceived
conducted
constructed
consulted
contracted
contrived
controlled
cooperated
coordinated
counseled
created
dealt
defined
delegated
demonstrated
designed
determined
developed
devised
devoted
diagrammed
directed
displayed
distributed
edited
effected
eliminated
employed
encouraged
enlisted
established
estimated
evaluated
examined
expanded
expedited
extended
fabricated
focused
forecast
fortified
founded
generated
guided
handled
harmonized
headed
implemented
improved
incorporated
increased
influenced
initiated
inspected
installed
instituted
instructed
interpreted
introduced
launched
led
lectured
listed
maintained
managed
modified
molded
monitored
motivated
negotiated
observed
operated
organized
oriented
originated
overhauled
participated
performed
persuaded
planned
pinpointed
prepared
presented
preserved

processed
produced
programmed
promoted
proved
provided
received
recommended
reconciled
recorded
recruited
reduced
reestablished
regulated
rehearsed
reinforced
renegotiated
reorganized
reported
researched
reshaped
restored
revamped
reviewed
revised
scheduled
selected
set up
simplified
solved
specialized
stimulated
streamlined
structured
substituted
suggested
summarized
supervised
supported
systematized
taught
trained
tutored
updated
used
utilized
volunteered
widened
worked
wrote

As you sharpen and energize your examples, using well-chosen verbs, using specific descriptions, and quantifying your achievements, you may be surprised to hear how competent you sound. Are you comfortable with your examples, or do they sound exaggerated? Resumes of entry-level people can err in both directions, sounding either underconfident or boastful. You don't want to take credit for successes that belong to your supervisor or to your entire team, but you certainly want to give yourself full credit for your accomplishments. To make sure you've described yourself honestly, imagine an interviewer taking an example from your resume and asking you to elaborate. If you'd feel you have to back down and qualify yourself, you may be exaggerating a bit. Usually, though, young people (especially women) tend to underplay their skills and achievements.

Be careful also in your use of numbers. If they don't make a strong positive statement, leave them out. If only two more people joined the glee club when you were president, best not to say "two people" (even though in reality those memberships were a real kudo for you). Does it sound any better put as a percentage? If not, look for another sort of result. Did the glee club have more concerts when you were president? Did more people attend them? If so, you can say something like: "Glee club increased in membership, number of concerts, and concert attendance."

10. Arrange your verb phrases in the most appropriate order. If you can, mention first under each experience the skills you'd most like to use in your next experience. Deemphasize less relevant information by listing it later in your item description and saying less about it. Leave out unnecessary information. If you have chosen a field, learn the language and the buzz words and include some of the jargon in your descriptions where appropriate. If you're open to several fields, keep your words more general. Don't try to convey too many ideas in each entry; instead, describe two or three ideas vividly. Feel free to leave jobs and experiences out if you're uncomfortable with them; you don't have to confess your mistakes and failures. A resume is not a confidential autobiography or a shopping list of everything you've done.

Basic Resume Content

After you've struggled with the heart of the resume—your experiences and the skills you've demonstrated—it's time to review the standard parts of the resume.

Who You Are and Where You Can Be Reached

Your name, your current address and telephone number, and your permanent address and telephone number should be listed above in a clear, easy-to-read fashion, with your name emphasized. States should be referred to by the two-letter abbreviation used by the post office. For example:

VICTORIA VARGAS

Current Address	*Permanent Address*
(until May 15, 1991)	122 Dean Street
Gardiner House	La Santa, NM 03358
Smith College	Telephone: (505) 555-1212
Northampton, MA 01063	
Telephone: (413) 555-1212	

Career Objective (optional)

A career objective (also called a job objective, career goal, employment objective, employment goal) is a brief statement indicating the type of work you are seeking and the range of skills you wish to use. It should give the reader some idea of your interests and career focus.

The experiences of students or new graduates are often scattered and underdeveloped and their resumes tend to look alike, so a well-thought-out job objective can pull a resume together and give it focus. The trouble is that job objectives are often so vague as to increase the impression of being scattered or so narrow as to be limiting.

> **Vague Objective:** *A challenging and exciting position where my skills and talents will be fully utilized in an organization that will offer me professional advancement.*

This objective contains little besides clichéd enthusiasm; it takes up space, sounds naive, and signals to the employer that you're not sure what you want to do.

> **Narrow Objective:** *A position in an international division of a investment bank that uses my computational skills and my fluency in French and Spanish.*

This is a fine example of a clearly defined job objective, but it limits the resume. Resumes with this objective must only be sent to investment banks with international divisions. It cannot be used to apply to a commercial banks or other financial institutions, for example.

Here are some focused job objectives that better walk the line between being too general and too specific.

> **Focused Objectives:** *A position in the communications industry using my reporting, interviewing, investigative, and writing skills.*
>
> or
>
> *A position in social or science research using my writing skills and quantitative background. Special interests include public policy and financial analysis.*

Like many college students, you may want to consider many sorts of entry-level jobs that will give you basic training in your chosen field, or you may be open to any job that will enable you to develop certain skills. You don't want to shut out possibilities because of a too-limiting job objective. In that case you may either:

1. Leave the job objective out entirely and use your cover letter to relate your job skills to the particular job/field/function that you are applying for at the moment (more about cover letters later); or
2. Develop two or three working versions of your resume, some with a job objective and some without. This approach gives you the opportunity to highlight the skills most appropriate to the different job areas you are considering.

Education

Because young people's jobs tend to last only for a few months and utilize more elementary skills, most new college graduates put the Education section of their resumes before the Experience section. Your educational history should be listed in reverse chronological order, beginning with your most recent (or anticipated) degree. Emphasize educational experiences that illustrate your interest and ability to handle the positions you are seeking. You might want to describe a major research project or independent study program that is relevant to your audience or has special significance for you. Include foreign languages (specify your level of competence). Do the same with computer background or any other relevant areas in which you have specific training or exposure. If you have taken courses that enhance your background but are not apparent from your major, list them in the education section. Example: "Additional emphasis in ________."

If your Grade Point Average is 3.2 or higher, you might want to list it. (In fact, some employers, such as banks, management consulting firms, and other organizations that are competitive and emphasize numbers, insist on seeing a GPA. They correlate the disciplines needed to do well in college—analytical and quantitative skills—with success in their field.) If your total GPA isn't so good, you might be able to point to certain years when you got a 3.0 or above; for example, "Dean's List, junior and senior years."

If you attended a college other than the one from which you graduated, list it second, and describe any special experiences there as you did above. Omit your high school unless you are a freshman or sophomore looking for a summer job or internship, or you had an unusual high school experience that is relevant to the career field you wish to enter. For example, you might wish to mention that you attended a high school for the performing arts, if you want to be an actor or a dancer.

Your extracurricular, volunteer, or public-service activities show employers the breadth of your personal interests and involvement with others. How you deal with them on your resume depends on how involved you were and whether the skills you learned are pertinent to the career you're pursuing. One way of handling such activities is to list club *memberships* in the Education section, but expand on *leadership* positions—captain of the tennis team, managing editor of the college newspaper—under the Experience section. Here are some ways of presenting the material in the Education section.

Linda wants to work in the communications office of a senator or representative in Washington, DC. In her Education section, she emphasizes her studies and her practical knowledge of government, lists her related research project and award, her computer skills, and indicates the breadth of her interests and abilities.

EDUCATION

SMITH COLLEGE, Northampton, MA
B.A. degree expected, May 1992. Government major, Philosophy minor. Dean's List 1990–1991. Selected as Jean Pickering Semester in Washington Scholar, Fall 1991. Wrote major research paper on the effectiveness of the televised presidential debates.

Literate in Pascal, XyWrite, and WordStar computer programs.

Student Government Association Senator, member of the residential house council, admission office student guide, lifeguard at campus pool, alumnae house fund agent. Studied ballet for twelve years.

Zoe knows she wants to teach math in a private school, and is certain enough about her objective to include it in her resume. She mentions her high school to show her familiarity with independent schools.

OBJECTIVE

To obtain a position teaching mathematics in an independent boarding school with the opportunity for additional responsibilities in dormitory supervision, activities coordinating, coaching, and student advising.

EDUCATION

SMITH COLLEGE, Northampton, MA
B.A. in Mathematics and Art History expected, May 1992.
Additional coursework in Education and Computer Science.
THE SHIPLEY SCHOOL, Bryn Mawr, PA
Graduated with honors, 1989. Member of the student government

In this case Zoe mentions that she attended a well-known private boarding school to show her familiarity with the sort of job setting she desires. Her education background may seem less rich than Linda's, but that's not the case. Later in her resume, Zoe elaborates on her college positions—treasurer of her dormitory, chairman of her college services organization—as demonstrations of her leadership capacity.

Here is how Alix, who wants a job in banking, highlights her teamwork and leadership abilities in her Education section.

EDUCATION

SMITH COLLEGE	Candidate for a B.A. degree, May 1992 Major: Economics Minor: Philosophy G.P.A. 3.5
ACTIVITIES	Smith College Varsity Tennis (1989–present): Currently ranked #1 doubles nationally; New England Champion #1 doubles, #3 singles; All Conference Team.

Dormitory President (1991–present): Elected to manage and maintain a seventy-five-student dormitory. Responsibilities include heading up dormitory council, appraising and implementing dormitory and college policy, and conducting dormitory meetings.

Dormitory Council (1990–91): Elected to the positions of Class Representative, Social Chair, and Athletic Representative.

Volunteer Tennis Instructor (1990–present): Instructed junior tennis players in college-sponsored tennis clinics.

Nicole is looking for jobs in business, marketing, or consulting.

EDUCATION

Smith College, B.A. in Economics expected, May 1989.
- Relevant courses: Accounting, Statistics, Calculus II, Corporate Finance
- Language: fluent in Spanish
- Computer proficiency: Lotus 123, BASIC, DOS, VAX
- Extracurricular activities: Marketing Director, AIESEC (International Association of Students in Business and Economics): Program Director, ODN (Overseas Development Network).

* * *

Francesca wants an entry-level position in a metropolitan or university art museum. She emphasizes her studies abroad and her language proficiency—good complements to her background in art history.

EDUCATION

Smith College, Northampton, MA B.A. May 1991
Major: Art History and Italian Language and Literature
Junior Year Abroad Program, Florence, Italy, 1988–89
Honors: Dean's List, 1989–90, G.P.A. 3.4
Language proficiency: Italian and Spanish
Middlebury College School of Italian Summer 1990

You'll see more of the resumes of Linda, Zoe, Alix, Nicole, and Francesca in the next section.

Experience

The Experience section is the heart of your resume. In this section you list the various positions you've held and describe them in some detail, using your action-verb phrases to show employers your most relevant skills, job growth, and results achieved. Generally, college students have five to nine entries in this section. Any position, paid or unpaid, is fine to list—volunteer activity, internships, major on-campus commitments, and summer, part-time, or work-study jobs.

There are three basic formats for this section:

1. Chronological, in which you list each of the experiences in reverse chronological order
2. Functional, in which you categorize your experi-

ence according to major skill areas that you know are of interest to the companies to which you're applying

3. A combination of chronological and functional

Chronological resumes are usually most suitable for college students and new graduates unless their backgrounds are very unusual. The chronological format sounds rather rigid, but much can be done to adapt it to your own needs and experience, as you will see. If you want more information on the functional and combination resume, check the books listed in the bibliography at the end of this chapter.

For each position you choose to list, you must include the job title, the name of the organization, the city and state, and the dates of your employment. By choice of format, you can emphasize the name of the organization, or your title.

Washington, DC, Brookings Institute, Research Assistant
Summer, 1991

or

BROOKINGS INSTITUTE, Washington, DC
Research Assistant (Summer, 1991)

Here are some general tips:

- You don't have to use the exact job title that the company gave you. Reword your titles so that they have as professional a cast as possible while still remaining accurate. "Administrative Assistant" sounds better than "secretary" or "typist." See the Experience sections that follow for good examples.
- When discussing college activities, translate abbreviations and explain names: Editor of *The Sophian* (biweekly college paper); President of AAAC (Afro-American Affairs Council).

- Rework your verb phrases until they're as dynamic and take-charge as they can be. Use numbers when you can, especially for quantitative jobs like banking: for example, talk about the size of your club's budget or the amount of money you handled daily as a bank teller. Again, search for results. Were you promoted? Did you get a commendation from your boss? Were you asked back next year?
- Avoid passive phrases such as "duties included . . ." or "responsibilities were . . ."

Notice how, in the following Experience section, Linda highlights her organization and communication skills and emphasizes her familiarity with government issues, the legislative environment, and the world of Washington in order to get that congressional communications job.

EXPERIENCE

STUDENT COORDINATOR, Smith in Washington Program, 1985
Organized seminars and special events for students. Wrote biweekly newsletters. Cowrote program handbook. Assisted students with summer housing and internship opportunities.
CONGRESSIONAL INTERN, Representative Nan Garlock, Washington, DC, 1985
Researched projects for legislative assistants. Answered constituent correspondence. Handled office mail.
PRODUCTION ASSISTANT, National Public Radio, Washington, DC, 1984
Worked in Election Unit and Washington Bureau. Assisted in daily operations, special coverage of presidential primaries, Democratic and Republic Conventions, and election night. Cowrote and edited election handbook.
SWIMMING COACH, Barton Barracudas, Barton, MN
Trained 125 swimmers for summer AAU competition. Or-

ganized biweekly dual meets. Led team to championships and best record in team history.

Linda's Experience section is a good example of the advisability of hanging around where the action is, even if you have to take a "gofer" job to do it. The congressional intern job may have been unpaid and may have involved little more than sorting mail. And for National Public Radio she may have volunteered to get coffee. No matter. She was on the spot where things were happening, and she made the most of her exposure in her resume. Notice how she quantifies and highlights results in her last entry.

Now let's see how Zoe presents her credentials in teaching and working with young people.

WORK EXPERIENCE

COUNSELOR, Deer Run Camp School, Foster, MT (Summers, 1989, 1990)
Supervised and motivated young adults in every aspect of their nonacademic lives. Helped students on a one-to-one basis in all academic areas. Taught in the classroom as a substitute. Mentored new counselors in the second summer.

GRADER, Smith College Mathematics Department (1989–present)
Hired and employed by the Math Department as a grader for Calculus I and Calculus II. Responsible for reading, correcting, and evaluating thirty to fifty papers a week.

ADDITIONAL EXPERIENCE

CHAIRWOMAN, College Service Organizations (Present)
Chair a fifteen-person board. Responsible for weekly agendas, facilitating meetings, motivating board members, and recruiting and appointing a new board, acting as a spokesperson for the Service Organizations.

DORMITORY TREASURER (1989–90)
An elected position responsible for collecting and budgeting $4000 each semester.

A key quality for teachers is responsibility, especially when combined with supervisory duties at a private school. Zoe has worded her descriptions in such a way that her ability to deal with responsibility is stressed in almost every entry. In the school camp description, she could easily have said: "Served as counselor and adviser to teenagers when their classes were over." Her wording is much stronger. "Supervised" and "motivated" are words that are sure to catch the eye of school administrators. In fact, a great many of Zoe's action verbs and key words relate to teaching: *supervised, motivated, taught, mentored, reading, correcting, evaluating, grader.*

Francesca leads off each item in her Experience section with the organizations she's worked for, instead of her rather lackluster job titles, thus highlighting her experience with art galleries. She also played with dates a bit to emphasize the position most related to her career choice. Technically in a chronological resume, her Student Affairs Office position, the most recent, should come first. But she pushed the gallery job up front.

EXPERIENCE

Dina Marple Gallery City, State
Assistant to Manager, Summer 1991. Oversaw, with assistance of artist and architect, the arrangement of sculpture in City Mall. Assisted organization and production of first city AIDS benefit. Assembled artists' work for summer exhibitions.

Office of Student Affairs, Smith College
Head Resident, 1991–1992. Served as liaison between administration and house residents (women specially

chosen to manage dormitories and counsel the students). Oversaw general welfare of 66 House Residents. Promoted awareness of social issues, including racism and substance abuse.

The David Brownfield Art Center City, State

Intern, Summer 1989. Compiled, catalogued, and documented museum records. Selected, handled, and hung artists' work for exhibition. Assisted children's tours and supervised follow-up activities.

Center for Ecumenical Ministry City, State

Camp Counselor, Summer 1988. Worked with underprivileged children in recreational atmosphere. Organized and initiated group activities and outings with limited funds and resources.

ACTIVITIES

Intercollegiate Athletics, Smith College

Varsity field hockey (Fall 1988, 1889). Varsity lacrosse (Spring 1990).

Sophomore Class Representative, Smith College (1989–1990)

Elected to act as liaison between house members and class cabinet. Organized class social activities and fund raisers.

Financial Aid Liaison, Smith College (1989–1990)

Was elected representative to financial aid office. Disseminated information to students regarding campus work and college policy.

Gold Key Guide, Admissions Office, Smith College (1989–1990)

Represented college to potential applicants. Led campus tours. Aided alumnae in recruitment efforts.

Francesca's Activities section is included here, following her Experience section, to show a contrasting way of handling extracurricular activities. Many people include them under the Education section. Alix (page 168) did so to stress her leadership and management skills, as well as her competitiveness—qualities important for a banking job. Francesca chose another placement because she wanted to get her jobs in the art world closer toward the front of her resume. Her college activities come later to demonstrate her general well-roundedness.

If you have had a number of different summer jobs, some related to your chosen career goal and others not, you can break your experience section into two parts, headed Work Experience and Additional Experience. This sort of arrangement is good if you're an artist, a performer, or are looking for a job related to the performing arts, where experience does not always come in neat time blocks. Under Artistic Experience or Theater Experience or Concert Experience, you can list the shows and performances, and under Additional Experience you can list your "regular" jobs.

To let an employer know that you have held other jobs you have chosen not to outline in detail, you might wish to use a phrase such as "various other positions included fast-food waitress, house painter, and lifeguard" or "other part-time jobs included cashier and dishwasher."

There are many variations on the theme. Play around with the organization with the help of your career counselor or career development office adviser until you get the presentation that suits you best.

Personal (optional)

Employers are interested in you as a person—your special interests, recreational activities, social service commitments, travel, nationality. In this section you may want to add material that will give your readers a sense of you as an individual and potential colleague.

* * *

Nicole's personal section was brief but interesting:

PERSONAL INFORMATION	Interests include the stock market, jogging, and biking. I biked from Mexico to Canada (Summer 1990).

What *Not* to Include on Your Resume

- The word "resume." There's no need to identify the document. Everyone knows what a resume looks like.
- Any mention of your age, race, religion, sex, national origin, marital status, or number of children. The government has outlawed discrimination in these areas.
- Any physical description (height, weight) or mention of your state of heath.
- Any listing of, or mention of, references. You may see a line on some resumes: "References available upon request." Today most employers assume that you have people to recommend you, and they'll ask you for them when they have determined they're interested in hiring you. (More about references in Chapter 8.)

Your Resume's Appearance

Your resume is your representative in a potential employer's office, so it should be neat, easy to read, and letter perfect—no inconsistencies, no typos! The computer/word processor and the laser printer are the best things that have happened to resume preparation in recent years; they can check your spelling, allow you to switch sections with ease, and give you a number of typefaces and styles to experiment with. Unfortunately, this means that resumes typed on old-fashioned typewriters will look less than competitive. If you don't have your own personal computer, ask to use a friend's or book time at your college career office or computer center. Or employ a friend to prepare your resume. Some copy and printing shops have a special resume preparation service, with staff to help you choose the right format, and so on. They might also offer advice on how to organize your material, but take their suggestions with a grain of salt; these people are usually not qualified career counselors. As you plan how your resume will look, consider the following:

1. *Length.* Employers find that many resumes submitted are too long. Banks and management consulting firms, in fact, will not read resumes that are longer than a page. Try to keep yours to a single sheet if you possibly can, without squeezing the layout or sacrificing margin space. If you've edited all you can and still need more space, a page and a half is acceptable in most cases. Be sure your name is on both sheets.

2. *Paper.* Use good quality white or cream-colored 8½ × 11-inch paper; purchase matching envelopes and extra blank sheets from the printer for cover letters. Do not use colored paper, even "conservative" colors such as light brown or grey. The type is harder to read on colors other than white.

3. *Layout.* Think of a resume as blocks of type with underlined or bold-faced headings and lead-ins. They should be neatly and consistently presented on the page so that there is a sense of unity and lack of visual distraction. There should also be plenty of white space: Huge, solid blocks of copy are hard to read. You might want to center your headings in a symmetrical presentation or position them flush left in an asymmetrical layout. The resume sections presented later in this chapter will give you some ideas.

4. *Grammar and Spelling.* Nothing will ruin your resume in the eyes of an employer more quickly than a typo—especially if you have said you're detail oriented. Have several people who are good with words read your resume for grammar, spelling, and typos; after sitting at

the computer all night, you may not recognize the errors. Put the text through a computer spell check. Double-check all names of companies, towns, abbreviations for states, and so forth.

5. *Consistency.* This is an extremely important factor in a professional presentation. Your resume should be consistent in use of typeface. If one heading is in boldface, for example, all other comparable headings should be in bold. Be consistent in the word forms that you use. If you capitalize the seasons (for example, Fall 1990) in one entry, you must capitalize them in other places as well. If you refer to Fall, 1990 with a comma between, you must do that in similar situations throughout. Decide ahead of time whether you'll abbreviate states, capitalize college courses (i.e., Philosophy of Religion, Advanced Organic Chemistry), and do so throughout. Do you want to use the form "1991–92" or "1991–1992"? Decide and use the same form throughout.

6. *Simplicity.* With the advent of the computer and laser printer, you will have a greater variety of typestyles to choose from—boldface, italic, underlined, and so on—but don't get carried away with graphics. Too many typestyles can look silly or distracting, and fancy designs and unusual presentations work only for graphic arts jobs or advertising, and even then only occasionally. Keep your resume simple and clear, and let the content speak for itself.

Your Resume Grows

Putting a resume together at the last minute needn't be a rushed, energy-depleting hassle if you're organized enough to start a resume file early in your college career and add to it as you acquire new experiences. Katherine is *very* organized. For several years she has been updating her resume material bit by bit on a master file on disc in her personal computer (it could just as easily be typed, sheet by sheet, and stuck into a manila folder). This file contains every job, position, membership, honor, and skill she can remember, no matter how minuscule or long ago. Katherine has divided her master file into five fields—counseling, business, nonprofit, hobbies/extracurriculars, and academic honors—to help her keep track of the skills she has developed. Describing the nature of the skills in each job or internship or volunteer experience helps her to get in touch with the skills that she has learned. She finds that once she has written about her skills on paper, it's easier for her to discuss them further, in a cover letter, for example, or on a job interview. Her complete master file looks like this:

KATHERINE FISHBURN

College Address:
Hopkins House
Smith College
Northampton, MA 01063
Telephone (413) 555-1212

Permanent Address:
P.O. Box 100
City, State, Zip
Telephone (804) 555-1212

Education

Smith College, Northampton, MA. B.A. expected: May, 1990. G.P.A. 3.75
Major: Psychology, with special emphasis in social psychology and women's studies.
Languages: Minimal French, BASIC, Pascal, Lotus, WordPerfect, XyWrite and other word processors.

Counseling

Student Coordinator and Peer Adviser, Career Development Office, September 1988–present. Served as student consultant in design of program. Coordinated the training and activities of five Peer Advisers. Designed and wrote advertisements and in-house teaching tools. Counseled students on resume and cover letters, career skills development, and conducted outreach workshops in student dormitories.

Co-Coordinator, Career Steering Committee, State Scholars Academy, 1988–1989. Initiated and launched an annual career newsletter targeted at state leaders in industry, nonprofit organizations and colleges. Wrote and edited articles on career development skills. Compiled the entries solicited by students and developed coding system to further identify each entry.

Administrative Aide, Career Development Office, Smith College, September 1987–May 1988. Prepared an internship database, updated library holdings and assisted staff with student relations.

House Liaison, Career Development Office, Smith College, September 1987–May 1988. Distributed information on programs and deadlines, reduced post-college phobia and introduced peers to the office's resources.

Business

Special Projects Intern, Clarke & Coburn, City, State, Summer 1988. Created monthly motivational sales program for city branch. Set goals and rewards for 80 employees with the cooperation of department managers. Provided support services for managers and sales clerks throughout set-up of program and recorded weekly progress.

Self-employed, Hometown, State, 1985–1986. Instructed students, ages seven to fourteen, in piano and music. Developed curriculum for levels beginner to experienced.

Other experience includes carpentry, sewing and repairing clothes and costumes, secretarial jobs, including word processing and database management, waitressing and other kitchen work.

Nonprofit

Advisory Council, State Scholars Academy, August 1988–present. Critiqued all publications for further improvement and aided staff in developing and enhancing programs to meet members' needs.

Scholars Academy Intern, State Scholars Academy, September 1985–August 1986.

»Editor, State Scholar: edited students' and professional educators' articles, designed and constructed layout and supervised final publication and distribution.

»Program Coordinator: planned and supervised eight summer-long educational programs, coordinated and accompanied annual Roots of Civilization tour to Greece. While there presented a quantitative research paper on Greek women and theater.

»Instructor/Counselor: taught self-awareness and self-presentation through writing and college application skills (interviewing and touring) to 100 high school juniors from across State. Represented these students at First National Transition Symposia in New York.

Hobbies/Extracurriculars

Co-Chair, Senior Ball Committee, Smith College, 1990. Coordinated activities of Physical Plant, Dining Services, President's Office and my committee, budgeted $500 for decorations for 1000 guests, negotiated with businesses for best price and with college departments for support, supervised quality control of four subcommittees, networked with similar student organizations, and decorated ballroom.

Librarian, Smith College Glee Club, 1989–1990. Supervised the distribution and collection of music for 80 members. Maintained database record system.

Eliminator of Confusion [stage manager], Smith College Glee Club, 1988–1989. Organized the activities of 70 Smith members plus any visiting choirs and accompanists. Largest production: full orchestra and 150 choristers. Besides these duties, served in any nonconventional capacity not covered by other Cabinet members.

Associate Secretary, Smith College Glee Club, 1987–1988. Handled attendance and absenteeism issues for the 40 Altos.

Gold Key Guide [admissions office representative], Smith College Admissions Office, 1987–1989. Conducted weekly tours of campus for prospective students and others. Hosted prospective students for overnight visits.

Energy Representative, Hopkins House, 1988–1989. Distributed information within house and motivated students to conserve energy, especially during conservation contest.

Soprano II, Smith College Chamber Singers, 1988. Trained four to six hours per week, culminating in week-long performance tour in England plus several local concerts.

Alto I, Smith College Chamber Singers, 1989–1990. Trained two hours per week, culminating in two-week performance tour of Sweden, Denmark, and Germany plus several local concerts.

Alto I, Smith College Choir, 1986–1987. Rehearsed four hours per week for several performance dates.

Handbell Choir, 1986–1987. Assisted in the formation, including writing charter and budget. Rehearsed four hours per week for several performance dates.

Academic Honors

Jill Ker Conway Scholar, 1988. This scholarship for $1000 is presented to one sophomore for proven industry, academic excellence and significant contribution to Smith environment.

Psi Chi, inducted 1988. National Honor Society in Psychology.

First Group Scholar, 1987–1988. Maintained GPA of 3.65 (A-) or better for the year.

Dean's List, 1986–1989. Maintained GPA of 3.33 (B+) or better.

Recently Katherine graduated and was ready to look for her first full-time job. Her career of choice right now is to be a conference or meeting planner for a corporation, and for that she needs to show experience in organizing, planning, communicating, and negotiating.

Below is the resume Katherine put together from her master file. It's divided very simply into "Education" and "Experience." Under "Education," she lists not only Honors (they look good to any employer) but also her Extracurriculars, because her positions in the glee club and the senior ball committee required complicated organization and management of money and details. She wanted to move that sort of experience to the top of her resume.

Since Katherine has several employers whom she has returned to, she emphasized that by listing her "Experience" chronologically by employer rather than by job title. Thus her succession of jobs for each employer is evident. And she was able to keep her final resume for the convention and meeting planner jobs to a single page.

KATHERINE FISHBURN

College Address:	Permanent Address:
Hopkins House	P.O. Box 100
Smith College	City, State Zip
Northampton, MA 01063	Telephone: (804) 555-1212
Telephone: (413) 555-1212	

EDUCATION

Smith College, Northampton, MA. B.A. expected: May, 1990 GPA: 3.75

Major: Psychology, with special emphasis in social psychology and women's studies.

Languages: Minimal French, BASIC, Pascal, Lotus, WordPerfect, XyWrite, and other word processors.

Honors

Psi Chi, 1989. National Honor Society in Psychology.

Jill Ker Conway Scholar, 1988. $1000 scholarship presented to one sophomore for proven industry, academic excellence, and a significant contribution to the Smith environment.

First Group Scholar, 1987–88. Maintained GPA of 3.65 or better.

Dean's List, 1986–89. Maintained GPA of 3.33 or better.

Extracurriculars

Librarian, Glee Club, 1989–90. Supervised distribution of music for 80 members.

Stage Manager, Glee Club, 1988–89. Largest production: full orchestra and 120 choristers.

Associate Secretary, Glee Club, 1987–88. Handled attendance and absenteeism issues.

Member of 3 other music performance groups, including competitive European touring group.

Co-Chair, Senior Ball Committee, 1990. Coordinated activities of Physical Plant, Dining Services, President's Office and my committee; budgeted $500 for decorations for 1000 guests; negotiated with businesses for best price and with college departments for support; supervised quality control of four subcommittees; networked with similar student organizations; decorated ballroom.

EXPERIENCE

Career Development Office, Smith College, Northampton, MA

Student Coordinator and Peer Adviser, 1988–89. Served as student consultant in design of program; coordinated the training and activities of five Peer Advisers; designed and wrote advertisements and in-house teaching tools; counseled students on resume and cover letters, career skills development, and conducted outreach workshops in student dormitories.

Administrative Aide, 1987–88. Prepared an internship database; updated library holdings; assisted staff in student relations.

State Scholars Academy, City, State

Co-Coordinator, Career Steering Committee, 1988–89. Initiated and launched an annual career newsletter targeted at state leaders in industry, nonprofit organizations, and colleges; wrote and edited articles on career development skills; compiled the entries solicited by students; developed coding system to further identify each entry.

Scholars Academy Intern, September 1985–August 1986.

»*Program Coordinator.* Planned and supervised eight summer-long educational programs; coordinated and accompanied annual Roots of Civilization tour to Greece.

»*Editor,* State Scholar. Edited students' and professional educators' articles; designed and constructed layout; supervised final publication and distribution.

»*Instructor/Counselor.* Taught self-awareness and self-presentation through writing and college application skills (interviewing and touring) to 100 high school juniors from across WV.

Clarke & Coburn, City, State (Retail chain)

Special Projects Intern, Summer 1988. Created monthly motivational sales program for city branch; set goals and rewards for 80 employees with the cooperation of department managers; provided support services for managers and sales clerks throughout setup of program; recorded weekly progress.

Here are two other complete resumes that show the effective use of different formats. Victoria is a junior. Although she has a good academic background, especially in languages, her jobs have so far been pretty much clerical in nature. Notice how her use of action verbs makes the most of those beginning library jobs.

VICTORIA VARGAS

College Address:
Cushing House
Smith College
Northampton, MA 01063
Telephone: (413) 555-1212

Home Address:
122 Dean Street
La Santa, NM 03358
Telephone: (505) 555-1212

EDUCATION

Smith College, Northampton, MA
Candidate for Bachelor of Arts degree in May, 1992
Major: Government (International Relations Concentration)
Minor: Spanish Literature
GPA: 3.2, Dean's List, 1990–1991

Additional Coursework: International Law, Latin American and European History, Macro-Economics, Art History, French Language and Literature.

Languages: Spanish (fluent), French (near fluent), Russian (1 year).

ACTIVITIES & ELECTED OFFICES

NOSOTRAS (Hispanic Students Organization)
Gold Key Society (admissions office representative)
Student Recruiter (admissions)
Pre-Law Society
Intercollegiate Varsity Crew Team
House (Dorm) President
Junior Class Secretary
Career Development Office Liaison
Dorm Fire Captain
Dorm Council
Freshman Representative
Dorm Gold Key Liaison

EXPERIENCE

Career Development Office, Smith College, Northampton, MA (September, 1990–Present).
Maintain, update, and file in Graduate School and Employer files. Ability to perform a variety of clerical tasks, attention to detail and accuracy very important.

Smith College Library, Northampton, MA (September, 1990–May, 1991).
Circulation and Reserve Desks. Compiled statistics; aided patrons in discharging and processing of books; aided in location of resource materials.

Harvard University Library, Cambridge, MA (Summers, 1989, 1990).
Circulation Division. Discharge and locate material; knowledge of Library of Congress and Harvard cataloguing systems; occasional supervision of area; strong interpersonal skills.

PERSONAL INTERESTS

Languages, Reading, Rowing, Swimming, Flute and Piano. Have traveled extensively and lived with native families in France and Spain.

* * *

Tanya, who has just graduated, has been exploring careers in publishing or arts administration. Her most responsible job was a volunteer position—editor of the college yearbook—and she makes sure it gets noticed as the first item in her Experience section, instead of listing it under Education or placing it farther down in the resume under Activities.

TANYA LOGAN

Temporary Address	Permanent Address
Duckett House	4 Center St.
Smith College	Seattle, Washington 10101
Northampton,	(615) 555–1212
Massachusetts 01063	
(413) 555-1212	

EDUCATION

Smith College, Northampton, Massachusetts
  Bachelor of Arts, May 1991
  Majors: Art History and Economics
  Languages: Reading knowledge of French, elementary Spanish
North Atlantic Cultural Exchange League, France, Summer 1990
Additional Experience in Macintosh Desktop publishing and computer processing

EXPERIENCE

SMITH COLLEGE MADELEINE (Yearbook), Northampton, Massachusetts

Editor, (1990–present) Negotiated contracts with a new publisher and photography studio. Interviewed, appointed, and trained a staff of twenty. Budgeted the $40,000 production of the yearbook.

Associate Editor, (1989–1990) Initiated a fund-raising campaign to supplement the allotment from Student Activity Fees to finance improvements in design. Launched a program to increase circulation and revenue through parent sponsorship.

Senior-Section Editor, (1988–1989) Organized, designed, and executed the largest single section of the yearbook.

SMITH COLLEGE MUSEUM OF ART, Northampton, Massachusetts (1990–present)

Assistant to Associate Curator of Painting and Sculpture. Researched artists associated with current exhibits, prepared documentation files on works in the collection, and aided in preparing works for exhibition.

WEST SIDE ANTIQUE MARKET, Seattle, Washington (1988–1989)

Sales Associate. Bought and sold European and American antique and estate furniture and jewelry. Wrote advertising spread for publication.

SMITH COLLEGE CAREER DEVELOPMENT OFFICE, Northampton, Massachusetts (1987–1988)

Graphics Assistant. Solely responsible for designing, producing, and distributing on-campus publicity.

SEATTLE MUSEUM OF ART, (Summer 1989)

Receptionist. Supervised weekend activities in the Museum.

ACTIVITIES

Departmental Liaison, Smith College Art Department (1988–present)

Chosen as a student representative to serve on faculty search committees, interviewed candidates, surveyed students, and conveyed the results to the faculty.

Gold Key Guide, Smith College Admissions Office (1989–present)
Chosen to guide prospective students and their parents around the college.

Class Representative, Smith College Dormitory Council (1988–1990)
Elected to act as liaison between the students in the dormitory and members of the Class of 1991.

Head of Freshman, Smith College Dormitory Council (1988–1989)
Elected to represent student concerns in the dormitory council and aided the first-year students in the transition process.

INTERESTS

Contemporary American Art, Graphic Design, Violin, Tennis, Aerobics

Cover Letters

Generally speaking, cover letters are letters that are prepared to accompany your resume when you are contacting a potential employer by mail. But to distinguish them from letters requesting informational interviews (Chapter 5) or door-opening letters (Chapter 6), we'll define a cover letter as a letter written to apply for an actual job opening. Many people make the mistake of replying to a want ad or responding to a job opening by sending a resume alone. This almost guarantees that they will not be considered. Employers, like other people, want to be approached in a courteous manner, and want to feel there's an enthusiastic, motivated human being behind the fact sheet. Furthermore, cover letters give you, the applicant, a great opportunity to introduce yourself, to show a little knowledge about the company or industry you're considering, and to point up a few of the relevant skills in your resume.

Some people write cover letters of only a few lines: "I am writing to apply for the job of ________, as noted in the *Boston Herald*. Enclosed is my resume." They know they have to write a cover letter, but make the mistake of covering the bare minimum. An effective cover letter is more than a mere add-on to a resume; it's a sales document in and of itself. A good cover letter is a companion and guide to your resume. It helps the employer make sense of your experience and relate it to his needs. And it gives a more personal picture of you than it's possible to give in a resume alone.

Preparing to Write Your Cover Letter

If you're answering a newspaper ad, or if you hear of a job opportunity from a friend or contact but are unfamiliar with the organization you'll be applying to, do some homework first. Before you sit down to write, find out the answers to these questions:

1. What does the organization make, do, sell, research, and so on? Phone the company for literature (page 140); use your network and see if you can talk to a friend of a friend who works there.
2. What does the job description or application form tell you about the organization and its current needs? Since advertisements are brief and the friend who gave you the tip can give you only the basics, try to get the name of someone at the organization (a personnel staffer or the person you'd be working for) and call him or her to find out what kind of job you're really applying for.
3. To whom should you be addressing your letter? To obtain the name (spelled correctly), title, and work address, simply call the organization's switchboard or personnel office.
4. What interests you about the opening? Take some time alone with a pencil and paper, and think about why this job possibility intrigues you. What have you

done that might show the reader that you already have some relevant experience, or have demonstrated the potential to learn the job quickly? Look over your resume, compare it with the job description, and pinpoint the places where the organization's requirements and your favorite skills overlap or are related.

Appearance and Tone of Your Cover Letter

Keep your cover letter to a single page of three or four paragraphs (see page 196 for business letter form). Your paper should be white or cream, and it's a nice touch if it matches your resume. But unlike your resume, your letter should always look handcrafted—not printed and certainly not photocopied. Type it (or have it typed) on a good-quality typewriter or print it out from a PC on a letter-quality printer.

Although each cover letter you write should be slanted to the person to whom it's addressed and his or her particular job needs, you certainly don't need to reinvent the wheel each time you write. Keep three or four standard versions on a computer disc, or photocopy each letter you write and revise it slightly each time you write a new one. Switch around paragraphs and emphasize one set of skills or another as needed.

Effective cover letters are personal and conversational; they should sound like you in your most mature and confident mood. See if you can convey your sincere enthusiasm without being overblown or gushy. Use words like "delighted," "pleased," "excited," "intrigued"; but think twice before you use "thrilled," "marvelous," "fascinating" or repeat the verb "love" too often. Be friendly but be careful of automatically assuming a chumminess with the person you're writing to. Have a friend (or two) read your letter over and comment on the tone, but make sure *you* feel good about it before you send it.

What to Cover in a Cover Letter

There are three different content areas in an effective cover letter, which can be outlined as follows:

First paragraph: State why you are writing. Talk about the position you're after and how you heard about it. Help your reader out by giving her all the details so that she immediately understands what you're talking about.

> **Incomplete Opener:** *I was delighted to see your advertisment in the* Boston Herald *because . . .*
>
> **Strong Opener:** *I was delighted to see your advertisement for marketing trainee in the* Boston Herald *(Sunday, May 20) because . . .*
>
> **Incomplete Opener:** *I was pleased to hear from Mr. David Canaday that there was a position available in your company for a marketing trainee.*
>
> **Strong Opener:** *I was pleased to hear from Mr. David Canaday, your company's production manager and the father of a good friend of mine, that a position for a marketing trainee has recently opened up in your department.*

Follow up your opening sentence with some information on what attracted you to this company or this job:

> *As a skier of eight years who's always looking for comfortable and stylish outfits, I noticed the arrival of Slalom ski clothes on the market in 1989, and was especially attracted by your refreshingly nonsexist advertising. After reading some of your company's literature, I'm excited by your team spirit philosophy, and like the idea of a small staff where people get to perform a variety of tasks.*

Next one or two paragraphs: What you can bring to the job. In this next section, focus not so much on your career goals but *on the employer's needs and how you can meet them.* This is sometimes hard for beginners to get; they're often very eager to talk about what they want from the job, what they want the company to teach them. It's better, though, to address the company's selfish interests here. Talk about what you can offer, which of your skills will be of value—in fact, use those words and phrases. Point to areas on your resume that will support your most valuable skills and interests:

Both team spirit and athletics have meant a great deal to me throughout my college years. As you'll see on my resume, I participated in three varsity sports and was captain of the volleyball team, which placed second in the regional competitions last year. I feel my ability to work cooperatively with others and to motivate them will surely be of value in this particular job.

If you don't have particular skills directly related to the job, point out those more generic skills all employers are looking for in beginners: perseverence, follow-through, ability to learn quickly, self-motivation.

In analyzing the job description your office was kind enough to send me, it seems that what you really need in a new marketing assistant is a "quick study"—someone who can take on new responsibilities and quickly figure out what needs to be done. As noted on my resume, I ran my boss's boutique singlehandedly in the summer of 1990 when she had a health emergency, and oversaw cash flow, the arrangement of new stock, and the relationships with suppliers. I even hired a temporary staffer. I was very busy but it was great fun.

Last paragraph: What will happen next. You have a choice of how to end your letter: You can sign off in a way that leaves it up to the employer to contact you, or you can state that you'll be calling to see whether he would want to interview you. The first choice seems a little safer and less of a risk; the second is a little more assertive. Do whatever is most in line with your intuitive feelings about the job and your personal style. If you say you'll call, however, be sure to do so. That you keep your word is important to employers—and to your own sense of self-confidence. If you're sending out many letters, it will be hard to call everyone; you might consider sending out a few letters at a time and following up with phone calls. Also, bear in mind if you're applying to companies in a faraway city, a statement about when you'll be in town will press them into a decision about whether or not they want to see you. Here are some ways you could end the letter:

I look forward very much to talking with you further about this position; I hope I will hear from you soon.

I hope I will have the opportunity to further discuss with you my qualifications for this position. I will call you early in the week of January 5 to see if we can arrange an interview.

I will be in Chicago the week of March 20–25. May I telephone you this coming week to see if I might meet with you?

How to Write the Perfect Job-Hunt Letter

Your job campaign will require that you write various kinds of letters along the way. For the sake of convenience we have divided them into three main categories: informational interview letters (letters asking for career advice); door-opening letters (letters requesting interviews from companies that you'd like to work for but who may have no jobs open at the moment); cover letters (letters of application for a job you know is available). They are targeted in a various ways, depending where you are in your career research or job hunt, and you'll find them described in Chapters 5, 6, and 7. The suggestions given there are by no means hard-and-fast; different circumstances require different approaches, so when you're writing your letters, it's a good idea to turn to each of the chapters mentioned for ideas.

However, most job-search letters do follow a particular physical format, and your ability to use it is an indication to employers of your maturity and professionalism. Here are the basic rules to follow:

1. Use good-quality 8½ x 11-inch bond paper, white or cream (matching your resume if you like). Do not use personalized stationery.

2. Try to keep your letters to a page in length with 1 to 1½-inch margins all around.

3. Use concise, energetic sentences and paragraphs. Be direct and conversational without being chatty. One way to identify circumlocutions and stiffness in your style is to read your letter aloud. If it sounds either pompous or hyperbolic, or you are uncomfortable with it in any way, change it. After you write your letter, edit it down so that every word counts. Pay particular attention to grammar and spelling. Remember, letters are your proxy in the offices of potential employers and they should represent you in the very best way, especially if you're claiming to offer writing skills.

4. Include your telephone number on your letter, even if it's on your resume, since the resume and the cover letter may become separated. You can put it under your address in the upper right hand corner, above the date, or you can put it below your signature (leave a couple of spaces).

5. Type your letter perfectly. Letters should always be personally prepared on an up-to-date typewriter or on a personal computer with a letter-quality printer. They should never look commercially printed or, worse, photocopied. They must be single spaced with double spaces between paragraphs. You may indent five spaces at the beginning of a paragraph or begin it flush left, but whatever

style you choose, be consistent. If your letter runs onto a second page, put your name and page number in the upper righthand corner (for example, "Martin / 2"). Be sure to position your letter on both pages so that there's more than just a line and a signature block on the second page.

6. In closing, stick to "Sincerely yours" or "Yours truly." "Cordially" may seem too chummy, "Respectfully yours" too servile. After the closing, leave five or six spaces and type your name. Sign your name above it in ink, exactly as typed—no nicknames.

7. Set up a chronological file for your career correspondence. Make a copy of each letter you write and keep it in the file, so you'll know when to follow up, whom to call, and what you have already said. On each letter jot down whether a resume was included.

For Further Reading

Faux, Marian G. *The Complete Resume Guide: More Than 200 Job Categories Keyed to Model Resumes.* New York: Monarch Press, 1988.

Jackson, Tom. *The Perfect Resume*, revised ed. New York: Anchor Press, 1990.

Lewis, Adele. *Better Resumes for College Graduates.* Woodbury, N.Y.: Barron's Educational Series, Inc., 1985.

McLaughlin, John E., and Stephen K. Merman. *Writing a Job-Winning Resume.* Englewood Cliffs, N.J.: Prentice-Hall, 1980.

Parker, Yana. *The Resume Catalog: 200 Damn Good Examples.* Berkeley: Ten Speed Press, 1988.

Yate, Martin John. *Resumes That Knock 'Em Dead.* Holbrook, Mass.: Bob Adams, Inc., 1988.

CHAPTER

8

Job Interviews

Opportunities for *bona fide* job interviews—appointments to discuss actual job openings that you might be suited for, in interesting organizations in fields you've been exploring—can occur at any time in the job-search process. Sometimes they come at the beginning, as a total surprise, before you've found your sense of direction or had a chance to do adequate research. Or they may come after months of waiting, when you've just about given up hope of ever finding the right job. Rest assured, though, that if you've done even half of the self-assessment and background research suggested in the preceding pages, you'll be way ahead of most of your competition. You'll have a good fix on what skills you're best at and enjoy most, and you'll be able to demonstrate them in your "success stories" from past work/school/volunteer experience. You'll at least be starting to read about the fields most interesting to you—assessing the possible rewards and difficulties in these areas, identifying current issues, targeting growth areas, and getting a sense of the kinds of entry-level jobs available. You may even have already researched certain companies.

The trick in any job interview, however, is to bring the

most relevant information about who you are, what you can do, and what you know to the attention of the interviewer in the short period of time allotted—usually a half an hour or forty-five minutes. Although a few people have the gift of thinking fast on their feet and spontaneously handling tough questions well, for most of us the best way to maximize this half-hour opportunity is through preparation and practice.

Another thing to know: Interviews usually come in pairs. Your first interview for most positions is a screening interview. Sometimes such interviews happen on campus when company recruiters come around. In this case, your second interview will be on the site where you will work. Or, both the initial and the follow-up interview can be given on site. More about second interviews later in this chapter.

The tips below will help you to make a success of your first interview even if it comes at the beginning of your job search, when you've just begun to do your homework.

Give Yourself Preparation Time

This is particularly important if you get a job interview out of the blue (but even if you've carefully set it up). See if you can buy yourself a few days or even a week to get ready for it. Say, for example, you're in the information-collecting stage of your job hunt. To your surprise, someone hears about you from a person you spoke with on an information interview, calls about a job vacancy, and says, "Can you come for an interview tomorrow?" Even though you might feel immensely flattered by this unexpected attention, don't feel you must say yes. Unless there's some pressing reason why you have to follow up right away (for example, the person is leaving town tomorrow night), it's best to postpone the interview until you've had time to prep. A good response: "I'm delighted that you called and I'll be glad to meet with you, but I really can't before Wednesday." Or "I'd be delighted to meet with you, but early next week would be better for me. Is that all right with you?"

Now that you've gotten yourself a few days' working time, you'll want to spend it collecting pertinent information, psyching yourself up, planning answers that you might give to the questions asked of you. Here's how to start.

Compile All the Information You'll Need

Pull together all the information you've collected on this particular company. If the company is new to you, turn to page 135 and use whatever information-gathering suggestions seem most doable in the time you have. You might want to make a quick trip to the library, call the chamber of commerce, or stop by the company for brochures, a newsletter, or an annual report. Call anyone you know who is now working for the company, who has worked there in the past, or who has a friend who works there. Call anyone you know in a rival company and ask what they know.

Find out all you can about this particular job. Call the personnel department and ask for a written job description for the job you'll be interviewing for, if they have one. If you're able to network your way to someone who knows about the department you'd be working in or the supervisor you might have, make the most of this great connection by asking some of the questions on page 143.

Review the current issues in the industry in general. Pull out any magazine or newspaper articles you've saved about the current state of the field. They might generate some questions that you would want to ask your interviewer. Be sure to get a good idea of the range of beginners' salaries in the field.

Set Yourself Up Mentally

Find out where you are about interviews right now by giving yourself the following "Interviewability Assessment." Undoubtedly you'll feel more confident in some areas than in others. Those "This is hard for me" answers will give you an idea of the areas to practice on and prepare for in the time you have before the interview. The friend or relative you'll select to practice your interviews with can give you especially valuable feedback; you may be far more effective in those areas than you think you are.

Interviewability Assessment

The following somewhat elusive qualities are the factors that interviewers will be using in order to assess (1) the quality of your interaction with them, and thus (2) your strength as an applicant for employment.

I. Check the column to the right of each quality that best describes *the degree to which you feel you manifest this quality now.*

QUALITY	This is hard for me	I score 50/50 on this	This is easy for me
1. Appearance, poise	________	________	________
2. Interest and ability in business, with a clear, in-depth understanding of whatever career field to which you are applying	________	________	________

3. Perceptiveness, alertness			
4. Personal energy and vitality			
5. Assertiveness (not passivity, not aggressiveness); leadership			
6. Uniqueness			
7. Awareness of world issues and how your career in a business would be affected by events external to the organization			
8. Awareness of self			
9. Broad range of interests, experiences			
10. Sense of humor			
11. Self-confidence			
12. Independence			
13. Sense of audience			
14. Ability to handle tension and stress—"equinimitas"			

15. Technical/ quantitative skills ________ ________ ________

16. Motivation to be successful in your work ________ ________ ________

17. Clear sense of how your gender will and will not be a factor in your career life—or at least the ability to handle such questions easily ________ ________ ________

II. For each item that you check off as "hard" for yourself, brainstorm with a friend or counselor some ways to "move to the right" on this quality. Do you need to *develop it more* or just *demonstrate it more effectively?*

Match your demonstrable skills and strengths with the requirements of the job. Once you get as clear an idea as you can about what this job would involve, sit down with your "success stories," your resume and/or resume master file, and your Inspired Abilities Assessment, and decide which of your skills and experiences might best convince the interviewer that you would be a strong candidate for this particular job. Consider your background, academic performance, interests, personal aspirations, and values.

As you think this matter through, keep in mind that you'll never be able to present everything about yourself to a potential employer in a single interview, and if you try, you may well confuse the interviewer. In order to position yourself in a clear and memorable way, see if you can identify three to five major themes about your candidacy. Write each theme on a separate index card, and back it up with specific examples drawn from your success stories and your resume. Again, try to show your achievements in progress, as a story, instead of just stating a job duty or a school office.

Theme #1: Good at making deadlines

Incomplete Example: Ad salesperson, summer community newspaper.

Much Better: Was able to get weekly commitments from over fifty local merchants as to advertisement size and copy, and positioning on the newspaper, by 5:00 PM each Wednesday.

Other themes could be "Good at handling money," "Good writer," "Good problem-solver." Other suggestions can be found on pages 158–159.

After you complete these index cards, carry them around with you. Read through them while riding public transportation or each night before you go to sleep. They will bolster your confidence, and you will eventually become so familiar with them that you will spontaneously offer them as examples and answers to questions during your interview. More about this later.

Identify the weaknesses of your candidacy. Undoubtedly there will be areas in your background that aren't entirely favorable—an uneven record, a borderline GPA, poor test scores, minimal work experience, being let go from a job. Don't let those problem areas dishearten you—everyone has some area she's less than proud of, and no employer expects a candidate to be perfect. In fact, your forthright and positive answers when questioned about these delicate matters can turn the tide of the interview in your favor. For this reason, you need to face any potentially embarrassing areas in your background and consider how best to discuss them.

You should know that some interviewers (mostly representatives of competitive, high-finance organizations or fast-track corporate training programs) are much more concerned about grades and GPA than others. Many employers won't ask you about your grades at all, or will ask you in the most general way.

Be ready to blow your own horn. Job interviews are really different in purpose and tone from the information-gathering interviews, where you were asking questions and seeking knowledge. Now it's time to really talk *yourself* up; you are competing for a real spot with other candidates, and cheerful self-confidence is very attractive to an employer who is looking for someone who'll take hold of the job with energy and enthusiasm. The trouble is, it's hard for women just out of college to parade their strengths in a straightforward way, because they often don't quite believe in them themselves. What if you didn't always make all those deadlines? What if you left that summer job in disgust halfway through? What if you're not so sure you're such a highly motivated self-starter? Most people have a fair number of false starts and wrong turns in their early life.

Bear in mind, though, that it's an all-too-human tendency to dismiss our successes as unimportant ("Oh, anyone could do that") and to dwell on our failures. No one's perfect, including those competing with you for this job. There are two main ways of keeping your confidence up during the interviewing process: Keep reading your index cards and your success stories, and practice answering interview questions with a partner until confident answers become second nature.

Switch from a college point of view to a business point of view. As you begin to think about your interview, your mind might naturally return to four years ago when you were undergoing those grueling college entrance interviews. But college interviews are different from job interviews in a subtle but important way, and you'll be much more attractive as a job candidate if you can grasp the difference and take a slightly different tack than the one that may have worked in the past.

Colleges and universities have a very different purpose from companies, and switching from one to the other calls for some refocusing. When you attend a college, you are both the consumer of education and the product of your college; furthermore, you are paying the college to educate you. Therefore (and this is especially true in small colleges), your well-being and intellectual growth are the main concerns of the faculty. This tends to foster a "me first" attitude on the part of students; at least to some extent, the college staff is there to help you solve your problems.

On the other hand, in any sort of organization where you're an employee, you're largely considered the means to an end, be it a quality service or product, or a healthy profit. *You* are the one being paid, and you are being paid to solve company problems. This means that your ambitions and goals will be less important to an interviewer than your possible contributions to their company. Many people, even those who have been working for years, don't really understand this; they feel it's the company's job to take care of them. Therefore, if you show some understanding of this idea, you'll be way ahead of most of your competition. As you formulate the answers to your questions, do so in a way that includes company goals. Instead of saying "I'd enjoy being a marketing assistant here," a more effective reply would be "I think I'd make a real contribution to this company as a marketing assistant."

Prepare Your Answers to Tough Interview Questions

Now that you've brought all your material together, it's time to prepare for the interview. One of the best ways to do this is to anticipate questions you'll be asked and plan out how you might answer them. Below are a number of questions interviewers often ask, grouped as to the kind of material they're designed to elicit. Following this is some advice on handling those "soft" areas in your background that might require some explaining.

Most-Asked Questions on Job Interviews

- Tell me about yourself.
- What are your major accomplishments?
- What experience do you have that's relevant to the job?
- What are your greatest strengths?
- What are you most proud of about yourself?
- Why should we hire you?

Interviewers who ask these questions are throwing you the ball in a general way to see what you will do with it, and also testing your self-confidence. These are perfect opportunities to sing your song, to set forth the themes of your candidacy and back them up with success stories. Choose one or two statements about yourself that that support the themes you've identified: "Well, I tend to bring a lot of energy to everything I do." Then back up this statement with a success story of how you worked longer and harder than you had to, pushed for a result when everyone else gave up.

Especially with the first question, don't wander off the track by thinking the interviewer wants a life history ("Well, I was born in Boise, Idaho, in 1968") or giving him details of your personal life (your relationship with your boyfriend, your family situation, your most recent vacation, or how many children you want to have). Unless the interviewer asks you specifically about more personal matters, keep all your answers company- and job-related.

If very general questions such as these come at the beginning of the interview, you might feel compelled to give everything you've got right away. Don't tell too much too soon. You don't have to tell *everything* about yourself. If the interviewer wants more, he'll ask for it.

- What were your biggest problems in college? On your last job?
- What is your greatest weakness?
- What has been your biggest difficulty (frustration) to date?
- Describe a difficult event or situation in your life and how you handled it.

These are tricky questions. You and the interviewer both know you're not perfect, so you can't pretend that your weaknesses don't exist. On the other hand, you don't want to be drawn into a situation where you unnecessarily reveal negative information about yourself. Here are three different ways to approach these questions.

1. Include among your success stories at least one in which you were asked to correct a work habit or modify a personality trait—and did so. For example:

Part of my job involved proofreading. I started by reading copy at my usual speed, which was really too fast for proofing, and my boss told me I wasn't catching enough errors. I worked hard to slow down and check every syllable, and I also began reading proofs aloud with a coworker. By the end of the summer, my boss told me I was finding more errors than the professional proofreader she hired the year before.

MESSAGE: "I'm easy to manage. I take criticism well, and I approach problems in a logical way."

2. On the theory that every character trait has both positive and negative aspects, choose one of your qualities that could have a negative side, and show how you've worked with that quality to maximize the positives. For example:

Well, I tend to worry a lot. This is because I take things seriously, I'm responsible, and it is important to me that I do well. In college, I've learned that I can turn that worry into positive energy. When I begin to worry, I immediately do something about the situation, and if I can't at the moment, I take a brisk walk. I find that as I've gained confidence over the last four years, I worry much less.

MESSAGE: "I'm a serious, responsible person. I'm learning to handle anxiety in a mature and positive way, and use it as a motivation for action."

3. Take a difficult situation (school or work) and talk about how you handled it as an example of how you solve problems—for example, analyzing the nature of the problem, talking to "experts" about it, trying on different approaches for size to find the one with the best fit, seeking out people for support.

Whichever way you choose to approach this question, be sure you devote only about a quarter of your answer to dealing with the negative aspects of the problem; use the other three-quarters outlining the solutions and turning the situation around into a positive. Any organization is looking for employees who can solve problems, and here you have a great opportunity to show your trouble-shooting style.

- Why do you want to work in this field?
- What will you be able to contribute to this field?
- What do you know about this field?
- What do you consider the most important issues in this field today?

Now you'll get to use all that research. Think about how your inspired abilities fit the needs of the field. Be prepared to talk about the most crucial problems currently facing the field, some general approaches you might recommend in dealing with them, and end up (as always) talking about how you feel you can contribute.

- What do you know about this company?
- Why do you want to work for this company?

Here's your cue to use the material in all those brochures, newsletters, annual reports, and word of mouth about the current problems of the company. If you have an idea of your interviewer's goals for her department, you can persuade her that you're the one to help her achieve them.

- What are your career goals?
- Where do you see yourself in five years?

Questions like these are meant to uncover how well your goals for growth align with a company's aims. But they're hard for new college graduates, who tend to be rather vague about what kinds of activities and responsibilities they'll like best, and also what sort of options companies will offer them. You don't have to have an iron-clad ten-year plan, but you need to offer something more definite than "Well, I'm not sure." Try to find out what the company does with people who start out in the position you're applying for. You might go to the library and look in *The Occupational Outlook Handbook*, put out by the Federal Bureau of Labor Statistics. It describes about 250 different jobs in detail. Check out the duties of more advanced positions in the field to which you're applying. Armed with that knowledge, you'll be able to explain what you'd like to do down the road. It's fine to respond to a future-oriented probe with "I'd like to know more about settling insurance claims or perhaps claims adjusting because I'm good at numbers." It's a simple answer, but it demonstrates openness plus a basic knowledge of the industry you're considering.

- Why did you choose your college? In retrospect, how do you feel about that decision?

Be prepared to field some questions about how you selected your college, and whether you liked your choice. If you went to a women's college, your interviewer may ask why you chose that experience. Or if your resume indicates a transfer, you may be asked about that. The interviewer wants to see how you make important life decisions, where you are about commitments, how you think ahead and plan. So talk about the various options you considered and how you evaluated them. Always talk about the positive reasons for any decisions you made. Don't say, "I left *X* University because I was miserable there." Rather say, "I chose to transfer to *Y* College because I became intrigued by psychology and the program there was much stronger."

- What do you think of the professors at your college?
- What did you think of your last job?
- What did you think of your last supervisor?

The purpose of asking questions like these is to identify chronic blamers and complainers, people who are unhappy wherever they go, and people who have trouble with authority figures. No matter what a beast your last boss was, find something nice that you can sincerely say about him, and say it. Keep your answers brief and positive.

- Your GPA is on the low side. Can you explain?
- You don't seem to have a great many extracurricular activities. Can you explain?

If you've done your homework, you've targeted those soft spots in your record and have decided how you can best address them. Do not blame your fate or other people or defensively reel off a list of excuses. Simply acknowledge the problem (25 percent of your answer) and then talk about the positive side of things (75 percent). For example:

This college was so much more competitive than my high school that it took me some time to catch up. I learned to prioritize, to plan my time, and I even joined a study group. Once I got into the swing, I gained confidence and did fine. You'll notice that my grades in the last two years are far better than earlier.

Other questions you might be asked:

- Are you willing to go where the company sends you? For how long?
- How will your liberal arts education manifest itself in the work you would do for us?
- Talk about your intellectual curiosity. How does it manifest itself? How would it be used in this field?
- How long will you stay with the company?
- How have you spent your time in college?
- Who is the most successful person you know? What constitutes this person's success?
- Do you intend to pursue graduate education? How? When?
- What makes you laugh? Why?
- Do you believe that females and males bring different or the same strengths to the business world?
- What do you do well outside of your academic work?
- What do you think is the most critical public issue of our time? Why? Would you intend to be involved in addressing the problem?
- What were your most difficult subjects?
- Do you think your grades are a good indicator of your abilities?
- If you were choosing a major again, would you choose the same one? Why?
- During your college years, how do you feel you have matured the most and why?

Fielding Out-of-Bounds Questions

Illegal interview questions touching on age, national origin, marital status, or plans to have a family are less frequent today than they once were. Smart interviewers go out of their way to avoid asking them, but if you happen on one who does, decide whether this person is just making small talk. If so (even though it's not required), you might want to reply to the question without making an issue of it. However, if you feel the interviewer is on a fishing expedition, try to get at the underlying reasons and answer them rather than exposing more about yourself than necessary by locking into the question itself.

By inquiring about your plans for marriage and family, for example, employers may be trying to find out whether you're serious about a career. A good reply might be, "If what you're asking is whether I'm committed to a career with this company, the answer is definitely yes. I want to grow, and I finish what I start."

The interviewer may also be wondering whether you'd consider a job in another city, or whether you're available for travel. Whether or not you know in advance that these are likely to be concerns with this job, be prepared to discuss them. More and more firms are requiring drug tests and various kinds of honesty exams from new employees; although these steps may seem intrusive—and they're certainly controversial—at the moment, they're legal in most cases. If you object to such tests, perhaps it would be simpler not to apply for jobs that require them. Likewise, certain government agencies and state universities ask applicants to sign a waiver stating they will not request to see any information gathered for their application. (This waiver makes it easier for the agency to get written references from former employers.) Don't apply to companies or agencies that make this request if you don't intend to sign the waiver. The interviewer may say he doesn't care whether you sign, but if you don't, there's a strong possibility you'll be screened out.

Consider Some Questions You Might Ask

Ideally, a job interview should be a conversation, not an interrogation. Feel free to ask questions of your own. (Many times questions seem to fit best after you've answered an interviewer's question.) Be sure, though, that the questions you ask are good ones, and you ask them because you really want to know the answers, not because you think you're expected to ask something. Here are ways to be sure your questions will be useful and strengthen your candidacy.

1. The better questions are usually those that flow from the content of the conversation. The interviewer gives you some information; you probe for more specifics or ask for an elaboration; the answer generates more questions.
2. Try not to ask the obvious kinds of questions that are answered in the company brochure; rather, show that you've done your homework by reading the annual report and letting the information there generate questions.
3. Never ask questions in order to try to show how smart you are, or how much you know, or to make the interviewer look foolish. The only legitimate reason to ask a question is because you genuinely want to learn the answer or to generate further discussion.

Kinds of Questions Job Applicants Often Ask

Although the best questions are spontaneous and appropriate to your own situation, it's useful to know the kinds of questions that are asked and the topics that are discussed at interviews. Choose the ones that sound most interesting to you, and ask them in your own words.

- What are some of the most difficult situations you're dealing with in this department now?

This can be a useful question to ask near the beginning of the interview, since it is designed to bypass the niceties on the job description and unearth the stickier situations you'll be dealing with on the job. As the interviewer explains his toughest problems, you can mentally flip through your success stories and find a couple that will show how you could help him solve those problems. Such a question also shows that you're willing to roll up your sleeves and be a troubleshooter.

- Are there particular qualities that you are looking for?

Again, this question is designed to bypass the formalities of the job description and inquire about the personal preferences and biases of the interviewer. As the interviewer outlines the qualities he prefers, ask yourself, "Does this sound like me? Does this sound like someone I want to become?" These questions are very important.

- How will I know if I'm doing a good job? How are employees evaluated and promoted?
- What has happened to people who have started with this job? What sorts of career paths have they followed?
- What are the characteristics of a person who has been successful in this job? Is successful in this company?
- What are the most challenging aspects of this job?
- Which of the major industry trends most affect this company and how is the company responding?
- How is this company doing financially?
- What makes this company different from others in the field?

- Can you describe the company's strengths and weaknesses?
- What would you expect me to have learned after a year on the job? What might I be contributing?
- Can you explain the overall structure of the department in which I would be working?
- Does this company (department) have any plans for growth or expansion? What are they? What kinds of talent will be needed?
- What is it like to work here? Describe the pace, the general attitude.
- How would you describe your management style? Is it similar to, or different from, other managers in the company?
- Why do you enjoy working for this company?

Handling the Issue of Salary and Benefits

Any job hunter is interested in the question of money, but it's best to allow your interviewer to bring the matter up first. There are all sorts of ways he might do this: He might mention the salary range in a *pro forma* manner first off in the interview as part of the job description; this tends to be the case when you're being interviewed by personnel. He might bring the matter up at the end of the first interview; if the interview has been lively and the fit is good, money talk at this time indicates you're a strong contender. Or discussions about salary may take place on the second interview, after preliminary screenings are done.

It's to your advantage to delay money discussions until later in the interview, when you and the interviewer have gotten a sense of each other and you know you're seriously being considered for the job. You will be worth more if you seem to fit in, and you'll have the confidence to negotiate a bit if you think the interviewer really likes you.

Some interviewers ask questions like, "What are you looking for in terms of money?" early in the interview process either because they don't know any better or to put you at a bit of a disadvantage. If this happens, see if you can delay the discussion by saying something like, "I'll be happy to talk about money, but why don't we discuss the job and see if there's a fit?" If they really press you, ask if they could give you the range in their budget for this kind of job. If they won't, indicate a range you'd be willing to consider. "High twenties or low thirties" is one way to say it.

It's also best to delay discussion of vacation time, health insurance, and other company benefits until the employer mentions them, or until you know the interview(s) have gone well and a job offer seems imminent. Although you may have gotten the rundown of the number of weeks' vacation time and so on in personnel, you'll learn more if you ask your particular supervisor about benefits. His offhand comments or body language may indicate that although three weeks is the company policy, no one ever takes that much in his department. That's important information!

If your interviewer reads down a list of what the company offers, listen carefully, but then ask for a brief outline of benefits or a booklet that you can study at your leisure. A low-paying job may be compensated for by tuition money for further education or a break on parking expenses for commuters in a busy city. Some companies offer "cafeteria-style" benefits; you assemble your own package from a number of choices, depending on your lifestyle. If child care is offered and you don't have children, for example, ask what the tradeoffs are for entry-level, unmarried people. The most important part of the package is the medical and dental insurance; study the literature on them well.

If Your Interviewer Doesn't Know How to Interview

Although there are many fine interviewers out there who are experts at assessing job applicants, there are a great many inexperienced ones as well, who have never been trained and don't have a clue about how to give you information or how to draw you out. Not-so-great interviewers are often found at companies that don't have personnel departments to screen job applicants or at small companies where the bosses do everything, including the preliminary interviewing. If you get someone who really doesn't know how to get at your abilities and talents, you'll have to help him out. It'll be up to you to politely but firmly make sure he understands what you're offering without overtly controlling the process.

Novice interviewers generally fall into three categories. Here are some ways to get around:

Interviewers who talk too much. Some managers will launch into a discourse about the job opening and various problems in the department without asking you much about yourself. Your major task here is to get your best assets in front of this long-winded interviewer. First, note any problems he's brought up and quickly think how your experience would help to solve them. When he pauses, say, "You mentioned deadlines. May I tell you how I've learned to deal with them?" Then tell a success story based on your previous work or school experience, about how you've managed to get jobs done on time. Repeat this technique, varying the content to fit the problems he's mentioned, until you've covered your main strengths.

Interviewers who interrogate you. Other interviewers go to the opposite extreme and grill you about your abilities and skills without divulging any important information about the job. In this situation, tack on a relevant query of your own to each answer you give: "I cope with deadlines because I start well in advance, and I do at least some work on a project each day so things don't pile up. Can you tell me what sorts of scheduling problems occur in this job?" This tactic turns a one-way interrogation into a conversational exchange. You and the interviewer become partners, not adversaries.

Interviewers who ask short-answer questions that shut off discussion. Some employers will make statements with a question tacked on that's not conducive to further conversation. For instance: "We have lots of pressure around here. Are you good at handling stressful situations?" The obvious answer is yes (no one in her right mind would answer no), but you also can feel almost as silly giving such an expected reply. Do it anyway (it's not your fault if the question was asked in a way that made the answer awkward) and expand on the subject, with a few short illustrations from past experiences or another success story. Ending with a question of your own ("What are the most stressful situations that occur on this job?") will provide you with more information and possibly clue you in to potential problems—insights that are vital to making the best career decision.

Practice, Practice

A day or so before the interview, you might write out your answers to the most commonly asked questions, not to memorize them but to generally plan out how you will respond to different approaches an interviewer might take, and to see that your themes are played and replayed a few times.

Then see if you can arrange a mock interview with a partner (a friend, family member, professor, or counselor). Choose someone who has good knowledge of your skills, and, if possible, some awareness of the career area that you seek. Using the list above, both of you choose about ten questions that you will prepare in advance of the session.

Set up an interview time and place away from distractions (people coming and going, ringing phones). You might even wear the clothes you plan to wear to your interview.

Ask your partner to choose any five of the ten questions you have prepared. She should then ask two more unexpected questions about events or issues that surface in your answers.

Bring two tape recorders with you, one to tape and play back the interview and the other to tape the feedback as you replay the first tape and discuss how the interview went. The mock interview could be about ten to twenty minutes; the feedback and critique about thirty minutes. Better yet, have the mock interview videotaped. Some college career offices or some career counselors can arrange for videotaping. Or borrow a friend's camcorder. You'll need another person, of course. It can be embarrassing to see and hear yourself being interviewed, but you'll learn a great deal, especially in the "postmortem" analysis.

Ask your partner to fill out and discuss with you the Interview Style Analysis below. It will give you additional insights about your interview style and how you present yourself.

Interview Style Analysis

Applicant ______________________ Interviewer ______________________
Date ______________________

Please evaluate the performance of this applicant—list *specific examples* whenever possible in the explanation section.

Circle the Appropriate Response	*Strongly Agree*	*Agree*	*Moderately Agree*	*Disagree*	*Strongly Disagree*
1. The applicant presented her stengths clearly, without hesitation. Explain: ______________________	5	4	3	2	1
2. The applicant responded fully to questions asked by the interviewer—used specific examples well. Explain: ______________________	5	4	3	2	1
3. The applicant appeared to be relaxed, comfortable, confident. Explain: ______________________	5	4	3	2	1

	5	4	3	2	1
4. The applicant appeared to be enthusiastic about both this job and the field in general.	5	4	3	2	1

Explain: ______________________________

5. The applicant avoided unnecessary verbal and nonverbal distractions (e.g., "ah," "you know," "ok," waving hands, slouching in the chair, looking around the room.	5	4	3	2	1

Explain: ______________________________

6. The applicant appeared prepared for this interview.	5	4	3	2	1

Explain: ______________________________

7. Name some *descriptive phrases* that come to mind to describe the *style* of this applicant.

____

Check with the applicant to see if these are the impressions she wished to make.

On the Day of the Interview

What to Wear

Here are some tips on appropriate interview clothing:

- Let the dress standards in the field you've chosen be a guide to what you wear on your interview. What's appropriate for retail sales may be a bit too high-fashion for banking. Look in the annual report and see what people are wearing; dress only slightly dressier than they do on a day-to-day basis.
- A suit or a dress is almost always most appropriate. Forgo pants unless you're interviewing for an archaeological dig or an active sports job.
- Consider the geographic location. New Yorkers dress differently from San Franciscans.
- Err on the side of formality rather than informality, but keep your outfit simple and elegant rather than showy. Limit jewelry to one or two nice pieces; no dangly earrings or rings on every finger. Wear a wristwatch; it looks professional.
- Some makeup will make you look more part of the work world, especially if you're used to the barefaced college look, but keep it low-key. Go easy on the eye makeup; nail polish should be light or neutral.
- Carry a medium-sized conservative leather handbag (no sports bags) and a briefcase containing extra copies of anything you might need—your resume, references, writing samples, artwork, transcripts. (Be aware, however, that in some fields, such as finance, an "unencumbered" approach is sometimes effective.) Put your handbag and/or briefcase on the floor while you're being interviewed, so that you won't be tempted to fool nervously with it.

On the Interview

You may not have had the time or opportunity to do all the activities and exercises suggested here. No matter. A modest amount of research and preparation will take you further than you think. What is most important is that you come across confident, honest, and eager. Here are some tips to make the actual interview go smoothly.

Give yourself a cutoff time (the night before the interview; three hours before) when you will stop your study and preparation. After this time, center and relax your mind. If you do meditation, now is a good time for it. Trust that your unconscious has absorbed the material and will give you what you need when you need it. If you continue to cram in facts while you're sitting in the waiting room, you may bring a panicky, anxious quality to your interview.

Arrive on time. Give yourself a half hour extra in case you get stuck in traffic or have mass-transportation problems, but should you arrive more than ten or fifteen minutes early, don't wait in the waiting room or you may seem anxious. Wait in your car or the lobby of the building until ten minutes before the appointed time.

Say hello to your interviewer in a confident, energetic way—no reticence or daintiness. Handshakes are important. They're part of your first impression. Practice your handshake in advance. Be sure not to offer your hand with the wrist up, as if you're expecting it to be kissed, or gather your fingers together into a fishy little point and slip it into the other person's grip. As you reach out your right hand, your palm should face the left and your fingers should be slightly separated. Grasp the other person's hand, palm to palm, lock thumbs, and shake briefly but firmly (do not pump). It's perfectly okay for you to initiate the handshake; combine it with a smile and eye contact and say, "Hello, I'm Julia Robbins."

Feel free to slow your pace of speech and relax. Many people tend to speak quickly when they get nervous, and then talking fast *makes* them nervous. Don't be afraid of silence; take a moment to consider your answers if you need it. You'll seem composed, thoughtful, and confident.

Finishing the Interview Strongly

Typically, at the end of an interview, the employer asks "Do you have any more questions?" Perhaps you have asked a fair number already, and find yourself saying rather lamely, "No." You might want to try a stronger ending that also gives you an idea of where you stand: "I want to thank you because you've answered most of my questions already. I've enjoyed talking with you, and I'm very much interested in the position. Could you give me a general idea of how my background fits in with this job?" This approach will be better received than asking baldly, "What do you think of me?" or "How did I do?" Such candor makes interviewers squirm.

Here's another gently probing approach: "When you make your hiring decision, I may be out of town. I'd appreciate hearing any reservations or considerations you have about my candidacy now." Both endings nudge the employer into sharing any concerns about you and give you a chance to answer them either on the spot or in your follow-up thank-you letter. These responses also show that you handle feedback with poise.

Finish with a question of your own, such as "When do you think you'll be making a decision?" or "What will the next step be?" Be sure to shake hands as you leave. A strong parting reinforces the positive impression you've just made—that you're a candidate well worth hiring.

Follow-Up

After an interview, be sure to send a thank-you note, as well as any materials the employer has requested (references, transcripts, writing samples, portfolio) within forty-eight hours. Keep the note short but sincere.

This communication serves several purposes. It provides you with an opportunity for further visibility as it places your name before the employer one more time. It gives you a chance to briefly remind the employer of your strengths or to clear up any misconception about your skills or qualifications. It gives you a chance to say anything that you'd forgotten to say or that occurred to you after the interview. And it demonstrates that you are a thoughtful, gracious person.

It's best to keep your note brief, type it rather than handwrite it, and keep a copy for your file.

Second Interviews

Second interviews usually give the company a chance to introduce you to the people you'd be working with, to allow the higher-ups to approve you, and to experience how you fit into the office setting. If you have been interviewed by a recruiter on campus, you will now be visiting the place where you'll be working. On your second interview, you'll probably meet a number of people, and may be taken to lunch. If you're coming from out of town, you might be entertained for an evening as well. Here are some tips on how to shine in this situation.

1. Prepare for your interview by researching the company in even more depth. If you haven't had a chance to before, check out the different company locations, the profit-and-loss picture, new areas of development—topics beyond your particular job or department. Think of a few questions that you want to ask during your interview to gain even more information.

2. Know that you might feel a bit hurried and confused when you're introduced to a number of people, one after another. Try to remember names, especially of the top people; you might take special note of any names mentioned in letters or other communication to you, and memorize those names and positions in advance. But don't feel as if you must remember everyone you meet; you're only human. Also, don't be afraid of repeating yourself as you go from office to office. Saying the same thing over and over may seem a little silly to you, but it won't be noticed by the others at all.

3. Second interviews can be mentally and emotionally exhausting because they generally take a longer time than first interviews, and there are more elements involved. Bring a candy bar along and take a few bites in the ladies' room for quick energy if you find you're wilting.

4. If you're asked to lunch, you're being informally tested on your general sociability and your awareness of the world around you. The night before your interview, read the daily or Sunday paper in the city where the job is being offered, so that you can enter into a discussion on current events and local issues.

5. When ordering lunch, wait for your host to order first, or order in the low- or medium-price range. Order easy-to-eat food, so that you can concentrate on the people instead of your food; steer clear of spaghetti that can stain your clothes or chicken on the bone, which is hard to cut. It's best not to order liquor, even if your host does, since it can dull your judgment a bit. The exception might be if you are interviewing for a job that involves heavy entertaining. In this case, order a glass of white wine or a spritzer.

6. Part of a second interview might be a group talk—you and some other people from the company. Keep yourself focused and clear by directing your answer to any question to whoever asks it. Don't try to figure out

who the more powerful people are and cater to them; treat any and all questions as of equal value, and answer them as they come.

7. If the company asks you to arrange transportation and accommodations and offers to reimburse you, show them that you'll be frugal with company money by keeping your expenses down. Arrange discount airfares if possible, but ride in coach in any case. Choose moderate-priced hotels unless they are located too far away to be practical. If you drive your own car, charge the current government rate for mileage. It's fine to charge food expenses, but don't include drinks, theater, or other evening entertainment.

A Word About References

References (or recommendations) are supporting statements about you and your work, prepared at your request, usually by former employers, supervisors, or professors. Most schools and companies will ask for three or four references; they might divide them into "business" and "personal." You may be asked to write the names of your references on a company's employment application, or your interviewer might ask for their names once he knows that you're really in line for a job.

Companies give letters of reference a fair amount of weight, so choose them carefully. They should be people who know and like you, who have a good understanding of and respect for your particular academic or work skills, and who can communicate well. Sometimes, for a variety of reasons, former bosses don't meet all these criteria, so think beyond them to other people who know you or have worked with you, such as a field-work leader, an internship supervisor, a community leader you've worked with on a volunteer project. You might even use someone in a company you've worked with other than your boss, someone who has a managerial title and knows your work.

Most managers and professors are glad to serve as references for young people, but they may not always remember your work all that well, or they may not be clear about what's involved in the job you're after. You'll want to give them all the information they need to write a good recommendation while taking as little of their time as possible. Here's how:

First, target the experiences on your current or former job, or the skills that showed up in your academic work, that would be most valuable to the position you're going for. Did you want your reference to mention your talent as a salesperson, for example, or your ability to think logically and get to the heart of a problem? What particular projects did you do for your reference that would highlight those abilities? Think in terms of transferable skills. Do you want your reference to bring out your abilities in organization, communication, decision making? What about pertinent technical skills—facility with a computer, for example?

Then phone or meet with each reference and ask if she would be willing to recommend you. (Always ask the person before you give out a name and address; and wait until you're asked before volunteering names.) If your reference seems enthusiastic about recommending you, say "Could you comment especially on my sales experience, and my part in that promotion that was so successful?" If you're not asking your reference to write a letter, tell her to expect a phone call from your potential employer. In closing, say you'll send along some information that should help in putting the recommendation together, and follow by mailing your resume; a brief description of the job you're after; a paragraph describing the skills and projects you want highlighted; and the name, title, and address of the potential employer.

If you're requesting your reference to write a letter, include a *stamped*, number 10 business envelope, typed with the name, title, and address of the appropriate person at the company you're applying to. Sometimes your reference will attempt to lighten her workload and ask you to write the letter. This is more work for you but you have the opportunity to shape the letter as you would like it to be. Discuss the matter with her before you write; ask what she'd like to say about you in the letter, and ask her if it's okay if you stress certain skills, abilities, and projects. After you write the letter, she might want to type and sign it herself or she may give you some stationery and ask you to do the typing. You'll then return it to her for her signature, or send it back with a stamped, addressed envelope, so that she can send it on to the employer or school directly. If you have a personal computer, save the letter. The next time you need a reference, it will be right there in your file. Also, ask her for some extra stationery so that you can run off a general letter to carry around with you on interviews.

It's a good practice to request a letter of recommendation whenever you leave a job; your supervisor will be clearer about your skills while they're fresh in her mind, and she might be hard to contact later. Such a letter can't be tailored to the kind of job you're seeking. But if the letter is positive, highlighting some skills that the potential job requires, it can demonstrate your value as an employee. Mention it only after your interviewers have shown a strong interest in you, as something that can demonstrate your abilities in the areas that concern them.

As your career progresses, you'll gain referrals from peers and from top people in your field. It's an excellent idea to keep a reference file with up-to-date names and addresses, plus notes about which of your projects and skills these people can best speak to. The career development offices at some colleges, including Smith, will keep your references on file for you forever. Ask your college what procedures you should follow to take advantage of this helpful service.

It's courteous to drop your references a line if and when you get a job they've recommended you for, and to keep them apprised of your career growth through notes and

Christmas cards. People love to know that a good word from them has helped launch someone on a new career.

For Further Reading

Danks, Lawrence J. *The Complete Job-Hunting Guide for College Students.* Englewood Cliffs, N.J.: Prentice-Hall, 1985.

LaFevre, John L. *How You Really Get Hired: The Inside Story from a College Recruiter.* Englewood Cliffs, N.J.: Prentice-Hall, 1986.

Medley, Anthony H. *Sweaty Palms: The Neglected Art of Being Interviewed.* Berkeley: Ten Speed Press, 1984.

Yate, Martin John. *Knock 'Em Dead with Great Answers to Tough Interview Questions,* fourth edition. Holbrook, Mass.: Bob Adams, Inc., 1990.

CHAPTER

— 9 —

Evaluating Your Job Offers and Getting the Deal You Want

If the interview runs overtime because the conversation is so interesting, if your interviewer begins to stress how great it is to work for his company, if he starts to discuss salary and benefits, if he asks for references and talks about a health exam—the chances are excellent that a job offer is right around the corner! Your interviewer may surprise you and offer you the job on the spot, or he may call you a few days later; at any rate, it's a good idea to have a response rehearsed and ready to use. You can use the same response, or a variation on it, for whatever offer you get. The best ones have three parts: an expression of pleasure that you've been offered the job, and thanks to the people involved; a request for time to make a decision; and a request to discuss any further questions that you have about the offer with your supervisor. A good response might be:

> *I'm delighted about this offer. Thank you! I'm flattered that you want me to work for your company. I would like a few days to think it over. Would it be all right if I called you in the meantime with any thoughts or questions I have?*

Take Time to Decide

It's best to anticipate an offer and have a response ready because it may be difficult for you, in the wake of being offered an exciting job, to ask for extra time to make a well-thought-out decision. Once a company has decided to make you an offer, they'll almost surely want you to accept the job right away and to start immediately. Even the wording of the offer is frequently designed to create momentum and sweep you along: "We'd like to offer you the position of marketing assistant at $29,000 a year. Congratulations and welcome! Can you start next week?" Part of the reason for the push is that they want to settle the matter—they don't like uncertainty any more than you did when you were waiting for the offer. Another reason is that of course they'd prefer you to accept the offer right away and on their terms.

You, however, have nothing to lose and much to gain by taking the time you need (a week is not too long) to consider this most important decision. Most employers will grant your request with good grace. If your potential employer seems impatient, hold your ground gently but firmly, *no matter how much you're sure you want the job.* This grace period is important to you psychologically and strategically. Here are some reasons why:

- You have a slight edge over your potential employer during this period—more than you'll have after you accept her offer. Up until now, you have been selling yourself to the company. Now you have something that she wants. Consider how you might use this advantage—to clear up any doubts you have about the job, or perhaps to negotiate a better salary/benefits package.
- Even if you've wanted this job very badly, you might find the psychological energy is different now that it's actually been offered to you. Doubts or second

thoughts might creep in. It's important to take time to process these thoughts, to live with them for a few days and see what they mean. For example, did you really want the job so much, or did you just want to beat out the competition? In your desire for the offer, were there certain negatives you blocked out of your mind? This chapter will suggest specific exercises to evaluate lingering doubts about a job offer.

- If you have mixed feelings about the job offer, you'll need time to clarify the positives and negatives, and perhaps gather more information.
- If the salary is not as much as you'd like, you can use the time to outline a negotiating strategy, perhaps lobbying for better benefits.
- If you have several job offers pending, you need time to decide which you'd prefer. You might want to use this offer to hasten along others who are still deciding, or you may want to use this salary offer as a bargaining chip to be matched or exceeded by another company. You will need at least a couple of days to decide on a plan of action.
- Asking for time is important for your professional image: You've shown your new employer that you're someone who makes considered decisions on her own time and is not to be stampeded.
- It's important for your own sense of self that you take the time to make the best-thought-out decision on this matter of great importance to your life and career growth.

Thinking Through Your Offer

Now that this job is actually yours, many thoughts and feelings are likely to flood your mind—positive and negative. Now's the time to take stock. Do all of those different reactions add up to a "Go for it" signal? Or is something holding you back? If you have questions and/or reservations, but you don't quite know what they mean, your company research, self-assessment, and job assessment isn't over yet. Here are a few different positions you might take with regard to your job offer, and some ways of working your way to a decision you feel good about:

You're delighted with the offer. It was your first choice. Obviously you're in an enviable position. Enjoy it! You've got what you want, and because you're riding the crest of your success, you probably won't feel inclined to go back and analyze just what's right about your new position. Still, if you want to ground those good feelings with a little reality testing, you might want to fill out the Job Offer Evaluation Grid (pages 238–239), and remind yourself of just what it is about this job that appeals. The more aware you can be of why this job is for you, and what aspects (if any) are not so appealing, the more ready you'll be to start your job with a realistic but enthusiastic frame of mind.

You're not crazy about this offer, but you think you'd better grab it. You feel you may not get another as good. You're especially apt to feel this way if you get an offer at the beginning of your job search process. If you've barely begun your networking and you're not really sure what's out there, you can easily succumb prematurely to the pull of a flattering offer. If you're further along in your search, and you've opened more avenues of inquiry, you'll be in a better position to evaluate and, if necessary, turn down a job that doesn't quite fill the bill.

But jobs that aren't quite right can also seem tempting if you've been looking for a while and/or you've reached a plateau in your job hunt. You may think, "I'll take this job—how bad can it be?—and keep looking." But wait. A new job absorbs a good amount of energy, even if your commitment is minimal. And it will take even more energy to fake it, to act as if you care about the job when in reality you're still looking around. It will be very difficult to make time for job interviews or field job-related phone calls when you're at work. You may feel yourself in an ethically untenable position if your boss and others in your new company invest time in training you when you well know you're planning to leave the minute something better comes up. It's a far sounder and more effective strategy to keep your energies and loyalties undivided and focused totally on your job hunt until you find a job you can truly commit to. If you're in a financial bind, temporary, part-time, or seasonal work will keep you afloat while you take the time you need for letter writing, networking, and interviews. If you have a suspicion that your career search has gone awry and you aren't getting the interviews or offers that you should be after several months of steady work, it might be time to meet with a career counselor or schedule a few intensive counseling sessions with your college career development office. A trained person might be able to spot the problem and correct it quite easily.

Meanwhile, fill out the following Job Offer Evaluation Grid. After you're finished, you'll have some good solid reasons for accepting the job—or turning it down.

There are lots of good opportunities on this job, but you're not as excited as you "should" be. You have reservations, but you're not sure what they are. What you need to do is to pinpoint what it is that's holding you back and gather more information by talking to people and by further visits to the company. To begin, fill out the Job Offer Evaluation Grid on the next page. If you have more than one offer, photocopy the grid and do several evaluations.

Job Offer Evaluation Grid

	Terrific	Good	So-So
The Job (tasks, duties, job description)			
Chances for Advancement			
The Company (size, reputation, financial situation)			
Physical Environment (building, offices, location, commute)			
Your Supervisor (reputation, personality fit, work style, skill at training new staff)			
Your Coworkers			
Company Culture and Politics (workplace, expectations, interrelationships, hierarchy)			
Salary/Benefits Package			

Not good	Unsure	Explain

Now let's take these elements one at a time. Obviously, if you've checked "Terrific" or "Good" in a particular category, that's not the aspect of the job that's giving you trouble. "So-so," "Not Good," or "Unsure" categories bear further scrutiny. Here are some approaches.

The Job. To troubleshoot in this area, take the description for the job you're evaluating and break the various tasks down into skill categories. Then go back to your inspired abilities assessment. How well do the skills on this job match up with the ones you wanted to develop? In other words, is this job going to teach you at least some of the things you said you'd like to learn? Or have you deviated from the priorities and goals you once set for yourself? If you have changed direction, why have you done so? Is this a conscious choice? There could be good and sound reasons why you've altered your course. On the other hand, perhaps you are being seduced away from developing those strengths, skills, and abilities that you intuitively know would be your best contribution. Has the promise of a good starting salary or the attractiveness of your work environment made a humdrum job seem more appealing? No job is perfect, and some tradeoffs are worth the compromise. Others are not. At any rate, you need to be clear just what you're getting and what you're giving up.

Another feeling you might have about the job itself is some worry that you might not be able to do it well enough. It may sound overwhelming in some way. Presuming that this job does involve using the skills you've chosen, your feelings of inadequacy may come from several sources: 1) you might tend to be somewhat underconfident in general; 2) the job may not have been explained well; or 3) you are being asked to take on an impossible task—to solve unsolvable problems or to become a scapegoat for people who can't face the difficulties in their department.

To get to the source of your worries, first think back on jobs and internships you've had in the past. Did you have feelings up front that the jobs would be hard for you, only to find that you warmed to the challenge and did fine? Did you have an unpleasant experience that may have temporarily injured your self-esteem? Perhaps you often approach new experiences with some trepidation. If so, the source of concern may be more in your approach than in the job itself. It may help to know that if you like and trust your supervisor and that person thinks you can do the job, you almost certainly can.

Perhaps, however, there is something about the job that you just don't feel right about. Perhaps you're unsure as to what you'll actually do all day, or you've been told you'll handle several projects that seem monumental as they've been described to you. What you need is more specific information, and there are two ways you can get it. First, make an appointment to see your prospective supervisor again, indicating that there are a few more questions you'd like to ask before you make your decision. During your meeting, try to get her to be as concrete as possible, breaking down the different parts of the job into specific tasks. Ask what you'd be expected to do on a typical day. If you'd be working on various projects, you might want to know approximately what percentage of your time you'd spend on each. You might say, "It seems like there are a great many parts to this job. How will I know what my priorities are? Will I have to give 100 percent to every part of it?" How does your boss react to these questions? Is she eager to think the situation through with you? Grateful that you've helped her clarify the job description for herself? Irritated that you're raising troublesome questions? Her response will tell you much about her management style. Another gambit: Call the people you know within the company and ask them more about this position. Do they know any people who have held this particular job before? What are they doing now? Would they be willing to speak with you? As you speak with your potential boss and others, you may find that your concerns will fade. On the other hand, it may become clear that a large problem does indeed exist. In this case, pass by Mission Impossible and wait for a job where you have a better chance for success.

The Company. If you have not had adequate time to research the company that's offering you the job, return to Chapter 6 and figure out how much research you have time for before you need to decide. Zero in on your particular area of concern. Is the company the target of a takeover? Is the department you're thinking of joining a strong part of the organization? See if there's some person you can call who could give you the information or link you up with someone who can. Naturally, people who work for the company already are your most valuable contacts at this time.

Physical Environment. Perhaps your reservations reflect a negative reaction to the place where you'll be working. Do the offices seem airless or smoky? Are you being offered a cubicle to work in when you need to be near a window or some greenery? If you're being offered a position in a city that's new to you, be sure to figure out the lay of the land and the location of your office within it before you accept any position. One young woman was very much attracted to a company that she knew was about to offer her a job. But she didn't know the area, and she hadn't yet decided where she would live. She got into her rented car, and drove a half an hour north, south, east, and west of the place the offices were, and she could find no neighborhood where she felt she would be at home. Since she didn't want to commute more than that, she turned down the job.

Physical environment is pretty much a given, and there's not a whole lot you can do if you dislike the company's location or offices. Think through what you can reasonably ask for, considering that you're just starting out. Perhaps you could ask for the cubicle next to the window; on the other hand, offices with windows may go only to senior people. Again, people who already work for the company are your best sources for information like this. At any rate, don't underestimate the power of the physical environment to influence how you feel about your job. For some people, a noisy workspace or a lengthy commute can consume valuable energy better used on the job. Everyone has their own preferences and levels of tolerance. What are yours? Does this job offer the kind of environment in which you can grow? If not, are the other aspects of the job worth the sacrifice?

Your Supervisor. Although many people at your organization will have an effect on your professional development, your immediate supervisor is most important to your success. Some managers are excellent at training new people, spotting and using their talents, and promoting them to higher-ups. Others may be threatened by young talent—or they may have personal problems that make them difficult to work with. Most supervisors are complex mixtures of positive and negative traits. The question then becomes: Is this particular mixture one that you can successfully deal with? If your doubts about this job involve your potential boss, it's essential to clarify them. Perhaps this person seems nice enough, but your intuition tells you differently. Perhaps you have more concrete reasons to wonder about the fit.

To get to the bottom of things, feel perfectly free to request another interview. Tell your prospective boss you feel you need a more specific picture of what it would be like to work in her department. Once there, ask questions like these: "Are you formal, or do you prefer a loose structure? How are problems usually resolved? Do people write memos or do they talk out their ideas? Is there an open-door policy? How are positive and negative feedback handled?" During the interview, notice both the manifest and latent content of the answers you're given. Is your supervisor easy with your questions? Is she anxious, indirect, irritated?

Another way to get a fix on your new boss would be to call someone who works for the company, and find out what happened to other people who had your job in the past. Were they promoted? Did they leave? (If so, why?) Were they fired? (If so, why?) What kinds of skills and personalities did they have, and how did they interact with the boss? It would be wonderful if you could speak to one of these people directly. If you do get negative feelings or bad reports about your potential supervisor, seriously consider turning down this job. No matter how wonderful the opportunity might be, a supervisor who rides you or stands in your way can make your life miserable.

On the other hand, you might have very good feelings about your potential boss, and be extremely excited at the thought of working with her. She may have an excellent reputation for "growing" young talent. Nevertheless, one word of warning: Don't make your eagerness to work for this person the *only* reason you take a job. She may well leave or be hired away, and in that case you'll be left alone in a position you're less than thrilled with.

Your Coworkers. If you have a good personality fit with your coworkers, a job can be a wonderful communal effort. If you don't, you can feel lonely, isolated, and misunderstood. Yet many people never meet their colleagues before they begin the job. Often just visiting an office and observing people interacting can give you a sense of whether these are "your people." However, you may have a real need to meet your colleagues before you accept the job, and if you do, be sure to ask. One woman was hired to supervise several part-time workers. It was her first management job, so she felt it was important to get a feel for the people who would be working for her. So she asked her boss to introduce her around before she made a final decision.

As you say hello to your new colleagues, notice how they react to you. Do they seem welcoming or anxious? Is there good energy in the office or do you sense tension and unhappiness? Make light conversation with your coworkers, inquire about their jobs and their feelings about the company. Do they seem relaxed and energized or overstressed and burnt out? Also, do they seem the type of people whose interests and values jibe with yours? Do they socialize after work and if so, how do they socialize? At a classical music concert? A baseball game? A bar? What is the ratio of men to women and how do they relate to one another? Are you comfortable with the social banter? Do you detect a style of humor, and are you easy with it? Feeling a part of the team can make an enormous difference in your enjoyment of the job, and how well you fit in has a great deal to do with whether or not you're promoted.

Salary and Benefits. If everything else about the job looks good but you feel the salary you've been offered is just too low, you probably have some leeway for negotiation (although not as much as a more experienced person). Here are some things to think about.

First, be sure you're familiar with the going rate for this sort of job in this industry in this part of the country. If you've done your homework and the offer you've been made still comes in low, you'll have facts and figures with which to negotiate. Write down your sources; don't rely on memory. Second, be sure to look at salary-and-benefits as a package. A good medical plan that includes dental and psychotherapy is worth hard cash in your pocket. Nonprofits traditionally pay low but offer employees perks such as six-week vacations. Private schools compensate for their low salaries by giving employees free tuition for their children. What is your company offering you? Tuition remuneration for further education? Free parking at the local garage? Relocation expenses? Check your contacts within the company to see whether it would be appropriate to ask for any of these things if the organization can't match your salary request.

If you mentioned a range or your company told you its spread for this kind of job, and you were offered the bottom of either range, chances are you can get the salary up a bit. Before you negotiate, decide on a figure that's the most you could reasonably ask for and another figure that you'd settle for. You might write these figures down and have them in front of you during your phone conversation.

As you begin your negotiations, remember always to talk in terms of what you're offering the company, not about your own financial needs. The company doesn't care about your rent or your husband's tuition. They want firm reasons why they should pay you more. To create an atmosphere where both you and the company can be winners, keep your attitude flexible and your mood light. Use phrases such as, "I was thinking more in terms of . . ." or "I'd be more comfortable with . . ." Steer clear of strident, demanding phrases such as "I need . . ." or "I won't take less than . . ." They're off-putting. Ask for as much as you think is appropriate, backing it up with industry figures and naming the skills you're offering the company. Reassure the person who will be making a decision to pay you more: "I am really excited about working for Acme, and I'm sure I can do an excellent job for you."

Be prepared to compromise at your midrange figure. If your supervisor seems disinclined to move at all, you can ask for a substitute compensation, such as relocation costs. If the company's final offer is still less than you think is fair, ask if you might have a job evaluation and a salary review in three months' time.

It's important not to be shortsighted where salary and benefits are concerned. Of course you need to be paid a wage you can live on with some degree of comfort. But in the end the skills and experience you gain will be worth far more to you than a thousand dollars more or less in your beginning salary. If the job seems to be one in which you can learn and grow, and you're excited about the opportunity, you might want to overlook a less-than-stellar starting salary.

The Timing Factor

Timing is the perennial wild card in the job search process. Sometimes job offers come just in time to solve all your problems; at other times, the spacing of interviews and offers seems specially designed by fate to drive you crazy. What do you do if you're offered a mildly interesting job when you're having your first interview for a really wonderful (but highly sought-after) job next Thursday? Can you delay in your decision on the first job in time to get to that interview? If you like the second job, how long can you string Company 1 along until Company 2 makes a decision? Having several offers at once can tug at you emotionally, too. It's hard to decide which job has most of what you want. Being up for several jobs at once is always anxiety producing, and each situation is so unique that there are no hard-and-fast rules, but here are several ideas to keep in mind.

1. Once you have a job campaign under way, keep the momentum going until you have accepted a job. Don't cut off other contacts or fail to get back to people when you feel a promising offer is coming your way. It may be very confusing to have several hot possibilities in different stages of development, but consider the alternative. If you've failed to develop some leads because you were sure you were going to be offered a great job—but the offer was not forthcoming—you'll really be disappointed.

2. Consider each job on its own merits, outside of the context in which it's being offered to you. If you are offered two jobs at once, for example, you might feel you have to accept one of them. But if your Job Offer Evaluations show that neither of these jobs is really right for you, it may be best to turn both of them down, difficult though that may be.

3. If you are in a time bind, do not hesitate to let your preferred company know. Don't be coy. If Company 1 offers you a job, call your interviewer at Company 2 and inform them of the situation. "I just wanted you to know that I've received a promising job offer, and I must let Company 1 know one way or the other early next week. But I'm also very much interested in the job I spoke with you about. Can you let me know the status of my application? When do you think you're making a final decision?" You can also use the salary offer from Company 1 as a bargaining chip to get a better offer from Company 2. If the second organization won't match the salary offer from the first, perhaps you can split the difference. If you use one offer to up the salary of a second, however, negotiating etiquette requires you take the second offer if the salary is matched.

4. Don't let the anxious pushes and pulls of being up for several jobs at once propel you into a premature decision. Try to live with the stress, and take as much time as you can to get the best offer from the best company. Employers may try to manipulate you by telling you you have to decide this minute. Usually you have a bit more leeway. You don't want to be discourteous, but your future is at stake. You are entitled to time enough to get the information you need to make your own best choice from the options available to you. If you aren't sure how much time is fair to ask for, consult with your college career development office or friends who are experienced in the working world. It's more than likely that your anxiety is internally generated, rather than imposed by the outer world. In the last analysis it's better to struggle with a number of offers than to have none at all.

For Further Reading

Zey, Michael. *The Right Move: How to Find the Perfect Job*. New York: Ivy Books, 1988.

PART FOUR

USING YOUR JOB TO CREATE FURTHER OPPORTUNITIES

CHAPTER

10

Starting Off Smart

Finally! That plum job that you've been stalking for the last month is yours, all yours. They made you a deal and you didn't refuse. Congratulations! You probably feel that you're on the threshold of a big adventure, with all the excitement, apprehension, and sense of challenge that entails. Those few days or weeks between your accepting a new job and actually beginning to work are usually an enjoyable time, empty of anxiety, where you feel successful and secure about your immediate future, but you don't have to prove anything to anybody yet. It's an ideal time for a short vacation; try to take a few days, especially if your job campaign has been busy and stressful. You owe it to yourself.

Even if you do take some time to rest on your laurels, though, you're bound to begin thinking about what's ahead, and your musings about your new job can likely be reduced to one common theme: "How can I perform this job in the most effective way?" And you'll continue to ask yourself that question every day, in one way or another, as long as you're doing this job. The way you answer it will make the difference between just doing a job and making your new position the foundation of a successful career.

What constitutes effectiveness on the job? It's an important question. Generally, there are two parts to job effectiveness. The first is the more obvious part. It consists of fulfilling the job description and reaching beyond it. It involves learning the skills necessary for the job, and executing your tasks in the best possible way: writing clear, accurate reports with correct facts and spellings; coordinating the different parts of the department meeting so all goes smoothly; designing the most time-efficient computer program; bringing a project in under budget—to cite a few examples.

The second part of job effectiveness is less tangible, infrequently discussed, and hardly ever included on your boss's list of priorities for the week. Nevertheless, it could be the major factor in career success. People skills—the ability to get along with others in the service of getting the job done—are a vital part of career advancement. One thing you're sure to notice when you've been on *any* job for more than a couple of weeks is that many people spend far more time getting their ego needs met than they do addressing the task at hand. A vice president may constantly write memos not because the information is so essential to his staff but because he needs to remind them who's in charge. A secretary might make a point of never typing your report on time unless you "ask her nicely," which means flattering her for ten minutes or more with each request. An account executive may insist that everything be done her way to the last detail because she feels insecure otherwise. "People smarts" means dealing with difficult people like this without being perceived as difficult yourself. It means figuring out where the power lies and learning how to work *with* it. It means knowing when to address interpersonal problems directly and when to circumvent them. It means being able to stand your ground when necessary and not allow yourself to be drawn into other people's misguided agendas. If this is beginning to sound like "office politics," that's exactly what it is. You're naive to think you can avoid them—but you will have an array of choices about how to participate, some far more positive and helpful than others. You can be sure that the part you play in the communal life of your organization will be noticed by higher-ups. Are you a glory grabber or a glory sharer? Do you draw strict boundaries around your job and never cross them, or do you pitch in and help your officemates during busy times? Are you the only one who can get a smile out of the curmudgeon in the corner office? Some people are naturally skilled in dealing with others, but some degree of "people smarts" can be developed by virtually everyone.

This chapter will walk you through the first days, weeks, and months of your new job. It will cover several issues common to people who are newcomers to the workplace, but will concentrate especially on developing "people smarts."

Your First Day

It's good to remember when you're feeling new-job nerves that you can only do any job one day at a time. So take your first day first. As you arrive, you'll be jumping into a river that is already flowing. Observe the pace of that flow. Is the office frantic? Humming productively? Or on the slow side?

First, Get a Fix on Your Workload

When you report to your boss, ask him sometime during your first meeting what tasks he wants you to concentrate on—for your first day and for your first week. If he gives you quite a bit, you can always ask, "Which of these projects would you like me to start with?" Write down what he says. Your notes from this meeting will provide a structure amid the confusion of your first week, when you're struggling to learn procedures and find out who people are. As you check the completed projects off your list, you'll have a greater feeling of accomplishment than you might if you tried to wing it. Also, ask your supervisor whether he wants to be the one to answer your questions. It's important that you feel free to ask all the questions you want, no matter how obvious or "dumb" they may seem; asking will save you the time and bother of correcting mistakes later. If your supervisor is busy, he might prefer to ask someone else to help you out.

Then Introduce Yourself

After you've gotten an idea of your work load for the week, make it your business to be friendly, receptive, and a low-key observer of people and procedures. Try to start fitting in with your colleagues right away; it's even more important than getting a fix on your new duties and doing a perfect job. One young woman, nervous about the complexity of her new job, spent her first two weeks closeted in her office, trying to sort it all out. When she emerged, she discovered people thought she was remote and unfriendly, a judgment it took her a long time to change. Besides, if your peers like you, they can show you the ropes.

On your first day, make it your business to meet everyone in your immediate work vicinity. Ask your supervisor or the human resources people to give you a list of all the names in your department, and also an organization chart, and start matching names with faces. Your boss may take you around and introduce you, but if that doesn't happen, or if your coworkers are too busy to approach you first, look for a lull, and introduce yourself. If people are out of the office on the day of your arrival, be sure you note that, and get to them on the first day of their return, or they may feel they're being overlooked. Ask your new office-mates what they do, and get a sense of how their job fits together with yours. As you pick up names on memos and messages, start to identify and locate the people out of your immediate vicinity whom you and your boss work with most closely. Make a special effort to meet them early on. If they are higher-ups, ask your boss to introduce you.

Once you make a few friends, you'll feel freer to ask questions that may seem elementary—how strict lunch hours are, where the supplies are located. Save up your own questions and ask several at once. If you're not yet generating your own work when assigned tasks are finished, volunteer to assist others. People who pitch in are usually much appreciated.

Your First Month

Determining Alliances

As the first weeks go by, you'll find that you'll be filling out first impressions and forming personal opinions of the people you work with. You'll be getting an idea of which people are effective or ineffective, sincere or phony, secure or underconfident, honest or devious. If the people where you work get along well, you'll still find yourself gravitating to like-minded people; if your office is cliquish, there may be pressure on you to take sides. During the first month or so, it's best to stay neutral and try to understand what's really going on in the company before you choose your allies.

As you get to know the staff, be pleasant to everyone, but align yourself with the positive people, not the complainers. Find who's the informal group leader among your peers; his acceptance signals to others that you "fit." In casual conversation with people, find out how long they have been at their jobs. The people who have been with the organization longer may be good ones to ask about the reasons for various procedures.

As people get to know you, the friendlier ones will come by to chat or ask you to have lunch. If this doesn't seem to be happening soon enough—and it may not in a large office—take the initiative yourself. Just approach a coworker, saying something casual such as, "I wondered if you'd like to have lunch on Friday. I would like to learn more about what it is you do." Over lunch, ask her questions about herself and her job. As long as you're sincere and supportive and don't seem as if you're interrogating them, most people will be flattered by your interest. After five or six lunches, you'll be surprised at how much you know about the undercurrents of life in your department. You'll also get a sense of which colleagues share your concerns, values, and business goals, and which you have the best chemistry with. These are the ones who will make your best allies.

Relating to the Company Hierarchy

You may have some initial uncertainty about whether to be friendly or reserved with the more senior people to whom your supervisor has introduced you. Watch others around you—your office culture will determine how to approach people a level or two above you. In large, bureaucratic offices, where formality is the rule, premature friendliness on your part may evoke a cool response. Even in small, friendly offices, it's best to maintain some distance initially; a definite pecking order may lie behind the apparent informality. A smile and a hello or a nod of recognition is an appropriate greeting even for an executive—but even if you're riding on an elevator or are in the ladies' room with a vice president, let her be the one to speak first, unless you're working closely together. If you have reason to speak to a higher-up who seems to have forgotten you, say something simple like, "I'm Helen James. We met on Wednesday. I'm new here."

Don't focus your attention entirely on senior managers, however. Having a friendly working relationship with support people, such as the receptionists or the mail room attendants, is extremely important. Because they serve the company as a whole, they see and hear a great deal and are potential reservoirs of information. If they like you, they can be allies in a crunch; if they don't, they can frustrate you in a thousand ways. Some people consciously or unconsciously curry favor with higher-ups while dismissing people whom they don't feel are of use to them. But employees with true management potential are those who are courteous, respectful, and friendly with all their coworkers, no matter where they are on the organization ladder.

High Profile/Shy Profile

If you're the kind of person who reacts to uncertainty or stress by trying to show how competent you are, take it slow and easy the first few months. No need to be a shining star right away. People who dazzle too soon may seem presumptuous or even threatening. Your brilliance may have delighted your college professors, but in the business world, you need to win people over to your ideas slowly, with persuasion and diplomacy, in a way that includes other people instead of shutting them out. Be an observer and note taker at first, not a mover-and-shaker.

One of the best ways to show your intelligence is by incisive questioning. If you find the office procedures hopelessly outdated, for example, find out how long the procedures have been in place, what purpose they serve, who finds them most useful. Be sure your attitude is sincere, not critical. As you begin to learn more, you may come to understand why these procedures have been retained.

Another way to get on the success track in a nonpushy way is to observe the work of your more successful colleagues. If you see someone complete a successful project, congratulate this person, and then ask—admiringly, not competitively—how she did it. Get on her team, if you can. This practice will help you recognize excellence, reduce jealousy and backbiting, and give you models to emulate in your own work. Your job for now is not to flood your department with suggestions for change but to learn the value of teamwork. Opt for leadership later, when you've gained the necessary experience and credibility.

On the other hand, you might be the kind of person who tends to hang back shyly in new situations. Far from threatening people, you feel you disappear. Start with a low-risk way to raise your company profile by checking and adjusting your body language. Shy people often minimize the space they take up by slouching, looking down, crossing their legs when they stand or tucking their elbows close to their body. Instead, stand or sit straight with your feet several inches apart and your elbows at your side but a bit away from your body. As you speak, try to use occasional hand gestures and to make eye contact. Smile naturally—but not in a forced way and not too often. Frequent smiles and head nods come across as underconfident and take away your personal power.

To get noticed for yourself and not as "Mr. Richardson's assistant," take the initiative occasionally in introductions; don't always wait for others to speak first. Keep it simple; you don't have to say much. "Hello, I'm Nicole Bennett" seems more mature and businesslike than "Hi, I'm Nicky." Make eye contact, offer a firm handshake, and say, "I'm glad to meet you." At meetings with higher-ups, a polite, confident self-introduction assures you a presence and a professional identity.

To appear less distant around the office, don't neglect small talk. Scan business publications and trade journals for topics of conversation. They make good conversation starters at company meetings or social gatherings. Listen, or look in the company newsletter, for bits of information about others and use them as conversational openers ("I hear you used to work in our department"). Ask people about their vacations or their children; they'll be flattered that you care. As you get to know people's interests, keep up with their individual concerns; send them an occasional, appropriate newspaper clipping or mention it in person to them.

Your Third Month

Do an Anthropological Study of Your Company

Once some of the easier parts of your job become more routine, you can devote some time to studying the culture of your organization; it's sure to be more complex than it first appears. Imagine that you're an anthropologist who is studying an unknown tribe; first you observe and collect data, then you interpret what you see. Make the goal of your study to answer the following questions: What does the company see as its purpose? What does it value? What kind of behavior is encouraged? How do things get done? Here are some exercises to make you more sensitive to the values and folkways of a company's culture.

1. Notice what your company's environment looks like. Is it low-key and elegant? Down-home and comfortable? Flamboyant and creative? How is the space arranged? If the executive offices are plush but the spaces of support staff are slightly shabby, this says a great deal about company values.
2. Study the culture's "costume" and its language. What do the successful people around you wear and what does it tell you? How do they talk with their peers? With their subordinates? Are certain people allowed to break the dress code? If so, what makes these people different?
3. Notice the people on the way up (your boss, perhaps) and ask yourself why they're making it. What kind of people are "heroes" or "stars" in your company? Do they have glamour? Guts? Dedication to detail? Super salesmanship? Are they conformists or renegades? How do they spend most of their work time? How do they embody company values?
4. Identify the informal sources of power and influence. They may not be the people at the top of the organization chart. A secretary who's been around for

many years may have more know-how, even clout, than a new big-shot manager. Find out where to go when you want to get something done, or when you want to key into organization news.

5. Observe your company's rituals—retirement parties, Christmas parties, birthday celebrations, formal and informal meetings. What company values and beliefs are being acted out? Are those values encouraged and supported by what goes on every day? An inconsistent company that pays lip service to certain values but contradicts them by its daily decisions creates undue stress for its employees. Workers in such an organization will start feeling unnerved without understanding why—and if the situation continues, the company's potential success may be undermined.

As you observe the culture, you'll get a clearer idea of the kind of game your organization is playing. Is it a gambler's business where high risks and creative talent are required? Does it stress enthusiasm, team spirit, and hard work? Or does it value attention to detail and the careful following of certain procedures? The next question to consider: "Is this the kind of game I really enjoy?"

Build a Network within the Company

The best bulwark against political difficulties—and you can be sure you'll have some in the course of your career, no matter how competent, diplomatic, and supportive you are of other people—is to have some allies in key positions at the company who know you and respect your work. If somewhere down the line, you're suddenly working for a dreadful person who is undermining your every move, it will do wonders for your confidence—and for your job security—if you have people who can advise and support you when the going gets rocky. This does not mean that you should manufacture interest you don't sincerely feel or force yourself to become fast friends with influential people whom you loathe; in fact, the network does its job only if you choose people you admire and respect and with whom you have good chemistry. It's far easier and more fun that way, too.

Fortunately, you can begin to build these important alliances while you do your anthropological research. In your information-collecting travels around the tribal grounds, see if you can get talking relationships going with the following:

- Anyone a step or two above you whose methods you admire and whose style you feel you could emulate
- A colleague who is familiar with what you do or who has a job that's similar to yours. Perhaps you can work out an arrangement that you would sub for each other in case of emergencies, and pitch in for each other during pressure periods.
- A company historian who has been around since the Year One. Get him to tell you stories from the olden days; he'll be delighted by your interest. Key to any anthropological study is hearing and understanding the myths, legends, and lives of heroes from the past. People like this are fonts of knowledge about company history, and can give you detailed overviews of the development of the industry as well.
- A person who's worked with, or for, your boss in the past but does not do so currently. She may be an invaluable source of confidential advice about your supervisor's more mysterious character traits and behavior. And she'll be outside of the political fray of your department, so she'll be more objective.
- Powerbrokers of any sort with whom you feel "in sync." These may be vice presidents or the lady who cracks the whip in the accounting office. One warning about getting tight with higher-ups—be sure to do it in a way that supports, not threatens, your boss.
- One or two "company prophets"—insightful observers

who seem to know what's going to happen before it actually does. It's good to be tuned into the company grapevine.

Ask for a Three-Month Review

Many organizations have a three-month probationary period for new hires before they're formally welcomed onto the staff; if this is the case with your employer, you'll be getting a review. If this is not the case, ask your boss for one anyway. Request him to outline for you what you're good at, where you could improve. Ask him if you've learned the job as fast as he expected and if you're doing what's necessary to get to the next step, whatever you and he have decided that is. Asking proactively for a review is a positive step for a number of reasons. It will favorably impress your boss that you actively seek feedback; it will give you concrete data on how far you've come and what you need to work on, and it will set some goals for you in the months ahead.

For Further Reading

Deal, Terrence E., and Allen A. Kennedy. *Corporate Cultures: The Rites and Rituals of Corporate Life.* Reading, Mass.: Addison-Wesley, 1982.

Kennedy, Marilyn Moats. *Glamour Guide to Office Smarts.* New York: Fawcett Columbine, 1986.

Schmidt, Peggy J. *Making It on Your First Job: When You're Young, Inexperienced and Ambitious.* New York: Avon Books, 1985.

CHAPTER

11

Your Professional Cornerstone:

Good Work Habits

"She's a real professional." This low-key compliment is among the highest accolades in the business world, and it's well worth working for from your first day on the job. But what does it really mean? There are many aspects to professionalism. It implies a thorough mastery of the knowledge and skills most important in your chosen career field, but it's more than that. In a broader context, professionalism means having the personal maturity and inner strength to take complete responsibility for one's job—no passing the buck. On the most basic level, it means you consistently show up, on time and prepared. For the professional, cancellations are rare; no-shows never happen; excuses don't wash. Commitments are taken on thoughtfully (professionals feel free to say no as well as yes), but once assumed, are carried through completely. When problems arise, professionals never deny them or try to unload them on someone else; they communicate about them with the people involved and openly seek solutions. Professionals candidly admit mistakes and set about to clean up any problems they caused. Professionals set their sights beyond their own personal ego needs and rewards to ask,

"What's best for this company? What's best for this field? What's best for all involved? What is the ethical thing to do?"

To develop a professional attitude, you need to acquire certain disciplines, and they change in nature as you grow in your career and take on greater responsibilities. For beginners, a useful way to begin to build a professional outlook is through practicing good work habits until they become second nature. Your goal as you start out, and to some extent throughout your working life, is *to constantly reassure your supervisor and your coworkers that you can be counted on to do your job thoroughly and well.* Your boss needs to know, when she goes to sleep at night, that with all her other problems, she can rely on you. One way to reassure higher-ups that your share of the work is handled is to get good results on time. This is the kind of discipline you have probably learned in college by studying for exams, writing papers, and meeting deadlines. Many employers like hiring college grads because they have mastered these disciplines, and you'll be pleased to know that they are already in your repertoire of transferable skills. But in the world of work, *how* the job gets done is almost as important as *that* it gets done. This is where many college graduates become confused on their first jobs. It might be useful at this point to take a look at some of the habits you may have acquired during your college years and see how they might need to be altered or eliminated on your job.

Some College Habits to Transform

Here are a few typically collegiate behavior patterns that may have to be altered on your first job.

"Me First" to "Company First"

It has been said before in this book, but bears repeating, that although your supervisor is an authority figure as your parents or your college professors were, your relationship with him will have marked differences. He will supervise your growth and learning, but your personal well-being is not his main concern. Rather, he will be more interested in what you can do for him and for the company. You are being paid to support him—to be a means to an end—and you will do much better if you remember this principle in any communications you have with him. You will do far better when making a personal request—for a raise, for instance—if you couch it in terms of the company's best interests, and not your own.

Responsibility-Avoider versus Responsibility-Taker

Many working people retain the attitude, from their days as reluctant schoolchildren, that their job duties are enforced upon them by higher-ups, and they're smart if they can manage to get out of them. Colleges, especially the smaller ones, allow students to retain that habit of "begging off." Some students are used to asking for endless extensions, making excuses, getting out of things. But in the working world, even with the best excuses, you're still accountable for your work.

Your boss may show genuine sympathy when you're ill, for example, but he'll still be concerned with how you rearrange your work so that deadlines are met. One way to shake the student image is to make it a practice never to present your boss with a problem without also presenting a possible solution. He may not agree with your strategy, but the fact that you're thinking about the greater good of the department will not go unnoticed. Almost everyone has job tasks that she loathes (hopefully not too many), and the professional way to handle them is just to bite the bullet, get them done on time, and keep your complaining as good-natured as possible.

Lone-Ranger to Team Player

Former students, especially from large universities, may be surprised at how closely their work and social habits are observed on the job. In college, how you lived and worked outside the classroom was of little interest to your professors; their first concern was your academic performance on tests, papers, reports.

In the work world, however, you're more carefully observed and evaluated every day—on your dress, the appearance of your workspace, how you approach problems, how you get along with people. The brilliant loner who sailed through college but relates poorly to others may be in trouble on a job. To become more of a team player, communicate with your boss and colleagues on a regular basis. Keep them briefed on the status of your projects, what your successes and problems have been, how you've handled them, and what help you need from others. This is part of reassuring them, of developing your reputation for reliability as a professional.

Last-Minute Star to Long-Range Planner

Because grades and academic success get the main emphasis in college, the student who crams and pulls through at the last minute with top grades is often admired and envied. But unless you work for the kind of company that admires renegades and risk-takers, if you procrastinate until the night before deadline, you will not be creating an atmosphere of security for your boss and coworkers. Businesses more often admire self-discipline and smart time management for long-term projects. Long-term, one-step-at-a-time planning allows for input from others, the communal ironing out of problems, and interim evaluations, which are important in most businesses.

The college world tends to focus its rewards on people who are bright in an academic way, but the business world will give you credit for a wider range of qualities, such as enthusiasm, intuition, common sense, emotional stability, and the ability to get along with others.

Promptness, Neatness, and All That

Yes, your parents told you already: "Be on time and keep things neat." They're right—but it's not as simple as that. There's many a modern twist to these old dictums about how to succeed in business.

Beyond Nine to Five

You might have been told the official office hours on your new job, but they could have very little to do with how long, and when, people really work. In deciding how to schedule commuting time, evening classes and so on, take a good look at the hours people around you are keeping. For example, if you arrive at the official time to find the office humming and messages piling up on your desk, you'll know that the informal arrival time is probably a half hour to forty-five minutes earlier. It's best to plan your arrival accordingly, or your absence will be noted.

On the other hand, if your boss arrives at ten, don't assume that it's okay for you to do the same. Higher-level people often work at their own discretion and need their staff present during regular hours when they're not available.

More important than the time you show up and leave is the perception that you're dedicated to your job. Concentrate on giving your boss the "you can count on me" message by being present, visible, and geared up to work, especially when things get busy. A good way to show that you're responsible is staying late, without a fuss, to finish a priority job.

If your personal schedule (school, a long commute, children) locks you into rigid arrival and departure times, you can demonstrate your dedication by skipping your lunch hour a day or two a week. Have a sandwich at your desk and get in some extra work while everyone else is out. Now and then, take a task home and leave the finished product on your boss's desk the next morning. Try to communicate sincerely to two or three key people that you're there to make their jobs easier, and they'll be less likely to focus on your arrival and departure time.

Maintaining Your Workspace

For some people, orderliness is as easy as breathing; others struggle constantly against mess and clutter. If you are one of the latter group, it's worth exercising a little discipline, for how you keep your workspace will naturally be noticed by the people around you, whether they admit it or not. How neat does your workspace need to be? This depends on a number of factors. The first and most obvious is the kind of work you do and the cultural expectations in your company and your field. A certain casualness with files and papers is allowed in academia (the absentminded professor syndrome), in the arts (where there's a belief that chaos aids creativity), or in certain other work cultures where people consider a certain amount of disorder proof of productive activity. But in banks, accounting firms, law offices, or other businesses that deal with financial matters, you may be required to keep your desk shipshape. In these organizations, higher-ups and clients can become extremely nervous at the thought of important documents buried in sedimentary layers on someone's disorderly desk.

A second consideration is whether your desk is a showplace for your company. If you work in a reception area or if your boss sees important clients in her office area, your desk space is not really your own. Your boss may want to make a certain impression, so you and your desk must measure up. Another consideration: officemates. Consider what personal habits you have that may bother them and try to effect a compromise. Office decorations are best when they blend in with the environment. In some cases this means a plant and an elegant framed photo or piece of art; in others it could mean a lively, humorous poster. Nevertheless, keep in mind that your office is a place for serious, professional activity; it is not your livingroom or your kitchen.

Bear in mind also that there's a difference between working clutter (papers strewn around while you're working) and real litter. Soda cans lined up waiting to be returned, stale coffee in paper cups from the day before, and cigarette butts piling up convey a "don't care" attitude, and may earn you unwelcome attention. If you like to order in your lunch, be wary of strongly spiced ethnic food that draws undue attention to the fact that you're eating in the office. And be careful of how you dispose of any food. Even fruit peels and cores can develop unpleasant odors. In college, it was okay if your room became a snake pit during pressure periods, but to your supervisor, an untidy office may look like an embarrassing eyesore or, worse, a mistake waiting to happen. If you're not naturally neat, make it a practice to take five or ten minutes at the end of each day to throw things out and straighten up.

Telephone Techniques

One of the duties almost invariably assigned to beginners is answering the phone for the more senior people around them. But few new employees realize that this often bothersome task is crucial to their firm's public image. Studies have shown that about seven out of ten people who stop doing business with a company do so because of the feeling they get from their first contacts, most of which involve telephone communication with junior employees. Despite this obvious fact, few beginning workers receive any training in telephone etiquette.

During the course of a busy day, telephone calls can often be seen as interruptions. That's why people who screen calls for their boss, who handle many complaint calls, or who must deal with many calls at once can develop a defensiveness that gives a very poor impression. Here are some suggestions for developing a professional manner over the telephone.

Treat every caller not as a disembodied voice but as a guest in your home. There's no need to gush, but do put a slight smile into your greeting. Ask your boss how she wants you to answer: "Marilyn Wilson's office"? "Ms. Wilson's office"? Depending on the formality of the environment, you might want to preface that with "Good morning" or some other greeting. There seems to be a trend these days toward using first names only, when answering the phone, as in "Acme Corporation. This is Nicky. How may I help you?" If you've used this approach in the restaurant where you worked in the summer, be careful about automatically transferring this greeting to a more formal environment. Listen to the people around you, or ask what degree of formality you should assume in answering the telephone. Keep in mind also that your use of your first name only may give the message "I'm cute but unimportant, I have no authority." (Listen the next time you're on an airplane—flight attendants may refer to themselves as Betty or Don, but pilots always use their last names.) Unless you've been specifically instructed otherwise, it's probably best to use your first and last name when you're identifying yourself over the phone. It gives you a serious presence, and the person you're speaking with the reassurance that they will be able to get back to you if they need to.

Never put a caller on hold without asking permission first. Say, "Would you hold a moment, please?" Pause a beat, then press the hold button. Get back to that person within thirty seconds if you can, with a "Thank you for holding." If you're handling several calls, quickly jot down the name of the person on each line—and then address the callers by name, if possible. It makes a great impression. If you have to keep the person on hold for a long time, apologize and acknowledge that this may be an inconvenience. "Sorry I've had to keep you on hold, Mr. Leavitt. My lines are a little jammed. How may I help you?"

When your boss leaves the office, always find out when he or she plans to return. If someone calls in the interim, a good response might be, "Mr. Cooper is out of the office right now, but he'll be back at 2:15. May I take a message, or may I help you?" Don't volunteer where your boss is unless you're instructed to do so, and don't promise he'll return the call.

If you're handling certain responsibilities for your boss, you need to be competent and intelligent over the phone so that people will trust you and not try to push past you to your boss. Perhaps you are organizing a luncheon, making travel arrangements, or greeting guests from another city. First, make sure to obtain all the information and authority necessary to do the job. Then get back to people when you say you will, deal with any problems right away, and, if necessary, call the participants and reassure them that all is going as planned.

Deal with angry callers, even the most irrational ones, by just listening. Don't become defensive or say, "That's not my job." Ask the name of the person who's talking. When the complainer has finished, you might say, "Thank you so much for bringing this to our attention, Mr. Jones. I'll see that someone gets back to you (name a day) at the latest." Then do look into the matter, even if it's not your problem. If dealing with complaints is a good portion of your job, ask for specific training in this sort of telephone work. A seminar on dealing with these pressured situations can make you a much more effective employee and reduce the stress for you. Needless to say, be very careful that your own pressures and tensions on the job aren't reflected in the way you're handling your telephone contacts.

Always take a little extra time to help someone. Try never to end a conversation by saying "I don't know" or "I can't help you," unless you give the caller an alternative. Assume a partnership with the caller, a "Let's figure out this problem together" attitude. Say, "Let me think a minute about who could help you with that." Or "You want to talk to Mr. Brown in the sales department. May I transfer you?"

Make it a policy to answer your phone by the second or third ring and to return phone messages within forty-eight hours at the latest, even if it's just to say that a decision has not yet been made. Never deal with telephone problems of any sort by not returning calls. If you need to confront someone, say no to a request, or deliver bad news, think about what you might say, get some help from a more experienced person, and face the music. That's being professional.

Telephone dilemmas may seem bothersome or intimidating, but they can give you great visibility. On the telephone, you're your company's public relations agent, diplomat, ombudsman. If you're good at your job, you'll shine. Never take your telephone skills for granted. If you're good at solving problems over the telephone, be sure to include them in your list of assets when you ask for a raise or a promotion.

Managing Paper Flow

Another major task usually assigned to beginners is opening and sorting mail and maintaining files—your boss's or your own. The paper—in the form of junk mail, faxes, and so on—that flows into an ordinary office these days can really inundate you, so an efficient method of handling paper can save hours of your time. Here's a basic approach for you to consider. You may want to make your own modifications on it as you become more familiar with the needs of your office.

First, consider that each piece of paper represents a task and requires action of some sort. Think of each piece of mail in light of your projects and interests. Your job is to set priorities for tasks with your supervisor's help.

If you're unclear about priority projects, ask your boss for advice. Have her designate those projects, major interests, and names of key people and watch for them as you sort through the incoming mail and interoffice memos. Set aside a certain time each day to handle paper. As you sort through correspondence, try to handle each piece just once.

Basically, you can do only one of four things with each item.

1. Throw it out. Direct-mail offerings and advertising or press releases of no interest to your department can go straight into the wastebasket. Put items you're unsure of in a pile with a note to your boss saying "Should I throw out?" If she wants to keep them, ask her to let you know.

2. Direct it to another staff member. Pass on any misdirected mail to its correct destination. Write FYI (for your information) or a short note if appropriate at the top of the papers you're referring, and put them in your "Out" box.

3. File it. Certain items, such as memos from personnel or monthly sales figures for a report, need to be kept in files close at hand (unless your supervisor wants to review them first). If the appropriate folder is within arm's reach, file it immediately. Otherwise, note on the paper where it belongs and put it in a box or folder marked "To file." Clear this box weekly.

4. Act on it. Some letters will alert you to a matter that needs handling. However, unless your boss has delegated specific tasks to you, always check with her before acting. If the response will take less than fifteen minutes, do it immediately. Items that require more thought, such as a reply to correspondence, should be placed in a box or folder marked "Action."

Once you've worked through all the mail, sort through your "Action" file. Rate the items *A*, *B*, or *C* in order of priority. Unless you're sure, ask your boss when she'd like these various tasks completed. Make "appointments" with yourself to do the jobs, and note them on your calendar.

Some items (a speaking invitation, a request for a written report) should usually go to your supervisor first for her decision. When she responds, ask her for a date for you to follow up. Note this on your calendar and keep the item in a folder marked "Holding File" until it's time to remind your boss.

Another desk organizer: Instead of jotting notes and numbers on slips of paper that can get lost in the shuffle, use a shorthand pad. Date it daily, and let it serve as a work log. Use the last five or ten minutes of the day to sort any random papers on your desk.

Negotiating Work-Life/Personal-Life Boundaries

One issue young newcomers are often unaware of is the importance of considering the impact of their personal lives on their work lives, and their professional image. An important question to think about when you begin a job is, Given the work environment and my individual personality, how much and what kind of personal information is it appropriate for me to share with my workmates? And there's a related question as well: When I have problems in my personal life, how can I manage my work life so that my job is not jeopardized?

In college, work and personal life tended to flow together, so these distinctions were more blurred. Therefore, there's a natural tendency among ex-students, especially engaging, outgoing ones, to treat their work colleagues as dormitory pals with whom they share the more intimate details of their lives. But there is a difference between personal friends and work friends, and you might not want to reveal certain things about yourself to people at work. Do you want it generally known in your office, for example, that you had a bit much to drink on Saturday night or that your date stood you up? Even a casual comment to a friendly boss that you and the person you've been seeing are becoming more serious may start your boss speculating: "Will she be taking time off during the busy season to plan a wedding? Will this relationship interfere with her commitment to her job? Will she continue to work here? Will she be moving away?" As a result, he may have second thoughts about supporting or promoting you.

It's not that you *never* want to share personal ups and downs at work. You're human and so is everyone else. It's just that certain personal information, if known, may have consequences, and you may want to think first before you allow certain facts about yourself to become general knowledge. You'll probably be making judgments every day about how to handle the work-life/personal-life boundary, and there are many ways that the two impact on each other. Here are three common situations where these considerations come into play.

Keeping Strong on the Job When You're Ill or Have Personal Emergencies

Consider this predicament (things like this happen to every busy person now and again): You've just returned to work after being out sick for four days with the Asian flu. Next week you've asked for, and been granted, a day off because your husband is graduating from school. This morning you wake up raring to go, only to find that your cat is sick and needs immediate veterinary attention. You're really feeling pressured, and questions flood your mind. What will your boss say when you ask for a few more hours off? Should you lie about the cat and say it's a plumbing leak instead? Is your boss going to think you're the kind of person whose life is constant chaos and therefore lose confidence in you? These are not frivolous questions. Again, it's a matter of reassuring the people around you that despite recent intrusions from your personal life, you're committed to your job and you have it handled. Here are some ways of addressing the problems.

1. Know that your boss is far less interested in the details of your personal problems than in how much time you'll be missing and whether you can get your work done on schedule. You don't need to say any more about the cat than "Sorry, I have to handle a personal emergency this morning. I'll be in no later than 11:30." But if you have the feeling that your boss is getting irritated at the amount of time you've taken—or *you're* uncomfortable and guilty about it—make it a point to discuss it openly with him at your first convenience.

2. How you approach your boss will depend to some extent on the pace of your job and the consequences, if any, of your previous absences. If you have a slow-paced job in an easygoing workplace, and you've been able to complete your work on or before schedule despite your days off, you might say to your boss, "Even though I've had to take time off recently, I want to reassure you that my work is up to date. Still, I'd be glad to stay late a few nights or come in on Saturday if there's anything you'd like me to do."

If yours is a more pressured environment and you have fallen behind, devise a specific plan for getting back on schedule. Then acknowledge to your supervisor that your recent illness and emergencies have caused problems, apologize if necessary, and present your plan. Ask for his suggestions.

3. Note your boss's reaction; it will give you insights about his personality and his regard for you as an employee. Was he understanding about the time you had to take, or was he concealing his irritation? Was he beginning to doubt your involvement in your job? The better you understand your boss's feelings and expectations, the greater your chances of negotiating personal time off without misunderstandings.

4. Be honest with yourself. If these incidents weren't truly urgent, perhaps you're bored or frustrated by the job. In this case, you need to confront work problems and stresses head on instead of trying to escape them.

5. If at any time you anticipate a personal crunch of some duration—you're planning a wedding, a parent is ill, you need a series of medical treatments—be sure to inform your supervisor beforehand and discuss how you can best mesh your personal and work life during this busy period. Covering up your whereabouts will only add to your own uneasiness and may arouse unwarranted distrust in your boss.

Making Personal-Life Changes Public at Work

You may be surprised to find that the impact of certain kinds of personal news—an upcoming marriage or divorce or a pregnancy—has more repercussions than you might have imagined. Timing of such announcements can be important. Although there's certainly no right or wrong about these things, here are some general guidelines to arrive at your own best conclusion.

1. Tell your coworkers the news only when you're comfortable having everyone know it. Gossip has a way of leaking out in the workplace, even if you tell only one person. It's also polite to let your boss be one of the first people to know.

2. Be sure your situation is definite before you broadcast it. If you confide in an officemate that you're considering marriage, you'll make yourself the subject of more talk than you may be ready for. Besides, if the situation doesn't materialize, your disappointment will be more public.

3. If you're concerned about people's reactions to your news, ask some discreet questions about how similar announcements have been received before. Seek out someone who has been in a situation like yours and ask her in confidence what, if anything, to watch out for.

4. After you do tell, keep your discussions about plans brief. You're at work to do a job; you don't want to look like your major focus has shifted elsewhere. Respond to coworkers' inquiries, but tell them only as much as you're comfortable with. It's best to share excitement or jitters with office friends after hours.

Arranging for Your Vacation

When college vacation time arrived, almost everyone—students and faculty alike—was on holiday at the same time. But when you're working, the company—and your job—continue throughout your vacation. Especially if you work in a high-pressured environment or in the kind of organization where hard work and long hours are valued, you may have to give some thought to the implications of how much vacation you take and when you take it. Whereas in college it was perfectly okay to talk publicly and often about how much you need a vacation and what a great time you're going to have, in a busy office it's to your advantage to make your absence as low-key as possible. Here are some ways to plan for a vacation that indicate a more professional approach:

1. Just because your company allows you, say, two weeks vacation, don't just assume that you can take it all at once, whenever you want it. Bear in mind that your vacation will inconvenience others, at least to some extent, and taking the full two weeks at busy season would not be regarded favorably. Watch company tradition: If the people around you, especially the higher-ups, take only one week at a time, it's best to follow suit.

2. Make an arrangement with one or two reliable co-workers to cover at least part of your job while you're away. Establish a pattern of reciprocal backup with an officemate by offering to assist him when he's swamped, or by asking a favor and later returning it. Doing someone else's job can be a valuable opportunity to try different skills and get to know different supervisors and colleagues.

3. Notify your supervisor of your vacation plans well in advance. One way to approach him would be to say "I'd like to plan some time off in about six weeks or so. Which of these dates would be best?" That gives your boss some opportunity to decide when he can best spare you. If you work in a pressured office, present a backup plan—who will be covering what parts of your job; what projects you'll get a head start on before leaving. If your boss indicates concern that a part of your job be completed before you leave, make sure it's done, even if you need to work overtime.

4. Try not to regale people with your vacation plans or tell them how glad you are to be going away. On the other end, be prepared for business when you return, and keep descriptions about your vacation low-key.

The situations in this chapter outline only a few of the more fundamental elements of professionalism. The expectations of professionals vary greatly depending on the field in which you're working, but being professional basically means seeing yourself as a serious, contributing member of your organization and your field, and acknowledging the fact that others depend on you to do your job thoroughly. Professional behavior conveys the attitude that you can be depended on, and while you're at work, the job and the company come first.

For Further Reading

Lakein, Alan. *How to Get Control of Your Time and Your Life.* New York: Signet, 1974.

Winston, Stephanie. *Getting Organized.* New York: Warner Books, 1978.

CHAPTER

12

Managing Up:

How to Get Along with Your Boss and Coworkers

When you walk into your new workplace on your first day, what will be most immediately apparent to you will be people doing objectively observable work tasks—attending meetings, preparing reports, talking on the telephone, typing and filing. As time goes on and you get to know the people around you, however, you'll begin to feel the undercurrents of work life as people's different personal styles cooperate or clash. You'll begin to get a sense of what motivates the people around you—what they need, what drives them, what makes them feel secure or insecure. People in general are largely unconscious about the forces that motivate them, even though these forces are very powerful. And when people act in ways that they don't understand or won't admit to, there is sure to be trouble. In fact, it's probably fair to say that the majority of business snafus are attributable to misunderstood motivations, thwarted intentions, or poor interpersonal communications.

Conversely, if you struggle to become aware of your own needs, drives, and motivations (to make the unconscious conscious, as psychologists say) and to carefully observe and listen to others, you'll be in a position to work with these unconscious forces in others. You can neutralize negative forces in yourself and the people around you, encourage positive ones, and give people the emotional supplies they need to get the job done. And you may well be promoted for your good "people skills." You certainly don't need to be a psychoanalyst to succeed on the job, but it's invaluable to have a healthy curiosity about what makes people tick.

Start with Yourself

You'll have many opportunities as you get into your job to become more aware of your unconscious needs and motivations. You'll get an especially good look at yourself when you observe how you handle mistakes, frustrations, and crises on the job, and how you handle successes as well. But you can begin right away to gain some insight into the kind of psychological team you and your boss might make by doing the following exercises. And you'll begin to learn a bit about your boss in the bargain.

It's common knowledge among industrial psychologists that people tend to look upon their work colleagues as a family, with higher-ups as parents, and peers as siblings. (Everyone does this to some extent, but it's more apparent, less hidden, in younger employees.) People then often behave in the workplace as they did their family of origin—rebelling against or yielding to authority, competing with or emulating siblings, whatever their individual patterns might be.

When you chose to accept your job, there's a good chance you did so because you felt a rather high comfort level with the person you'll be working for. Or it may be that you accepted the job despite some vague feelings of discomfort about your immediate supervisor. Keeping the idea of family patterns in mind, you might wish to explore the source of those comfortable or uncomfortable feelings. Here are just a few of the unconscious expectations you might have of your boss as you begin your new job. If you have trouble getting the idea, check for clues in your family relationships. Which family member does your new boss most nearly remind you of?

If Your Boss Is . . .	You Might Be Looking for . . .
An older man	• the supportive father you never had • the supportive father you did have and wish to reexperience • the charismatic, authoritarian father to whom you want to prove something • the wise old man or guru who will teach you all you need to know
A younger man	• The jolly older brother who brings you along and shows you the ropes • The competitive older brother you long to get the better of • The attractive man who may be a potential romantic interest
An older woman	• The nurturing mother you never had • The nurturing mother you did have and wish to reexperience • The glamorous, charismatic woman who will draw you along in her wake • The wise old woman who will impart to you all her knowledge
A younger woman	• A sister or best friend with whom you can share your feelings

Most likely, you'll have your own unique variation on this theme. Write it here.

Once you have a notion of the role in which you've cast your boss, you'll be in a position to decide, as you get to know him, which parts of it are realistic and which are not. Many frustrations and irritations people experience on their jobs have to do with unrealistic expectations that come from superimposing the family pattern onto the work situation. The people at work are like your family in a way, but there are enormous differences, and it's important to tease out these distinctions.

It might also be interesting, as you get to know your boss, to try and figure out how you fit into his or her family construct. One young woman named Debbie was hired right after college by a very successful independent management consultant, a man who was approaching retirement. There was an excellent personality fit between them—she was bright and learned quickly, and understood just what was needed in his business. Then tragedy struck, and the man's only child, a daughter Debbie's age, was killed in an accident. While her boss grieved the loss, Debbie, who was naturally compassionate, did what she could to take up the slack. Then she discovered her boss wanted to spend more time with her, talking about personal matters. He gave her expensive gifts and offered to fund her graduate education. It became clear to Debbie that she was being asked to fill the place left by her boss's child, and she wisely realized that she was neither willing nor able to do that. Because she recognized the pattern, Debbie was able to continue to give support and enjoy the positive side of the working relationship while gently setting limits and making it clear to her boss that she could not replace his daughter.

Get to Know Your Boss

If you become aware of what you might be asking for, subliminally, from your supervisor, and recognize it for what it is, you will become freer to get to know him in a broader way. You can get beyond "What can he do for me?" to "What is his place in this organization? Which of his talents are valued here?" This kind of perspective will help especially when clashes and disagreements occur between the two of you.

The best way to get to know your boss is to listen and observe. Watch him when he's with higher-ups. (They will most likely see his most competent, professional side, since people naturally show their bosses their best face and allow their less acceptable moods out only with subordinates.) Watch him when he's with his peers. And when he's with *your* peers. How does he function in meetings? Does he have a special role in the group, and if so, what is it? After you've been working for a few months, run down this list of possible descriptions of your boss and his place in your organization. Check the one that seems most similar, or create your own.

___ 1. Well-regarded, on the way up, a typical example of success in this organization
___ 2. Struggling to make it, but must iron out some problems in personal or management style
___ 3. Not too much power, but performs an important function competently
___ 4. An eccentric, different in style from most in the organization, but tolerated or respected because of unusual talent or experience
___ 5. Other ______________________________
____
____

Below are more exercises that might help you get to know your boss by pinpointing his strengths and weaknesses and encouraging you to think about their consequences to you and to your organization. Select the positive and negative qualities in the table below and check any that apply.

Possible Strengths of Your Manager

Strength	*This Quality Is . . .* Valued by Boss Him/Herself	Important to Organization	Important to You
Loyal to company			
Loyal to peers			
Loyal to subordinates			
Enthusiastic			
Intelligent			
Self-aware (realistic idea of own strengths and weaknesses)			
Good problem solver			
Reliable (makes deadlines, keeps promises, etc.)			
Good follow-through (returns phone calls, follows projects to completion)			
Good with detail			
Good with people (deals with "people problems" even-handedly and without delay)			

Personally engaging, glamorous, or charismatic

Other:

____

____

____

Possible Weaknesses of Your Manager

Weakness	*This Character Trait Is . . .*		
	Known to the Boss Him/Herself	**Noted by Higher-Ups**	**Especially Irritating to You**
Disorganized			
Inconsistent (changes mind often about what's important)			
Volatile (moody, gets upset about minor matters)			
Poor communicator (gives unclear direction)			
Closed-minded (wishes to do things his way even if another way would be more efficient)			
Handles authority poorly			
Other:			
____________________			
____________________			
____________________			

Once you have a more or less realistic idea of your supervisor's strengths and shortcomings, you'll be in a better position to see where you fit in—how you can help your supervisor better do what he's already good at and shore him up in areas where he's weak. This is the secret of "managing up."

Managing Up

Most first-time workers automatically and naturally expect their supervisor to provide them with clearly directed, supportive management and a flexible structure in which to learn. And ideally, they're absolutely entitled to it. In the real world, however, there are many managers who are good at surviving in an organization but haven't a clue as to how to manage their employees in an effective and respectful way. In addition, there are many more supervisors who perform certain management tasks well, but manage other tasks poorly. If you work for a boss like this, your first reaction may be anger and disillusionment that you are not really being managed properly. After those feelings calm a bit, your best course is to figure out how to manage your boss. This is what "managing up" is all about. Probably in the best boss-employee relationships, as in the best marriages, a little people-management is done by each partner.

What Do Bosses Really Want?

The most important thing to learn in order to "manage up" is what your boss wants from you. Not what she *says* she wants from you (you've probably already discussed that or it's in your job description), but what she *really* wants from you. The kind of support bosses really need (and it's different in every case) is mostly unconscious and almost always unspoken.

Case in point: Gale was hired as the assistant to a public relations account executive whose clients were mostly in the beauty industry. Gale's boss was glamorous, entertaining, and affable. She was well known in the industry and personally liked by all her clients. She specialized in long lunches in which she chatted up her accounts, and Gale was left back at the office to train and manage herself. When Gale was reviewed at her three-month probation period, she was shocked to find that her boss felt she was not making the grade and that she was considering letting her go!

The point that Gale did not pick up on while she was waiting to be managed was that her boss was great at the public parts of her job but poor with details. She had no organizational ability and a poor head for details, and she really counted on her assistant to clean up after her, to finish projects that she started, and remind her of things she forgot. Like most bosses, she wasn't self-aware or self-revealing enough to say to a new assistant, "Look, I'm extroverted but scatterbrained, and I always leave things in a mess. Your job is to straighten out my mistakes without making them public, never challenge me about my disorganization, and in general, make me look good." All Gale's boss was aware of was a vague insecurity that her office wasn't quite in capable hands as she went about the business of entertaining, and she felt she might need an assistant who was more on-the-ball.

Fortunately, Gale was given another three months, and, by talking with her boss's former assistant, she was able to get some advice on how to manage her disorganized supervisor.

What would your boss tell you about her needs if she could? "I'm out of good ideas and I'm panicked about it. I need you to give me some"? Or "When I go into a tailspin, I need you to listen, not chatter"? To get a fix on those unconscious needs, listen well, especially when your boss is upset, and try to see just what message she's giving you.

Here are some techniques for managing a variety of difficult bosses:

The Volatile, Irritable Boss

If your boss tends to fly off the handle for little apparent reason, and you tend to be the recipient of his bad moods, try these suggestions for "managing up."

Observe the timing of the blowups to try to get a fix on the reasons why they happen. Do they occur most frequently before a client presentation? After a private meeting with his managers? Does he seem overawed or intimidated by anyone? Is he in a political pressure cooker? Is he valued in the company, or do many of his accomplishments appear to go unnoticed?

Compare your style with your boss's. Maybe you're a person of few words under pressure, whereas he needs to open his steam valve. Or you fret over details and he doesn't. Or you're breezy and offhand; he's less casual all around. These differences can be annoying during pressure periods. You might try to lower tensions by adapting to his style as much as possible.

Try supportive statements. If he's gearing up for a presentation or speech that's well researched, say so. If he's been well received in the past, remind him of that. Don't overdo it; a simple phrase will do. Other tension-easers:

- The light touch: If a little teasing or joshing is a normal part of your relationship, a touch of it now might brighten your boss's mood. Keep it light, not personal, and skip it if you're unsure.
- The work break: You can try to calm a frenzy by saying, "Everything seems to be piling up at once. Could we take a minute to see what needs doing first?"

- The reassuring backup: Your boss may be nervous about things you're supposed to be doing. Say something like "Don't worry about this or that; I have it under control (or done). Go ahead and prepare your speech for tomorrow."
- The frank offer of assistance: Look straight at your boss and ask, "Is there anything I can do right now to help? I don't mind staying late."

Your boss's moments of tension are no time to try to be right, grab credit for yourself, or expect reassurance from her. They're a time to assume a bit of maturity—and this will reflect well on you.

The Disorganized Boss

If you work for a scatterbrained person, you need to be super-organized. Use the following suggestions to nudge your boss subtly toward a more structured approach. Use a light touch; if you come across as too pushy, she may be more embarrassed and irritated than grateful.

Take the initiative. Ask your boss to meet on a regular basis, perhaps every other day for starters, to discuss priorities and details, and to update each other. The meetings needn't be long, but preferably make them first thing in the morning. It's up to you to set the agenda and see that the meetings take place. If your boss is a postponer, don't wait for her to summon you; stay near her door until she's ready to talk with you. Make notes on topics discussed, decisions made, and keep them in chronological order.

Be an advance planner. When you get word about an upcoming deadline, note, for example, when meeting rooms must be reserved, hotel reservations made for visiting clients; check them for accuracy with your boss. Then make notes on your calendar or slip reminders into your "tickler file." Fit these memory-joggers into your agendas for regular meetings with your boss.

Keep a phone log. If you answer the phone for your boss, as phone messages come in, write them on lined paper (with a carbon copy underneath) and keep them in chronological order in an open binder on your boss's desk. Then use your copy of the log to remind your boss about phone calls at your regular meeting: "Have you had a chance to get back to the hotel manager? Shall I call for you?"

Stay on top of details. Keep copies of everything. If your boss loses an important letter or memo, you should have a backup. You may want to retain originals of important documents and give your boss copies. Devise an easy, readily accessible filing system for the originals. You might want to store them, with the most recent (or top-priority) material on top.

Constantly remind your boss of upcoming events. Type or write her schedule for the following day—appointments, decisions needed—on an index card and leave it on her desk at the end of the day so she'll see it first thing in the morning.

Don't be too hard on yourself when mishaps occur—and they certainly will with a disorganized person. If you're a perfectionist, you'll be tense all the time. Don't panic. Relax into the job and enjoy the challenge.

The Too-Talkative, Overly Personal Boss

Bosses who love to talk and who are always telling you about their trips to the store, their spouse, and their children can drive you crazy when you're trying to concentrate on your job. Before you decide to cut such conversations short and "get back to business," it's good to realize what a person like this is trying to accomplish. Your boss's chatter may be her way of warming up the workplace, building trust and team spirit, and feeling connected to the people around her. Listening to her isn't a waste of time; it's an important signal that you're a reliable ally.

Besides, there are plenty of advantages to working with a talker. Chatty people reveal themselves more readily; you don't have to guess what they're like or what they want. If your boss sees you as "her kind of person," she'll probably be a good source of important company information. She'll also be more likely to give you growth opportunities and promotions. On the other hand, if you appear impatient and uninterested in chatter, she may think you're cold and she might look somewhere else for a protégée. You also may give the impression of someone who's too uptight to relax and take a few minutes for small talk. Don't feel you have to reciprocate by sharing details about *your* personal life. Simply listen uncritically, acknowledge her feelings, and offer a supportive response: "It must be hard when the first child leaves for college" or "It's so irritating when that happens!"

If your boss is a nonstop talker, tends to waste time, or gets distracted from important deadlines, it's part of your job to gently try to keep her on track. Since you have her attention, take the opportunity to discuss the day's schedule or get feedback on your work. Instead of cutting her off suddenly ("Well, I've got to get to work"), look for a break in the conversation and say something like, "Oh, before I forget, I was supposed to remind you that we should begin thinking about the promotional campaign soon. What are your priorities this week?" or "To change the subject a minute, I wanted to get your thoughts about that report I prepared." To get a block of quiet time to work, consider coming in early a couple of days a week, or staying late after she's left for the day.

There are many other difficult personality types among the supervisors out there, some far worse than these. Every personality has a positive and a negative side. The trick is to use the positives to your advantage and find your own way around the more annoying ones. The truth is that everyone can use a little managing from time to time, and if you manage your boss—and the other people around you—graciously and tactfully, you may find yourself a highly valued employee.

Hitting It Off with Your Coworkers

The point was made at the beginning of Chapter 10, that few skills are more valuable to you than your ability to get along with and work with your peers. Certainly the new competitiveness in American business has stressed all the power, energy, and motivation to be found in teamwork. But work colleagues, like siblings, are also competitive, and some companies motivate by stressing competition for raises and promotions. Which is more important—teamwork or competition?

The answer is that these two concepts, although they emphasize different values, are not at all mutually exclusive. Every sports team, for example, has its "stars" who both compete and cooperate with other team members. As a newcomer, though, your first task is to find your place within the group. Study the work attitudes of the people around you and learn to adapt to the company style. Here are some suggestions:

Determine your organization's goals and make them your own. Successful people are adept at determining what top management wants and delivering it, even if they're occasionally disliked by peers or subordinates. Ask yourself what your firm's real goals are (you may have to read between the lines) and what you can contribute. One company might value people who can cut costs; another might favor managers who meet deadlines, no matter what; and a third might cherish creative flair. The more your style meshes with your department's, the greater your chances are for success.

Know the rules for getting ahead. Know, too, that the rules may be unstated, political, and not as "fair" as you wish they were. For instance, higher-ups in your organization might admire a certain amount of raw competitiveness and approve of whip cracking to control staff.

Be people-smart. Most high achievers know they can't pull off major projects by themselves. They're usually experts in enlisting others' help. Observe the abilities and preferences of your peers so that when you go to your boss with an idea, you can also suggest how to parcel out the work. And build your own support network by acknowledging the good work colleagues do, asking for help when you need it, and returning the favor.

Seize your moment. Take full advantage of the times you shine. False modesty undercuts your leadership image. Instead, stand proudly in the spotlight and bring others in with you if it's appropriate. Come promotion time, there's nothing wrong with showcasing your own achievements.

The best team players and competitors can work amicably with people they don't like and tolerate situations that are "unfair" in order to meet company goals. Equally important, they're fully aware of their own power and use it judiciously but without apology.

What do these general principles of competition/cooperation look like when they're played out in real-life situations at your workplace? Here are some typical sibling-rivalry situations that may arise with peers, and some suggestions about what to do.

The Colleague Who Undercuts You

Envy is just as widespread in the workplace as it is in the world at large. Often an insecure colleague will try to puncture the balloon of a newcomer who's successful by talking against her with other colleagues or even with the boss. If this happens to you, try these guidelines for coping with the situation.

Start by making a written list of all the measurable results you've achieved so far on the job. This should boost your confidence and help you clarify the issue in your own mind.

Determine her motivation. Why would this particular person have it in for you? Are you competing with her for a promotion? Does your hard work make her lesser performance seem more obvious? Are you, as a newcomer, challenging old habits to which she's become accustomed? Have you unintentionally slighted her? Are there rumors of cutbacks in your department? Or other motivations for her behavior? Assess her relative power in the office. Just how much influence does she have with your boss, and where does it come from?

Have a talk with the person involved. Try to deal with your offending colleague directly. Do you work with her on a regular basis, and have you personally sensed her animosity? If so, talk with her about work-related issues. Avoid mentioning any rumors you may have heard; she'll probably deny them anyway, and you may end up involving those who brought the problem to your attention. Put aside any resentment for the moment, and approach her sincerely. Say that you've noticed some coolness and discomfort between the two of you, and you'd like to talk things out.

Ask if there's anything you do that disturbs her, any way you could work better together. Listen to her responses, repeat them back to her, and urge her to be as specific in her suggestions as possible. By no means let her draw you into a fight. If you feel your irritation level rising, end the conversation by saying, "Thank you. I'd like to think about your suggestions. Can we talk more later?" As you consider what she's said, read between the lines. How do you threaten her? Is there any way in the coming weeks that you can acknowledge her, flatter her, get her to feel you're both part of a team, not adversaries?

Have a talk with your boss. If your boss seems to be acting differently toward you and you think it's because of what this person has said, you might want to approach him directly to find out the source of his suspicions and strengthen your relationship with him. Ask questions centering on your work: "Is there anything I'm doing that I shouldn't be doing? Are there any improvements I need to make?" If your boss asks why you initiated this conversation, you might mention you'd sensed that you weren't completely trusted, and you'd been wondering why. Let your boss be the first to mention any gossip about you. That way you'll find out what he really heard, and you'll be in a far better position to rebut any false statements. You may want to talk with your boss even if your relationship with your colleague improves; your supervisor holds the keys to your success, and you don't want anything to jeopardize mutual trust in this area. After these talks are behind you, concentrate on doing a top-notch job.

The Officemate Who Steps on Your Territory

Another common problem is the colleague who tries to grab your glory, either by copying you (writing a memo when you do, requesting a meeting when you do), or by acting proprietary about projects, or by trying to cut you out of the information loop.

Bolster your confidence by asking for some feedback from your boss. Ask him to identify the areas in which you're doing well and those in which you need improvement. Then ask yourself if his comments throw any light on the problems you're having with your colleague.

Request a talk with your offending colleague to talk about how your jobs fit together. In a nonaccusing way, state what you feel the problem is: "The other day when you handed the completed project to Mr. Barton, I felt that I had been bypassed. Since this was a joint project, it's really important that we make sure each of us has equal input." Go on to discuss how your jobs differ and how they overlap. See if you can agree upon some procedures for dividing tasks, working together, and communicating better.

In the following weeks, be sure to give your colleague positive feedback when things are working well. If your mutually agreed-upon procedures are violated, be sure to mention it promptly and tactfully. Don't let resentments build. Keep the talk you had with her confidential; try to solve the problem between the two of you. If the problem is not resolved, you might want to ask your boss to act as mediator.

The "Old Guard"

Very often newcomers find themselves in conflict with members of the "old guard"—people who have been working at the organization for a long time; who often seem wedded to slow, inefficient procedures; and who may be somewhat threatened by, and defensive with, new people. Go very slowly with such a person; remember that he has the seniority and if you take an antagonistic attitude, you may lock yourself into an adversarial position that will be hard to reverse.

Try to find out why this person has been kept on. Is it because of his years of loyal service? Because he's approaching retirement? Or because he's well connected? Or he may be valued for his integrity, or because he does one important facet of his job extremely well.

Try to cultivate a friendlier relationship with him by taking a personal interest. Ask how he started with this company, how it was different then, who his bosses were, why he stayed on. Some people with long tenure are reservoirs of accumulated company wisdom. If you treat him with respect and attempt to defuse his defensiveness and suspicion, he may give you insights into key people, the culture, even save you from costly mistakes.

Ask him to explain those "inefficient" procedures. They may have a sounder basis than you suspected. If he senses you're not trying to undermine him, he might be more amenable to doing rush jobs as a favor to you. Thank him warmly if he does. If he won't deviate from set routines, learn to factor his slower work pace into your schedule; you may become a more efficient, precise planner as a result. Be aware, also, that higher-ups will notice how you learn to work with, or around, the set-in-his-ways type of person.

The above strategies are designed to give you a general idea of how "people problems" are handled in a professional manner. They by no means cover the many kinds of situations you'll encounter. Enough advice! What you need now is experience. Jump in, get started, see what kinds of situations arise. You're sure to be confused and at sea for a couple of weeks—maybe even a couple of months. Transitions throw us off kilter, but they're great growth periods. You'll be leaving behind your experiences as a child and as a student, and encountering the kinds of challenges that will shape you into a professional in whatever field you choose. As your self-confidence and sense of contribution grows, you'll find it's a journey well worth making.

For Further Reading

Bern, Dr. Paula. *How to Work for a Woman Boss.* New York: Dodd, Mead & Company, 1987.

Grove, Andrew S. *One-On-One with Andy Grove: How to Manage Your Boss, Yourself and Your Coworkers.* New York: G. P. Putnam's Sons, 1987.

Hochheiser, Robert M. *How to Work for a Jerk: Your Success Is the Best Revenge.* New York: Vintage Books, 1987.

Iaconetti, Joan, and Patrick O'Hara. *First-Time Manager: A Step-by-Step Approach to Mastering Management without an M.B.A.* New York: Collier Books/Macmillan, 1985.

McCormack, Mark H. *What They Don't Teach You at Harvard Business School: Notes from a Street-Smart Executive.* New York: Bantam Books, 1986.

Stewart, Nathaniel. *Winning Friends at Work.* New York: Ballantine Books, 1985.

APPENDIX

A

Information Sources for Profit-Making Organizations

Following is a list of bibliographies, directories, and other reference books that contain listings of profit-making organizations and information about them. This list is just a beginning. Always check the dates of the books you use; anything more than five years old is likely to contain out-of-date information. Ask your librarian for the most recent volume.

Business Information Bibliographies

These are books that list business-information books, articles, and printed material.

Association Publications In Print. Annual. List of printed and audiovisual material by subject and issuing organization. Useful as an aid in obtaining ephemera such as newsletters.

Business Information Sources. Daniells, rev. ed. 1985. Comprehensive standard source of material, newly updated.

Directories In Print. Annual. Identifies specialized directories of all kinds. Good for finding organizations and companies in specialized areas.

Encyclopedia of Business Information Sources. Wasserman, 1983. Unannotated listings of sources grouped by industry, source, and product or service.

How To Find Information About Companies. Washington Researchers, 1983. Lists primarily governmental sources of business information—which are a goldmine. Includes annotations.

Directories That List Companies

These directories give such information as: names of corporations, most of which are publicly held; addresses and telephone numbers; types of products; divisions; annual sales volume; total number of employees; names of the corporation's bank, legal firm, accounting firm; names of the top executives. The directories may have several listings: alphabetical, geographical, and product type. Read the introductions in the front of the directories to see the kinds of companies that are included and the kind of information given.

Dun & Bradstreet Million Dollar Directory. 4 v. Annual. Alphabetical listing of companies with assets over a half million dollars. Includes geographical and product-based indexes.

Directories of Companies Required to File Annual Reports with the Securities And Exchange Commission. Annual. A listing, primarily of 10-K reports, which may be obtained from the Securities and Exchange Commission.

Moody's Manuals. Multi-volume. Weekly update, plus annual bound volume. Contains summaries of company histories, subsidiaries, locations, products, with much financial data. Divided in volumes by genre and how traded. Use with *Standard & Poor's Corporation Records*.

Macrae's Blue Book. Multi-volume. Annual. Listings of companies by product. Use with *Thomas' Register*.

Standard & Poor's Register of Corporations, Directors and Executives. Annual. Alphabetical listing of companies, public and private, with indexes by location, product (SIC) code, and of executives.

Thomas' Register of American Manufacturers. Annual. Directory of manufacturers arranged by product. Includes catalogs for many. Use with *Macrae's.*

Directories That List Only Privately Held Companies

Companies that are privately owned and don't sell stock to the public may be more private about the information they wish to release. Many of them are listed in the large corporate directories, but if they aren't, check for them in these.

The Top 1,500 Private Companies. 1983. Listing with brief information and ranking by sales, products, employees, and number of locations.

Ward's Directory of 49,000 Private Companies. Good source of information on companies that may not be in *Standard & Poor's* or *Moody's.* Includes subsidiaries and divisions.

Directories of Subsidiaries

These directories contain information on companies that are owned by other companies and therefore may not be listed separately in the larger directories.

America's Corporate Families and International Affiliates. Dun & Bradstreet. Identifies over 22,000 companies—U.S. parents with foreign subsidiaries and foreign parents with U.S. subsidiaries.

Directory of Corporate Affiliations. Annual. Useful for finding parent companies that produce annual reports.

International Directory of Corporate Affiliations. Annual. Identifies foreign parent companies along with subsidiaries in addition to U.S. parents.

Who Owns Whom: North American Edition. Dun & Bradstreet. Gives the ownership of subsidiary and associate companies and how they fit into their umbrella corporations. Covers

U.S., Canadian, and foreign parents with U.S. or Canadian subsidiaries.

Directories of Foreign-Owned Companies

Principal International Business. Annual. International volume of the Dun & Bradstreet series.

Directories with Specialized Kinds of Information About Companies

These directories may include biographies of a company's top executives or in-depth information about a company's history.

Reference Book of Corporate Management. 4 v. Biographical information about top management of companies. Arranged by name of company.

Standard & Poor's Corporation Records. 5 v. Good information about company history, activities, products, mergers, and financial activities. Use with *Moody's.*

Standard Directory of Advertisers. Annual with quarterly supplements. Listing of companies with top officers and agencies handling their advertising accounts.

Directories of Business Organizations and Associations

Business Organizations and Agencies Directory, 2nd edition. 1984. Guide to trade, business, and commercial organizations. Gives much information.

Encyclopedia of Associations. Annual. Basic sourcebook with good information about associations of all kinds. Gives description, address, phone number, membership, publications, annual meetings, and so on.

National Directory of Trade and Professional Associations. Annual listings by special interest, size, and budget.

Directories of Special Interest to Job Hunters

Career Employment Opportunities Directory. 4 v. 2nd edition. 1985. A listing of companies and agencies that hire and train college graduates. Volume 1 contains listing for liberal arts and social science majors; Volume 2 for business majors; Volume 3 for engineering and computer science; and Volume 4 for science. Not comprehensive but very helpful. Use with *Peterson's.*

College Placement Council Annual. 3 v. A directory of companies hiring college graduates. Volume 1 includes job search fundamentals; Volume 2 lists companies hiring trainees in business administration, liberal arts, and the social sciences; Volume 3 will interest graduates in engineering and the sciences. Use with *Career Employment Opportunities Directory* and *Peterson's.*

Everybody's Business. 1980. Billed as "the irreverent guide to corporate America," this provides informal profiles of 317 large American firms. Also includes fascinating bits of information about industries.

Peterson's Business and Management Jobs. Annual. Describes companies and agencies that hire different types of graduates. Use with *CPC Annual* and *Career Employment Opportunities Directory.*

Peterson's Engineering, Science and Computer Jobs. Annual. Similar to *Peterson's Business and Management Jobs.* Also well-indexed and up-to-date.

Indexes of Business Journals and Papers

These will lead you to articles on companies, industries, trends, mergers, and so forth. Look under the name of the company or industry being researched.

Applied Science and Technology Index. H.W. Wilson. Good source for technical information.

Business Firms Master Index. 1985. An index of specific directories.

Business Index. Information Access. 16 mm. film. Contains citations to last five years of articles in business journals. Updated monthly.

Business Periodicals Index. H.W. Wilson. Printed index to business journals. Monthly with annual bound volume. Use with *Business Index*.

Guide to Special Issues and Indexes of Periodicals. 3rd ed. 1985. In-depth listings of special issues of journals with such information as directories and statistical data. Use with *Special Issues Index*.

Infotrac. Information Access. Laser disc service indexing around 1000 business and general periodicals, plus *The New York Times* and *The Wall Street Journal*. 1982–date.

The New York Times Index. Biweekly with annual bound volume. The most complete index that gives some information as well as the citation.

Newspaper Index. Information Access. 16 mm. film. Updated monthly. Index to *The New York Times*, *The Wall Street Journal*, as well as other papers.

Predicast's F. & S. Index of Corporations and Industries. Weekly with monthly and annual cumulations. Best source of current information on companies and industries.

Special Issues Index. 1982. Identifies special issues of journals. Use with *Guide to Special Issues*.

The Wall Street Journal Index. With annual cumulation.

Guides to Industry Trends, Analyses of Industries, Rankings, Forecasts

Black Enterprise's Top 100 Black-Owned Businesses. Annual special issue which summarizes the top black-owned one hundred businesses.

Dun's Business Rankings. Annual. Ranks companies by sales and employees, product, and geography. Good for locating leaders in fields.

Fortune Double 500. Special issues of *Fortune* magazine, which rank and analyze top five hundred industries and service companies. In May and June.

National Stock Summary. Twice yearly. Contains stock information; also includes current company activities.

Standard & Poor's Industry Surveys. Quarterly. Forecasts and summarizes by industry.

U.S. Industrial Outlook. Annual. Produced by the government, contains forecasts by industry for the coming year. Analysis of job gains and losses, trends, and so on.

APPENDIX

B

Resources for Researching Nonprofit Organizations

Directories

These contain listings of organizations and agencies with brief information about them: address, top official, brief description of activity.

Corporate Foundation Profiles. 3rd ed. 1983. Although aimed at grant seekers, this can also be used by job hunters. Gives good information on foundations established by corporations, including staffing and whether a part of the corporate structure or a separate entity.

Encyclopedia of Associations. Annual. Invaluable for identifying organizations of all kinds. Includes complete address and brief description of activities, publications, annual meetings, and so on.

Foundations. 1984. This is Volume 8 of the American Organizations series. Gives in-depth and historical information about America's major foundations.

The Fourth of July Resource Guide for the Promotion of Careers in Public, Community, and International Service. 1987. The Middle Atlantic Placement Association. Special Project for Public and Community Service.

Foundation Directory. 10th ed. 1985. Contains good, brief information on foundations nationwide. Includes assets, officers, availability of grants, and whether annual reports can be obtained.

Good Works: A Guide to Social Change Careers. 3rd ed. 1985. Written for the job seeker, this describes organizations, their goals, recent activities, availability of internships, types of jobs, and contact people. Emphasis on groups interested in human betterment.

Internships. Annual. Includes many nonprofit organizations in such fields as the arts, museums, environmental interest, religious-sponsored, public interest, and social service. For graduates and undergraduates.

National Trade and Professional Associations of the U.S. Annual. Gives full address, brief information on activities of groups, along with size of staff, publications, and so forth. Excellent source for nonprofits in trade and professional areas.

Official Museum Directory. Annual. A listing of museums in the U.S. and Canada. Gives personnel, fields collected, publications, and so on.

Research Centers Directory. 10th ed. 1986. Academic and private research facilities. Information includes governance, funding, scope of research, staffing, and publications.

Social Service Organizations. 1978. 2 v. Another part of the American Organizations Series, this gives historical background on various nonprofit organizations.

Taft Directory of Non-Profit Organizations. 1987. 1st Edition.

U.S. Government Manual. Biennial. The directory of governmental agencies with descriptions of duties, locations of offices, and top officials.

U.S. Non-Profit Organizations in Developing Assistance Abroad. 1984. Identifies private organizations, gives executive personnel and financial status, goals and areas of operations.

World of Learning. Annual. Worldwide coverage of higher education institutions, museums, and other cultural institutions.

Newsletters

The following publications contain information and listings of jobs in some nonprofit areas.

Artsearch. Monthly with occasional supplements. Performing arts classifieds nationwide, including jobs in administrative, production, and internship areas. Use with *National Arts Job Bank.*

Chronicle of Higher Education. Weekly. Lists of jobs in all areas of academe—teaching, administrative, and fellowships—as well as articles on the field of higher education.

Community Jobs. Monthly compilation of nonprofit jobs and internships. Nationwide in coverage.

Federal Career Opportunities; Federal Jobs Digest; Federal Times. These three cover the areas of Federal employment with job listings and articles on the employment picture. Includes overseas listings.

National Arts Job Bank. Covers all the arts. Use with *Artsearch.*

Books

These may help focus on the various types of nonprofit organizations.

Careers in the Nonprofit Sector. 1986. The Taft Group.

Careers in International Affairs. Focuses on job possibilities for college graduates with nonprofit groups in international policy and affairs. Extensive information about the organizations, job requirements, number of employees.

Guide to Careers in World Affairs. Similar to the above but also includes information on internships.

International Jobs. For those interested in international affairs or working overseas, this has sections on various kinds of nonprofit organizations.

Invest Yourself. A catalog of volunteer opportunities. Although primarily a list of agencies using volunteers, this can pinpoint job ideas in the nonprofit service sector.

Making the Community Your Career. Published by the periodical Community Jobs, this is a list of sources of information on jobs with organizations interested in social change.

The Overseas List. Opportunities for living and working in developing countries, for organizations interested in improving conditions there.